WOMEN, GENDER, AND THE PALACE HOUSEHOLDS IN OTTOMAN TUNISIA

WOMEN, GENDER, AND THE PALACE HOUSEHOLDS IN OTTOMAN TUNISIA

AMY AISEN KALLANDER

UNIVERSITY OF TEXAS PRESS
Austin

Requests for permission to reproduce material from this work should
be sent to:
    Permissions
    University of Texas Press
    P.O. Box 7819
    Austin, TX 78713-7819
    http://utpress.utexas.edu/index.php/rp-form

♾ The paper used in this book meets the minimum requirements of
ANSI/NISO Z39.48-1992 (R1997) (Permanence of Paper).

LIBRARY OF CONGRESS CATALOGING-IN-PUBLICATION DATA

Kallander, Amy Aisen, 1978-
    Women, gender, and the palace households in Ottoman Tunisia /
by Amy Aisen Kallander. — 1st ed.
        p.   cm.
    Includes bibliographical references and index.
    ISBN 978-0-292-74838-5 (cloth : alk. paper)
    ISBN 978-1-4773-0213-2 (paperback)
    1. Women—Tunisia—History.   2. Tunisia—Kings and rulers—
History.   3. Tunisia—History—1516-1881.   4. Tunisia—Politics and
government.   5. Courts and courtiers—Tunisia—History.   I. Title.
    HQ1792.K35   2013
    305.4821096110903—dc23
                                                        2012046684

doi:10.7560/748385

In memory of Linda Sherif
1969–2010

CONTENTS

vii

ILLUSTRATIONS

FIGURES

TABLES

NOTE ON TRANSLITERATION

I have followed a standard approach to all Arabic terms that relies on a simplified version of the *International Journal of Middle East Studies* guidelines, namely, excluding diacritical marks aside from the *ayn* (ʿ) and *hamza* (ʾ). This is applied uniformly, including proper names that often appear in French transliteration such as Kheireddine or Hussein ben Ali, which are rendered Khayr al-Din and Husayn ibn ʿAli. With weights and measures, I have opted for the awkward addition of the letter "s" at the end of the singular to facilitate reading for those unfamiliar with the Arabic language. Foreign terms are briefly defined in the text, with those frequently used also included in the glossary. The orthography of the archival records respects the original texts, which were written in a combination of classical and colloquial Arabic.

All weights, measures, and prices are given according to the units utilized in the eighteenth and nineteenth centuries. Though there was some regional variation, the approximate metric equivalents for Tunis are listed in the glossary.

Unless otherwise specified, translations from Arabic and French sources are my own.

CHRONOLOGY

1229–1574	Hafsid dynasty
1517	Ottoman conquest of Egypt and Tilimsan (Algeria)
1556	Beginning of Ottoman rule in Tripoli
1574	Ottoman conquest of Tunisia
1591	Soldiers revolt; one of the deys is included on the *diwan*
1598–1610	ʿUthman Dey
1610–1635	Yusuf Dey
1613–1631	Murad serves as bey, granted title of pasha; his descendants maintain the position of bey for the remainder of the century
1631–1666	Hammuda Pasha ibn Murad
1666–1675	Murad ibn Hammuda Bey
1675–1686	ʿAli ibn Murad Bey
1686–1696	Muhammad ibn Murad Bey
1690s	Intermittent fighting with Algiers over rule in Tunis
1702	Ottoman envoy Ibrahim al-Sharif arrives in Tunis to quell political problems
1702	Numerous political marriages between the Murad family and its dependents
1705–1735	Husayn ibn ʿAli nominated dey and bey, with sultan's recognition
1710	Governing position becomes hereditary
1711	Qaramanli family begins governing in Tripoli
1728	ʿAli Pasha divorces his cousin Hafsia, breaks with his uncle (Husayn ibn ʿAli), and makes a claim to govern
1735–1756	ʿAli Pasha returns to Tunis from Algeria and governs
1740	Assassination of Husayn ibn ʿAli
1756–1759	Muhammad al-Rashid Bey returns from Algeria; assassinates cousin ʿAli Pasha

1756 (approx.) Trakiya bint ʿAli Pasha marries her father's cousin ʿAli ibn Husayn

1759–1777 ʿAli Bey

1763 Muhammad Saghir ibn Yusuf (1691–1771) writes *Al-mashrʿa al-mulki*

1764 Circumcision festivities for Hammuda, Suleiman, Mahmud, and Ismail

1776 Family marriage celebrations, including one for Amina bint ʿAli Bey and her cousin Mahmud

1777 Ceremony of investiture at which his son Hammuda is granted the title of pasha and begins governing in practice

1777–1814 Hammuda Pasha

1782 Death of ʿAli Bey

1814 ʿUthman Bey

1814–1824 Mahmud Bey

1822 Death of Amina bint ʿAli Bey (wife of Mahmud Bey, mother of Husayn and Mustafa)

1824–1835 Husayn Bey

1827 Death of Fatma Mestiri, wife of Husayn Bey

1830 French occupation of Algiers

1835 Qaramanli governors in Tripoli deposed by sultan

1835–1837 Mustafa Bey

1837–1855 Ahmad Bey

1839 Death of ʿAziza bint Mahmud Bey, wife of Suleiman Kahia

1855–1859 Muhammad Bey

1857 *ʿAhd al-Aman* or Fundamental Pact establishes mixed courts in Tunis

1859–1882 Muhammad al-Sadoq Bey

1861 Fundamental Laws or constitution implemented

1864 Major uprisings throughout Tunisia; Muhammad al-Sadoq Bey suspends the constitution

1869 International Financial Commission takes control of finances in Tunis

1873–1877 Khayr al-Din serves as prime minister

1881 French colonial occupation of Tunisia; bey continues to govern in name only

ACKNOWLEDGMENTS

As is often true, this book is the result of a long trajectory, and I have benefited from considerable intellectual and institutional support. I would like to thank Matthew J. Connelly for introducing me to the history of northern Africa and for his gracious and unfailing mentoring over the years. My understanding of Tunisia, its place in Ottoman provincial politics, and the French colonial world owe much to the erudition of Edmund (Terry) Burke III, Beshara Doumani, Omnia El Shakry, and Tyler Stovall, who generously contributed their time and advice towards improving this project. Omnia went out of her way on multiple occasions to show her encouragement.

A number of friends and colleagues have read different portions of the book, providing valuable feedback: Julia Clancy-Smith, Emily Gottreich, Robert Lang, Asma Moalla, and the late Donald Quataert. Julia Clancy-Smith in particular has been an unfailing proponent and intellectual role model for organizing the disparate details of Tunisia's social history into a global context. My familiarity with the Tunisian archives and the particularities of Ottoman-era terminology has greatly benefited from conversations with Fawzi al-Mustaghanimi, who along with Mabrouk Jebahi provided welcome company at the archives and national library, as did Bacem Rzouga in Nantes. For sharing her own research in many conversations about Tunisia, my appreciation goes to Silvia Marsans-Sakly, and to Ilhem Marzouki for her passion for women's rights. Thanks are also due to Abdelhamid Henia, Sami Bergaoui, and the Diraset research group at the University of Tunis.

There are many families in Tunisia who have adopted me over years of research and writing, opening their homes and providing much more than food, tea, company, and conversation. These include the late Nabiha Jerad, Jnaina and Rim Fitouri, Naima and Mahrez Chinguiti, and the Kheriji-Elouafi family. Asma Moalla has been hospitable, encouraging, and generous with her time. A special note of gratitude to Ahmad al-Jalluli and Faycal Bey, who shared the history of their families.

Research for this project has been funded by the American Institute for Maghreb Studies, the Fulbright Foundation, the Fulbright Commission in Egypt, and the U.S. Department of Education through a Center for Arabic Study Abroad (CASA) III fellowship. Various portions were presented at conferences, where Brian Catlos, Kenneth Cuno, Nara Milanich, and Ruby Lal provided valuable feedback as co-panelists and organizers. The staff at the National Archives in Tunis have been especially amicable and accommodating, as have those at the National Library and the Centre des Archives diplomatiques de Nantes (CADN) in France. Both James A. Miller and Thomas DeGeorges facilitated scholarly engagement with the Tunisian academic community when they served as directors of the American research center in Tunis (Centre d'études maghrébines à Tunis [CEMAT]), where Riadh Saadaoui has made many years of research more enjoyable. At Syracuse University, thanks to Joseph Stoll, who prepared the genealogies, drew the floor plan, and designed the maps, and colleagues such as Subho Basu and Norman Kutcher for their interest and insight. I am grateful to Jim Burr for his persevering support of this project and to Julia Clancy-Smith and one anonymous reader for their careful reading of the manuscript and constructive responses. Nancy Moore greatly improved the quality of the prose with her meticulous reading. My parents, Jeff and Judy Aisen, have always supported and promoted my scholarly endeavors, as well as their timely completion. Finally, Mona and George not only have been a source of motivation and inspiration, but George meticulously read and commented on this manuscript a number of times, considerably improving the result, though all errors are my own.

WOMEN, GENDER, AND THE PALACE
HOUSEHOLDS IN OTTOMAN TUNISIA

FAMILY FOUNDATIONS
OF OTTOMAN RULE

Part I

In the summer of 1776, the governor of Tunis celebrated the wedding of three of his children: his son Hammuda, his daughter Amina, and a second daughter (whose name is unknown).[1] For months before that, women in the family, their domestics, and slaves were busy gathering the various articles for the trousseaus of the two brides, including diverse clothing and decorative linens, much of which was embroidered with silver thread. As they prepared for the days of festivities, 400 loaves of bread were baked, 1,800 *ratl*s of honey were transformed into impressive quantities of *zlabia* (a sweet made of fried dough), and an additional 1,100 *ratl*s of pastries were made from honey, dates, and almonds. Fruits, vegetables, and fowl were brought to the palace, and butchers were hired to slaughter nearly one hundred cows. Altogether, the expenses for these items totaled to at least 6,500 piasters and were intended as much for internal consumption as for public display.[2] Through these marriages the governor—or bey, the Ottoman title that became the family surname—made a series of political alliances, just as his own marriage had done. Hammuda married the daughter of an important religious notable, Amina married her paternal cousin, and the second daughter married a prominent minister. The banquets celebrated the establishment of new households headed by these couples, publicly announced the connections between the governor's family and the religious elite of the capital as they consolidated family ties, and secured loyalty among the palace inner circle.

Just a few years earlier, the daughter of Austria's Habsburg monarchs had celebrated her nuptials with the grandson and heir apparent of France's Louis XV. This union between Marie-Antoinette and the future Louis XVI was a strategic alliance, which was typical under the Bourbon dynasty (1589-1792), intended to secure the recent cooperation between these two erstwhile opponents. As the young bride and her 57-carriage cortège traveled across Austria in April and May of 1770, she was feted with banquets, town celebrations, dance performances, and fireworks. After a highly ritualized border crossing, she was conducted in a large procession to Strasbourg for the first official celebrations. Soldiers saluted as they entered the city through a triumphal arch constructed for the occasion and adorned with the arms of France and Austria. That evening, the city's chief magistrate and cardinal held an official reception, ending in a display of fireworks and a public banquet with fountains of wine and roast oxen. Additional fireworks, flowers, and speeches commemorated the arrival of her convoy in a series of small villages as they journeyed northward, towards Louis XV's royal hunting lodge.

When she finally arrived at Versailles, her ladies in waiting dressed her in a gown made of the traditional bridal cloth of silver and adorned with masses of white diamonds, while the groom wore a gold suit that was valued at 64,000 livres. Approximately six thousand aristocratic spectators gathered to watch the family procession travel through the ornate salons of the palace. Following a religious ceremony in the king's chapel, the signing of the marriage register, and additional formal introductions, the immediate family dined in a gilded, candle-lit room under the eyes of thousands of guests seated in its surrounding lodges. The wedding entertainment continued for another nine days and nights of banquets, dancing, an opera, a ballet, and a display of fireworks for a crowd of around two hundred thousand guests.[3]

While 'Ali Bey (1759-1777) was the fourth consecutive governor of Tunis from the descendants of 'Ali al-Turki, he certainly did not claim a royal pedigree to the tune of the French monarchs, nor could he boast of a palace to rival that of the Sun King. If he replicated on a smaller and less opulent scale European courtly norms, he was equally attentive to the precedents set by the imperial family in Istanbul because the governors consciously aspired to belong to an early modern political elite in which power was a family prerogative. At these courts, the conspicuous consumption demonstrated in bridal gowns, trousseaus, and lavish banquets was a claim to status, and marriage was a central institution for consolidating elite identity and securing diplomatic, economic, and social alliances.

As governor, king, sultan, or shah, official political sinecure was the prerogative of men, yet the celebration of weddings is only one example of women's contributions to diplomacy, palace economics, and the representation of power. For most early modern states, family was the most salient political model, and government administrations were structured as households, lending political weight to a multitude of domestic matters. From within their palaces, the wives, daughters, and concubines of rulers had an enviable position of access to the sovereign and the center of power. The modern distinction between public and private affairs is of little value in making sense of these familial states whether during the seventeenth-century Dutch Golden Age or in France's nineteenth-century Bourbon restoration and Napoleonic empires. While rarely governing in name, these "servants of the dynasty" organized and orchestrated political factions, promoted and opposed contenders to the throne, and engaged in foreign relations.[4] The overlap of domestic and political spaces meant that the ruling households of the governors of Tunis and their counterparts within the Ottoman Empire shared a number of traits with the early modern dynasties of Mughal India (1526–1858), Qing China (1644–1911), Safavid (1501–1736) and Qajar Persia (1794–1925), and European courts such as the Bourbons and the Habsburgs.

This book argues for the centrality of family to the political and social history of Tunisia in the eighteenth and nineteenth centuries. While family as a metaphor of the state and patriarchal models of authority are certainly relevant, the focus of this book is on the ruling family and the transformation of its relationship to government, especially in the nineteenth century. This approach has the benefit of incorporating women into the historical narrative, demonstrating their contribution to the decision-making process and the legitimation of hereditary rule. As family dynasties were common across the Ottoman Empire, such an analysis permits comparison with different provinces and the imperial center as well as with the equally family-based monarchies of Europe, India, and Asia. Comparisons with dynastic states are not meant to imply equivalence; though to a certain extent autonomously governed, Tunis was a province of the Ottoman Empire and not an independent nation-state. As clearly delineated in the first chapter and reiterated throughout, Ottoman political, cultural, and intellectual references remained salient at least until the beginning of French colonialism.

At the same time as the beys presented themselves in terms of early modern courtly references, they were acutely attentive to the local context, with both men and women striving to earn acceptance into provincial social circles. This is not to argue that they were nationalists or that they identified exclusively as Tunisian, as neither term held much weight during the period in question. As references to the courts of Mughal India and Bourbon France intimate, class identities carried more salience than ethnic or racial ones. This book situates the beys among numerous currents and understands their lives through the lens of multiple literatures: early modern court culture, Ottoman provincial history, feminism, colonialism, and consumerism.

The palace, with its dense population, luxury spending habits, and convenient location in the suburbs of the capital just a few kilometers from the port of Tunis, was a major economic hub within the province and its largest employer.[5] Wedding festivities were an explicit incarnation of how courtly habits such as sustaining a community of servants, slaves, and domestics were dependent upon local resources: agriculture, transportation, and artisans. On a daily basis, each palace household required enough provisions to feed an entourage of dependents, personnel, and soldiers, with additional resources devoted to charities.

Tunis—the provincial capital, and the Arabic name for the province—was a small domain of the Ottoman Empire in terms of both population and size. Its borders, defined roughly by mountains to the west and by the Mediterranean in the north and east, contained fertile agricultural land in the central plains and an expanse of desert in the south. With a population around one million in the eighteenth century, it was relatively urbanized, with towns such as Sfax, Monastir, Gabes, and Binzart sprinkled along the coasts (see Figure 0.1).[6] The holy city of Qayrawan (founded in the seventh century) and the Zaytuna mosque in the capital were both centers of learning, attracting scholars from Morocco, Algeria, and Egypt. Merchants and scholars followed the annual pilgrimage caravans westward for brief or extended stays in Cairo and the cities of the Hijaz. Religious brotherhoods such as the Shadhiliya, Qadiriya, Tijaniya, and Rahmaniya in its villages and towns connected Tunis to cities across the region from Fez, Tripoli, Constantine, and Algiers to Alexandria, and Cairo (see Figure 0.2).

Ties between rural and pastoral communities transgressed any political borders between Algeria and Tunisia, as did extensive commerce and contraband.[7] The temperate climate, diverse terrain, and extensive coastline allowed for a strong agricultural base, producing wheat, a variety of fruits and vegetables (particularly olives), fish, sponges, and coral.[8] Active merchant communities in Tunis and Sfax exported agricultural products such as olive oil, wool, wheat, and coral to Alexandria, the island of Malta, Marseilles, and Livorno, and in the nineteenth century they went as far as Glasgow and Odessa. In addition, there was a considerable volume of illicit traffic towards Algeria and the Italian islands.[9] Tunisians controlled the particularly lucrative trade in caps called fez (known locally as *sha-*

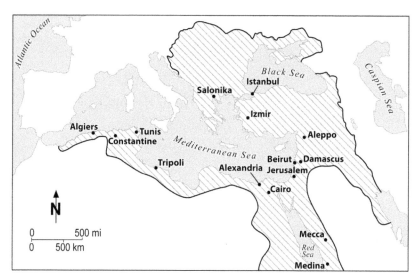

FIGURE O.I. *Map of the Ottoman Empire, circa 1600.*

shia) that were exported to the Ottoman ports of Izmir and Salonika and on occasion to Persia and the Balkans.[10] Caravans traversing the Sahara brought slaves, spices, and gold.[11] The small province was thus linked by commercial, intellectual, and religious ties to urban centers and international ports across the region.

Incorporated into the Ottoman Empire in the sixteenth century, Tunis remained part of the sultan's domains until the beginning of French colonial rule three hundred years later. By the late eighteenth century, its governors were able to balance their allegiance to the sultan and adherence to imperial policy with considerable autonomy in the management of quotidian affairs. The imperial government was largely decentralized, delegating provincial administration to local notables, whether to facilitate the incorporation of new territories, as was the case in the Balkans, or to compensate for limited communication with inaccessible and distant regions such as Mount Lebanon or Tunis.[12] While in certain locales such as Jerusalem or Damascus a few families dominated social, political, and economic affairs alongside appointees from Istanbul, in others, such as Tripoli under the Qaramanli governors (1711–1835) and Egypt under Muhammad ʿAli Pasha (1805–1848) and his descendants in the nineteenth century, the governorship was a hereditary monopoly. The particular expression of provincial autonomy that coexisted with, or relied upon,

FIGURE O.2. *Map of the province of Tunisia.*

family rule that developed in Tunis was concordant with a system of Ottoman governing in which the prominence of local elites became "the rule in practically every part of the Ottoman empire."[13]

The eminent families that made up the ruling classes in the provinces often emulated the lifestyles of the sultan and his ministers in Istanbul, building palaces, making expensive charitable donations, and extending their household networks into commercial activities.[14] This was not viewed as a breach of etiquette or usurpation of imperial authority as long as a balance was maintained between political stability and respect for the imperial order. But the eruption of revolts, heated factional disputes, armed confrontation, or shifts in regional or international politics provided impetus for the reassertion of central authority. This was demonstrated when a succession dispute led to the replacement of the Qaramanlis of Tripoli in 1835 and when the sultan dispatched foreign minister Fuad Pasha to Mount Lebanon in response to the prolonged communal violence of 1860. Where Tunis departs from such patterns is the extent to which one family monopolized the provincial government—and not just wealth or social capital in the province—for two centuries. Their officially sanctioned longevity allowed for a strong association between the ruling family and the government.

This dynasty in Tunis began with Husayn ibn ʿAli al-Turki (1705-1735), a soldier whose political career dates to the late seventeenth century. At that moment, control of the capital was shared between the military, officials nominated from Istanbul, and the descendants of a previous governor. Husayn ibn ʿAli climbed the ranks, serving in the entourage of important governmental figures and promoted to be head of the cavalry, positions that allowed him to establish connections to the governor's family, and the military. Though some contemporary sources believed that he was Corsican, others said he was the son of a Greek man who was successful at assimilating into the provincial elite, becoming a "Turk by trade" or a professional Ottoman.[15]

The 1690s were marked by political and military turmoil since internal feuding destabilized the government and Algerian troops invaded the province to quell the situation and install an ally in government. Ibn ʿAli combined political acumen with military skills to defend the capital from being brought under Algerian suzerainty and assert his authority. A military council selected ibn ʿAli as bey, a position subsequently confirmed by the sultan, and in 1710, he was able to make the position hereditary. His descendants still served as provincial governors when France occupied the

FIGURE O.3. *Bardo entrance, undated postcard, author's personal collection.*

province in 1881, transforming it into a colony (though they maintained a nominal position in the colonial bureaucracy through independence in 1956).

By the late eighteenth century, the governor of Tunis and his family had firmly established their residence in the town of Bardo, the seat of power that they inherited from their Hafsid predecessors (1229–1574). A few miles from the capital, the private home of the ruling family was also the center of political life in the province (see Figure 0.3). It often included at least three generations, maternal relatives, and greater degrees of extended family with each generation. The palace was staffed by washerwomen, instructors, nannies, doctors, guarded military contingents, and an elite slave corps. The walled palace grounds with five turreted watchtowers enclosed a small city where numerous palace retainers and employees had their homes, all of which benefited from the Bardo markets and mosque. Entering the city, one European noted that

> we pass between the sentries of the entrance-gate, and have before us a long, straight road, just broad enough for one carriage. Imposing marble palaces rise on the left, built of costly material, partly in the Renaissance, partly in the Oriental style. [. . .] These are the palaces of the princes of the reigning house, and of the minister. [. . .] And opposite these magnificent residences, a few steps from their gates, we see a long

row of common shops with an arcade in front, a true Eastern bazaar for the inhabitants of this town of palaces.[16]

While the immediate family and their entourages reached around fifteen hundred, the total population living at Bardo may have been closer to four thousand at its peak.[17]

Bardo contained a tribunal presided over by the bey that functioned as the highest court in the province. To accommodate public access to its chamber with the intimate affairs of the state, the palace consisted of a series of guarded entrances and separate courtyards. The primary entrance was flanked by cannons and wide enough for carriages to pass through into the main courtyard where litigants awaited the bey's justice. As an accessible part of the palace interior, its staircase, adorned with marble lions, became an emblematic reference for palace visits (see Figure 0.4). Only those on official business could pass through

a second great gate, where some attendants of the court were visible, and we were obliged to get out [of our carriage]. We walked through this gate, and entered a high arched way. [. . .] This led into a much cleaner and more elegant court, ornamented with green glazed tiles, with paintings, and with various coloured marbles; in the midst of

FIGURE 0.4. *The first courtyard and the lion staircase, undated postcard, author's private collection.*

which sprang up a fountain. A broad arcade with high but simple pillars ran round it.[18]

As foreign visitors took care to detail, the costly marble used to pave the courtyard and its surrounding columns were part of the presentation of grandeur, as were the decorative tiles adorning its walls. Wood lattice friezes hung below its vaulted ceilings, just as ornamental sculptured plaster and calligraphy were engraved over doorways.

This careful attention to décor was featured in the Schönbrunn Palace in Vienna, where works of art, architecture, design, and luxury items such as Chinese lacquer contributed to monarchical legitimation, reflecting how the Versailles Hall of Mirrors, with its marble walls, painted ceiling, bronze decorations, and mirror-clad arched windows, actualized royal investments in the palace as spectacle.[19] Early modern rulers used their wealth to distinguish themselves from their subject populations, legitimizing their authority in elaborate royal ceremonials. Royal weddings formed a perfect occasion to mobilize the resources of royal families, dressed in their finest and serving vast buffets. As the anecdote about Marie-Antoinette demonstrates, these performances were staged for the benefit of notables, elites, and the public hoping to get a glimpse of the dauphine as her carriages passed through the countryside. Despite the comparable opulence of European ruling houses, even those who recognized that Bardo was "a Versailles, or rather a Windsor of Tunis" still insisted that it was a "thoroughly Oriental palace."[20] The luxury of the Ottoman harem fascinated Europeans so that the harem became a sign of difference, and Bardo presented the "picture of oriental scenery."[21]

THE HAREM AS PALACE HOUSEHOLD

Alongside its public and political purposes, the palace was a residential space. According to most definitions, the inhabitants at Bardo constituted one family. The governing families all shared a single ancestor ('Ali al-Turki and later Husayn ibn 'Ali), constituting a lineage, and they all lived at Bardo, though in separate apartments. Yet the concept of the household, which comprises all the residents under one roof, is more useful for understanding domestic relations at the palace with its numerous nonkin and multiple generations. Organized into the smaller conjugal units that iterated a typical family structure, they were all financially dependent on the bey and his access to the government treasury for monthly stipends and provisions. The family model is a useful way to understand the paternal authority that the governors exercised over their male and female relations, ministers, and the general population and the filial respect the latter demonstrated in return. Patriarchal structures provided women an arena in which they could contribute to family finances through their access to resources and labor power. The marriages of the bey's daughters sealed social alliances and provided occasions to demonstrate his benevolence and largesse.

Family hierarchies were evoked as a metaphor for government organization. Terms such as father, uncle, or brother were used to denote respect, deference, affection, and not exclusively blood relations, so that defining the contours of the family is a messy task. Familial ties were created through naming, residence, or sharing breast milk. For example, when the governor Husayn Bey (1824–1835) married a wealthy widow, her son from a previous marriage, 'Allala, moved to the palace with her. 'Allala was raised alongside Husayn's other sons and treated as their equal, for example, receiving the same stipends and clothing, and archival documents list him as their "brother." Though not a descendant through the male line, palace accountants referred to him as 'Allala Bey, a title reserved for the direct line of male descent within the family. His marriage to one of Husayn's daughters, Hafsia, in 1821 confirmed these indices of filiation and reaffirmed his proximity to the ruling family.[22]

Mamluks, the elite palace slaves, could also marry into the governing family, despite their subservient origins. Taken from the empire's borderland regions such as Greece, Albania, Moldavia, and the Caucasus or in maritime raids in the nearby Mediterranean, these slaves were brought to Tunis as children, raised in the palace, and trained for military or administrative careers, providing contingents of the palace guards and the majority of its ministerial personnel. Female slaves could similarly become the wives and concubines of the beys. While only a few slaves sealed their ties to the family though marriage, the majority were treated comparably to palace children with whom they grew up. Male slaves occasionally took the names of their patrons, and female slaves were provided with dowries when they married.

The incorporation of slaves into household structures was a relatively common early modern practice. Well-off families in the capital and prominent landowners often purchased slaves from the trans-Saharan trade to work in agriculture or as domestics. Their labor contributed to the functioning of these households, and both in Tunis and beyond they were an important sign of conspicuous consumption and a mark of status. Slaves staffed the upper echelons of the Ottoman military and filled a number of prominent ministerial positions in Istanbul and the provinces. In Bengal, if not other parts of Mughal India as well, most elite families owned slaves whom they raised as kin.[23] Slaves could be given as gifts, creating ties between households, a practice that we will see later was also current in Tunis.

Though the discipline of history traditionally privileged the ruling elites as agents of change, to the detriment of the working classes, rural communities, and economically or socially marginal groups, such a narrow perspective routinely excluded women from the functioning of the state. In this respect, an exploration of the governors of Tunis as a family can both incorporate subaltern populations and contribute to the elaboration of women's history. Palace women were social, economic, or political actors from within their homes where they managed a large staff, conducted business with artisans and skilled workers, and distributed alms to the poor. As power built upon physical proximity to the sovereign, a privilege allocated to select ministers and palace women, gender segregation facilitated women's access to the center of state. Though they rarely left the palace, women were active politicians on a variety of levels, contributing to social welfare and increasing the prestige of the dynasty.[24] As servants of the dynasty, or diplomatic wives, these women exercised power in various informal ways.

Feminist scholars rightly insist that women's political activities have often gone unrecognized as a result of the modern gendering of a public sphere as masculine and the concomitant relegation of women to an apolitical domestic space. Their engagement in government, commercial activities, and social welfare problematizes the stark separation of public and private space and furthers the process of locating a specifically modern genealogy for this division. Though Middle East studies has come a long way in recognizing the importance of domestic space and how the lives of elite women elucidate economic, cultural, and political questions, the study of political power in Tunisia remains limited to the study of men.[25]

Royal palaces shared more than the taste for extravagant furnishings, with elements of architectural design such as multiple doorways and sequential courtyards to distinguish between outer and inner spaces. The arrangement of space communicated the power of the sovereign and his distance from the profane, even when his quarters were not called a harem. The women's quarters at Edo Castle of Japan's Tokugawa shogunate (1600–1868) were located in the Great Interior, separate from the outer spaces, where ceremonies were held, and the middle interior, where administrative affairs were handled. Confucian divisions of gender at the courts of Qing China (1644–1911) and Korea's Chosŏn dynasty (1392–1910) were symbolized by their inner and outer spaces with women's residences in the interior facilitating their access to the sovereign and their ability to intercede in factional politics.[26] For India's Mughal emperors, gender segregation itself was a sign of prestige and a claim to imperial status. Seclusion was one way in which Mughal women "were of critical importance in the establishment of imperial traditions and imperial grandeur, indeed an intrinsic part of the becoming of a (grand) monarchy."[27] Royal women in both Muslim and non-Muslim dynasties occupied separate spaces from men, as gender segregation was a common feature of hereditary governments in which the sovereign and royal family were considered sacred.

The depoliticization of domestic life was suggested by Europeans imagining that the harem was filled with beautiful, passionate women who typified the sensuality associated with the Ottoman Empire. Similar to scholars and amateur Orientalists touring Istanbul or Cairo, Europeans in Tunis did not hesitate to project elaborate fantasies onto the lives of Bardo's women.[28] They had "no other way to pass their time than at the pleasure of the *harem*"; in other words they were "preoccupied only by imagining and putting to practice anything that can arouse, sustain, and increase the mutual passion of the two sexes." Alongside these tantalizing scenarios, life in the harem was seen as a "sort of perpetual imprisonment that would be torture for a European woman."[29] Its ultimate symbol of difference for Europeans meant that the harems were depicted as "prisons lined with gold."[30]

While only the wealthy could provide separate quarters for women, Europeans mainly socialized with the upper classes, whose lives they took as representative of all women. In contrast to the palace, the average family was monogamous and had fewer children. The typical home contained only a single generation, and size limitations meant that gender segregation was neither possible nor practical. Since at least the nineteenth century, suspicions about what went on within the family have concerned colonial bureaucrats, Orientalist scholars, and Western feminists preoccupied with the plight of Arab and Muslim women. The abuse, repression, or general subordination to a husband or father justified generations of paternalistic concern from missionaries, feminists, or proponents of colonial expansion.[31] The enduring image from travelers' depictions of women's lives has continued to inform popular understandings of the harem as an instrument of the sequestration and subservience that typified family life, Islamic law, or Islam, alternately constraining women's rights and summarized in the trope of the prison.[32]

Women's status within the family (and within the domain of personal status or family law) remains integral to scholarly studies of Muslim women and a prevalent theme of Western liberal discourses and human rights agendas in their approaches to the Arab and Muslim world.[33] The family is considered a microcosm of larger society and representative of cultural, racial, or religious differences, making a better understanding of the complexity of family life, even among the elite, important for illustrating how women were and can be complicit in and benefited from patriarchal structures. A comparison across geographic regions makes it evident that such patriarchal bargains are not specific to Islam, regardless of its specifically local iterations. If the trope of woman as victim no longer informs scholarship on Muslim women, there remains an aversion to serious analysis of family life, particularly within the study of Tunisia.

FAMILY HISTORY

One of the three marriages in 1776 united the governor's daughter Amina to her paternal cousin. Orientalists and colonial-era ethnographers later viewed this arrangement as the typical Arab marriage, in sharp contrast with the exogamy of Western, European, or Christian family practices. Even radical studies of the family as an agent of vast economic and social change have been quick to presume a divergence between Western (or northwestern) Europe and the archetypical Middle Eastern family based on scant empirical data.[34] Over the past few generations, scholarship on the family in the Middle East has aimed to discredit such a stark dichotomy and the association between Middle Eastern families and polygamy, high rates of repudiation, and the central role of kinship to culture and tradition.

While initially informed by quantitative approaches to describing family life and European or American models, newer studies of the family stress its potential for informing global analysis of social and political questions. To access the importance of the family, scholars insist on broadening the definition of kinship to recognize that in much of the world, households included extended family and nonkin, such as slaves, boarders or servants, wet nurses, and nannies. Pioneering work has been done in Latin America, with scholars arguing for the relevance of family as a social institution. The efficacy of family connections in facilitating access to resources was particularly the case among the elite, for whom "kin networks were a fundamental basis of economic and political power."[35] Instead of arguing for a particular family structure as the motor of progress, recent studies reiterate that family is relevant to state building and to the understanding of social, economic, political, and cultural phenomena in a variety of global contexts.[36] This may offer particular advantages for the study of the Middle East, as an analysis of the family can build upon scholarship on Islam, gender, and modernity, connecting macro- and microprocesses and combining materialist and discursive frameworks.[37]

Alan Duben and Cem Behar were early pioneers in debunking the myth of Middle Eastern difference by demonstrating that in Turkey, the typical family was small and monogamous, often consisting of a marital couple and their children, though there were exceptions among the elite.[38] Studies on the family in Tunis similarly reject the notion that the plurality of marital practices can be subsumed under one typology. Leïla Blili Temime's work contextualizes the role of tradition and Islam to counter Orientalist images of the "Muslim family" as inimical to European ones. She argues that while polygamy was rare even among the elite, it served reproductive purposes, the demands of agricultural subsistence, or demographic imbalances and was not meant to fulfill men's sexual desires.[39] Scholars concur that class endogamy was common, as were repeat marriages between the same two families, though patrilineal-kin marriages were not in the majority among elite families.[40]

By rejecting the negative associations of Middle Eastern or Arab difference, these studies offer important demographic data to emphasize the similarities between family structures in the Middle East and Europe. Comparing the practices of urban elites across geographic regions similarly demonstrates the significance of class on family life. Hardly an anomaly, marriages within the family, including among first cousins, were a regular occurrence in the British royal family up to the era of Queen Victoria (1837–1901) and even more frequent among the Habsburgs. Other features, such as marriage or concubinage with slaves, common in the Ottoman Empire and its provincial courts, were normative under India's Mughal dynasty.

A number of studies on working-class or bourgeois families allow for comparison across socioeconomic and rural-urban divides. Middle-class Damascene women constituted a significant form of human capital and participated in various investment strategies that helped their families navigate political and economic change. When rural Mount Lebanon was hit by economic hardship, strategic adaptation occurred at the family and not at the individual level. Once women were allowed to work outside the home, their incomes helped preserve family land, so that land ownership became a more important sign of masculinity and family honor than did women's seclusion. Whether the wives of enterprising Cairene merchants who participated in their husbands' businesses around 1600, or women's agricultural labor among peasants in nineteenth-century Egypt, sexual divisions of labor did not preclude women's contributions as specific individual roles fluctuated in response to economic demands.[41] Even among lower-class families in occupied Palestine or Cairo's shantytowns, women have found ways to invest their gold in the education of their children or microcredits to support their families.[42]

Though patriarchal, Islamic institutions have proven flexible in practice, particularly regarding women's rights and family life.[43] Saba Mahmood's hypothesis that feminist scholarship has been constrained by the liberal emphasis on the individual, obfuscating instances of women's agency within their families, is certainly worth considering for the early modern period.[44] Viewing women within the context of their family reveals it as a space of opportunities as well as limitations, as it was for men constrained by responsibilities and obligations towards their wives and children. Taken together, these studies demonstrate that there was no single standard family model or blueprint for gender relations, thanks to the dynamism of family structures particularly in response to major processes such as the incorporation of local economies into global capitalist markets.

Such instances of women's economic activities argue for the need to reconsider the standard narrative of political and economic change in Tunisia's nineteenth century and the view that women were marginal. If less can be determined about working-class or rural women, among the upper classes, women participated in commercial activities and protected family resources by preserving the integrity of family property through the strategic use of religious endowments.[45] The palace offers a telling example of the commercial relations and labor of wealthy women who filled their time with productive activities such as "sewing, knitting, washing, or ironing."[46] They owned rental and commercial properties and agricultural estates, and whether managing these through a representative or commissioning luxury items from local artisans, women at Bardo were involved in a range of economic sectors. In fact, at royal courts across the globe, women contributed to the family business of governing by forging alliances with political factions, advising the sovereign, and participating in the spectacles of consumption that reaffirmed the class status of their dynasties.[47]

Far from being a particularity that distinguished the Middle East, the social, economic, and political importance of the family holds true across the globe, just as the overlap between family and politics was not purely an attribute of monarchies or empire. While hereditary sovereigns were often represented as fatherly figures, modern nation-states have also deployed images of paternal concern and meddled in family affairs. By the end of the nineteenth century, bourgeois family ideals informed debates about gender roles and normative sexuality, becoming a central site for defining modernity and national identity in Europe and its colonies. The Dutch policed domestic arrangements in attempts to ensure that proper racial and class inheritance would be transmitted by the women raising its future citizens, while in the British Empire, "the Victorian family came to symbolize modernity, economic solvency and the rise and success of the nation-state."[48]

Though the specific definitions of the ideal family differed, intellectuals in the Ottoman Empire and Qajar Persia expressed their ideas about social reform in terms of gender roles and family metaphors. Debates about companionate marriage or women's education focused on the family to represent imperial, national, or racial identities.[49] India offers but one well-known instance of how women were emblematic of progress and became iconic figures of an authentically national culture during the anticolonial movement.[50] Though the examination of women's status as a narrative of social problems and attack on Hindu culture were informed by national aspirations and the constraints of British colonial rule, the controversies they generated become global events.[51] While purporting to deal with women's place in the family or the nation, these conversations reveal much about masculinity, men's desire to assert control over the family, and the place of the family within discourses of modernity.[52]

That such intellectual conversations about family and modernity crisscrossed Europe, the Middle East, and the Mediterranean should be of little surprise when Italian anarchists ran schools and theater troupes in Egypt, and Iranians and Indians worked as translators for European Orientalist scholars.[53] While they held divergent beliefs about government, civilization, and women's status, they often agreed about the centrality of the family to social reform. Deliberations over women's rights focused on their situation within the family, making the home an object of scrutiny, and domestic practices a way to compare nations, civilizations, or cultures. Framing these transformations as a global experience and not as something uniquely imposed by colonial rule contributes to decentering modernity from its relation with European experiences while incorporating the insights of subaltern studies and postcolonial theory.[54] The modern understandings of the state, and republican states in particular, erroneously envision it as entirely distinct from hereditary rule and familial models of authority, concerned only with public affairs and not the private matters of family life.

In Tunis, the position of the governing families underwent significant transformation over the course of the early modern era, from the consolidation of family authority to their marginalization from the center of power. Despite the physical separation of their suburban palace from the crowds of the capital, the Bardo family was an agent of modernization and not a passive casualty, even if efforts to organize government institutions reduced the informal role of the ruling family within the bureaucracy. In the long run, the relation between ruling families and the state proved responsive to external forces, whether local or global, often to the detriment of dynastic authority. In Japan, Persia, and the Ottoman Empire, extensive reforms were undertaken in the nineteenth century, including administrative reorganization, investments in education, and experiments with representative government. For Tunisia, such projects were initiated around the middle of the nineteenth century and continued under French rule, and so colonial modernity was less a point of rupture than a reorientation of the process.

Across the Middle East, in its urban centers and rural villages, women contributed to the financial security of their families through labor, production, inheritance, and investment. They were prominent actors in the social networks that began in the home. Far from stagnant, the attributes of domestic life shifted according to stages in the life cycle and in relation to external change. By the late nineteenth or early twentieth century, bourgeois reformers and nationalists began to view the family as contained within the home, reconceptualizing it as an apolitical, private space. While many argued that women's role in child rearing was a patriotic duty, this gendering of the private sphere had the effect of depoliticizing women's lives. The study of the family explains local responses to global processes and their impact on women's lives and gender roles. Following the ruling family in Tunis over two centuries as a study in political history offers an example of its consolidation, prominence, and later displacement and demonstrates the malleability of family structures and the transformation of its role in government.

This book situates the women at Bardo within early modern court culture and elite family history to expand the scope of studies on Tunisia beyond the nation-state framework. It places scholarship on Tunisian women within the dynamic fields of feminist theory, women and gender studies, and colonial studies. Adopting a comparative context furthers recent efforts to globalize the Ottoman Empire and understand the relation between the Middle East and Europe through more than colonial binaries, as suggested by Clancy-Smith and Khuri-Makdisi. Tunis, like Alexandria, was a Mediterranean coastal city with a cosmopolitan population that included Europeans long before foreign occupation. Throughout much of the eighteenth and nineteenth centuries, any number of Italians and French could be found at court, not to mention Ottoman Greeks, Albanians, and Moldavians. Their interactions, shifting alliances, and contributions to elite culture have often been disregarded by nationalist scholarship, with its reliance on immutable ethnic categories, whether in the Balkans, Turkey, or Arab countries.

Conceptualizing the ruling class to include those who lived and worked in the palace, as well as those who maintained social and commercial relations with the governing families, avoids binding individuals by national or racial origins and allows these identities to alternate with religious, corporate, village, or family bonds. Similarly, the complex nature of the palace households and an appreciation for all the diverse individuals who composed them demonstrates how they interacted with one another and the ease with which they adopted or adapted to local practices.

I emphasize the Ottoman context to counter two trends that dominate Tunisian history: one equating autonomy with national independence, and the other insisting on the specificity of North Africa as distinct from the Middle East. The impetus to view the province as independent of the sultan has a largely colonial genealogy. After the 1830 conquest of Algeria, French consuls, out of expedience, consistently treated the governors of Tunis as sovereigns. Though this occasionally contradicted English diplomacy in the region, the French preferred negotiating with a local governor over dealing with the sultan. The insistence upon the autonomy of the province fueled claims of the empire's weakness, implying that Istanbul was unable to control much of its territory. Colonial-era scholars similarly separated Tunis from Ottoman politics under the premise that hereditary governorship failed to correspond to the classical model of provincial governance.

Nationalist historiography in Tunisia tends to view the Ottoman period as an inconsequential or irrelevant preface to the establishment of the proto nation-state under Husayn ibn 'Ali. This includes examination of the progressive "deturkification" of the government after the seventeenth century, replaced by supposedly Tunisian elements.[55] Popular histories of Tunisia similarly circumscribe much of the Ottoman period, renaming it after the governing families in the province as "the Muradite state" and "the Husaynite state."[56] The emphasis on provincial-cum-national dynasties opposes a Tunisian identity to an alien Turkish one, blaming the latter for European colonization or underdevelopment. Privileging colonial relations, European historical trajectories, and narrow definitions of modernity, Tunisian history is defined by its lack of capitalism and as a mutation of European models, in which Tunisians themselves have little agency.[57] Such focus on the nation contributes to the denigration of Ottoman political culture, ignores the rich cultural amalgam among the elite, and obscures the depth of commercial, religious, and intellectual connections to other parts of the empire.

When studies of Tunisia go beyond nation-state borders, they often include the neighboring North African states of Algeria and Morocco under the rubric of "the Maghrib." The populations of all three contained a majority of Muslims, and were predominantly Arab, yet this demographic basis belies the specificity of the numerous Imazighen (Berber) populations in Algeria and Morocco and their struggle to claim a visible role in politics and national culture. If they were all part of a single polity in the century following the initial Arab conquest and again from around the tenth through thirteenth centuries (under the Fatimid, Zirid, and Almohad dynasties) and later colonized by the French, they did not constitute a coherent space since political borders have existed between these countries for much of the last eight hundred years. Most scholars recognize that the concept of the Middle East grew out of imperial interests and Cold War policies, but there is less scrutiny about the supposed unity and homogeneity of North Africa or the Maghrib.[58]

Though there are exceptions, edited volumes and textbooks written on Ottoman and Middle East history often concentrate on Turkey and Anatolia, Greater Syria, and Egypt, to the detriment of everything to its west.[59] Without explicating why to prioritize the rubric of the Maghrib, the focus on the shared histories of these three North African nation-states seems to concentrate on colonial experiences.[60] In addition, it is worth examining the impact of French colonial rule on other Arab countries, namely, Syria and Lebanon, not to mention French colonies in

West Africa and Southeast Asia, or neocolonial states in general. Placing Tunisia in a global context does not ignore the relevance of its North African neighbors but takes a necessary step in decentering colonial experiences from the unfolding of modernity and the defining of scholarly paradigms.

Despite a set of common Ottoman and regional references, there was certainly much about the elite of Tunis that was unique to its geographic and economic position and political culture. While it shared elements of elite culture with other Ottoman provinces, Muslim states, and European monarchs, this borrowing did not preclude the development of specifically local practices. Tunisia was unique within the Ottoman context to the extent that the sultan sanctioned hereditary government for almost two centuries under the descendants of Husayn ibn 'Ali. They maintained this privilege much longer than the Qaramanlis in Tripoli and for generations before the ascent of Muhammad 'Ali Pasha in Egypt, despite profound political and economic transformations, both local and regional. While the governors of Egypt also embarked upon a considerable reform program in the nineteenth century, Tunis was the only part of the Ottoman Empire to experiment with constitutional rule in the 1860s.

The comparative analysis of elite women's political participation illustrates that dynastic power in the early modern world was built through more than a male line of descent or titles to office. Palaces were complex domestic spaces, the site of economic activity, and the seat of political power, so that at the highest levels of state and empire, family and marriage were political. Though nation-states initially sought to exclude women from political office, reducing them to representations of national culture, family remains relevant to modern political ideologies. The ideal family serves as a model for debates over gender roles, national identity, and a range of social questions. Taking a global approach to the transformation of relations between ruling families and the state in Tunis shows the relevance of palace families to political histories, includes women and gender in narratives about male political culture, and frames modernization as a global process and one that is relevant to the Ottoman and French empires, the early modern and colonial world.

CONTENT, SOURCES, AND STRUCTURE

The book is divided into three sections that combine chronological and thematic approaches, beginning in Part I with the period from the Ottoman conquest to the early eighteenth century. The three chapters forming Part II deal with the mid-eighteenth and early nineteenth centuries, and the final section covers the reform era of the mid- to late nineteenth century and the beginning of colonial rule. Each chapter engages different themes that locate family politics at the forefront of a comparative history of court cultures, in their deployment of marriage alliances, the practice of gender segregation, elite women's political participation, paternalist practices of government, and the invented traditions of colonial rule.

The earlier chapters illustrate how the family established itself within the province through a set of common early modern elite practices. Part III traces intellectual deliberations about government and women's contribution to family status that accompanied the process of modernization. Instead of viewing the period as merely a precursor to colonial occupation and the nation-state as emphasized in precolonial or nationalist histories, this narrative moves away from images of stagnation and dependency to insist upon dynamism. Finally, framing the transformations to the palace in Tunis as typical of early modern courts helps locate modernity as a global process.

Chapter 1 (with the Introduction, forming Part I) examines the common dynastic strategy of marriage alliances and more specifically their role in the expansion and consolidation of Ottoman power. These approaches were adopted by provincial elite in the empire's urban centers, such as Aleppo and Cairo, leading to the integration of Ottoman administrators and local notables. In Tunis as well, family connections and marriage alliances were central to the establishment of authority and its extension beyond the capital, creating political continuity between the two major ruling houses of the Ottoman period. Beginning with the Ottoman-Habsburg rivalry in the western Mediterranean and the Ottoman conquest of Tunisia in the sixteenth century, the chapter provides a cursory overview of the first century and a half of Ottoman rule, positing that the familial is political. By focusing on marriage as an element of state building in which the entire family participated, the chapter lays the groundwork for recognizing how women acted through the family in the development and consolidation of political authority. Finally, it considers how a contest over succession (a common source of dynastic strife) led to the mobilization of household networks. A number of insights on family relations are provided by the prominent eighteenth-century Tunisian chronicler Muhammad Saghir ibn Yusuf (1691–1771), in a work that so smoothly integrates family, marriage, government, and the major events of the era as to show the futility of separating family from politics.[61]

Part II of the book (Chapters 2–4) explores the nature of family rule and women's contribution to social status, economic activities, and public welfare. Concentrating on the family who governed Tunis during this period, Chapter 2 describes basic household structures, the diversity of palace personnel, and the organizational role of the household to portray the overlap between domestic and administrative functions. Offering a microhistory of food and diet, a material culture of life within the palace, I rely on a corpus of approximately sixty registers of palace treasury expenses compiled annually between 1755 and 1843. These volumes offer an inside perspective on the functioning of royal households and are an important source for re-creating the daily lives of the palace's inhabitants.[62] These records are supplemented by the bey's personal spending accounts covering much of the nineteenth century and about thirty account books dealing with categories of expenses such as troops, uniforms, provisioning of guests at the palace, and inventories of food and jewelry. Food played a prominent role in early modern social life, when royalty from Persia to England distinguished themselves from commoners through sumptuous feasts or the construction of elaborate sugar sculptures and wedding cakes. This chapter uses food and diet to suggest similarities between the governing families of Tunis, local elites, and other Ottoman urbanites in Istanbul and Damascus.

Chapter 3 presents gender segregation as a key organizational principle of palace architecture and a sign of power common in Qing China, Mughal India, and Safavid Persia. In each case, far from marginalizing women, the spatial configuration of the palace gave astute and determined mothers, wives, and concubines the opportunity to influence dynastic history. Certain women such as sultan Suleiman's wife Hurrem, the Qing empress dowager Cixi, or Marie-Antoinette of France attained enough power to become the targets of the political opposition. Women in Tunis also contributed to palace factions and occasional rivalries; these political and diplomatic activities are discussed in relation to the hierarchies of harem life and women's daily routines. The chapter suggests preliminary conclusions about the similarities and differences between women's lives and family structures within the palace and in the province of Tunis, showing their relevance to women's history more generally.

While ceremony, display, and conspicuous consumption featured prominently among early modern court protocols, wealth was also utilized towards charitable ends. In the Ottoman case, spending not only meant privileged access to luxury goods and competitive gardening but also represented the renovation of urban landscapes through the construction of elaborate public facilities and pious endowments. In Aleppo or Cairo, elite Muslim women utilized their wealth philanthropically and contributed to the status and prestige of their families. Chapter 4 continues the discussion of palace expenditures to illustrate how networks of distribution were used to create patronage, provide public services, and allow the ruling family in Tunis to interact with the local population to alleviate poverty and perform the Islamic duty of charity. The chapter combines the palace financial records with those of the tax-collecting expeditions and endowment records from the national archives and the ministry of state domains. It portrays how family events such as weddings and circumcisions were opportunities for hosting banquets, passing out money and gifts, and building upon patriarchal models of masculine financial responsibility through these acts of benevolence.

The two chapters of Part III concentrate on the nineteenth century by considering the political implications of European colonialism, intellectual exchange, and increased travel in and around the Mediterranean. Improvements in transportation and communication coincided with the Ottoman reform program (the Tanzimat), the Arab cultural renaissance (or *nahda*), constitutional rule, and colonial occupation, all of which transformed the position of the family as the state modernized. Chapter 5 examines how the shifting balance of global power placed new restraints on the governors of Tunis, their families, and the familial nature of rule. The Ottoman reform era, the Arab intellectual renaissance, and the experiment with constitutional government in 1861 progressively altered the relation between family and government in Tunis. As bureaucrats and intellectuals reconceptualized the nature of government and the responsibilities of the sovereign, they defined legitimacy in terms of reason or merit. Particularly through the modernization of the financial administration, these ministers sought to respect the family position in government while ensuring that the state was less invested in competitive displays of wealth. In the process, they transformed spending from an asset of governance into a sign of individualism that threatened communal security.

Over the second half of the nineteenth century, accounting practices underwent a series of revisions, particularly visible in the extant financial records. Chapter 5 utilizes a dozen registers from the Tunisian archives covering two- to five-year periods from 1840 to 1860 and materials about the constitution and lists of stipends. Though members of the foreign diplomatic community could claim only varying degrees of local knowledge, Chapters 5 and 6 incorporate archives of the French foreign ministry (in Nantes and Manuba) to illustrate French policy in the province from the conquest of Algeria in 1830 through the first decades of colonial rule in the 1880s and 1890s.

Chapter 6 is situated in the first decades of French rule in Tunisia (1881–1956), which coincided with a resurgence in European imperial competition. While the republican government distanced itself from the spectacles of consumption that stigmatized its monarchical predecessors, it created new venues for the dramatization of state power epitomized by the Universal Exposition of 1889. An elaborate festival hosted in Paris by the ministries of commerce, industry, and the colonies, the fair celebrated science, technology, and consumption while formulating a popular racism based on a hierarchical ordering of peoples. Depicting the French empire in familial terms as an expression of paternal concern for colonial children justified colonial domination and reconciled the seeming contradictions between republicanism and imperialism. Since Tunisia was the first major colony of France's Third Republic (1871–1940), this chapter suggests how practices elaborated in Tunisia, such as the reliance on hereditary government and the creation of royal traditions, served as templates for patriarchal rule in French Morocco (1912–1956) and Syria and Lebanon (1920–1946). While the exposition underscores how material means continued to represent state power and the centrality of colonialism to modern national identities, it demonstrates that the disentangling of family from political life was a complex process on both sides of the colonial divide.

In the critique of France's role in colonial Tunisia, I build on French colonial history and the notion of republican imperialism as well as the history of women, gender, and the family in French political life in the nineteenth century. Family ideals were the topic of Orientalist justifications for colonialism and the site of modern reform projects, yet empire itself was based on patriarchy. Hardly a remnant of early modern governance, in the French case, the civilizing project continued to be a central part of French national identity until 1962. The accumulation of colonial territories contained elements of competitive consumption and display, reminiscent of the material basis of monarchies, and both the French and the British invested in ceremony as they invented traditions in the colonies. The triumph of a bourgeois republic was thus facilitated by exporting patriarchal (and arguably aristocratic) models of government to the colonies to reveal the integral role of colonialism in creating modernity and the continued importance of familial politics for the modern state. This chapter teases out the contradictions between the imposition of patriarchal norms of colonial subjectivity and French efforts to perpetuate the gendering of space to exclude women and the family from politics. While gendered critiques of consumption were deployed to indicate the inadequacy of local government, the French perpetuated the ceremonial role of the bey while limiting his access to state resources. These financial constraints further reduced the bey's authority even within the palace.

The combination of archival records, financial registers, diplomatic correspondence, and narrative sources attempts to counter the limitations posed by each set of documents. As account books, the palace expense registers contain certain lacunae; to begin with, it is not possible to ascertain whether they represent intentions or actions or a combination of the two. When total costs are recorded, prices per unit are often missing, as are the amounts purchased. They include ingredients for baking but not complete recipes; they indicate the costs of clothing while revealing nothing on style or design, and they suggest who received money but not what they subsequently did with their cash. In short, while these detail the material and structural contours of palace life and the organization of the government, they reveal much less about the meanings people attributed to them. I supplement these with the writings of Tunisian historians such as ibn Yusuf for the eighteenth century and Ahmed ibn Dhiaf for the nineteenth century. Both men had connections to the palace and the ruling families that provided intimate knowledge of political affairs, forming valuable but partisan accounts.

European (and occasionally American) tourists, merchants, and diplomats visited Tunisia as early as the seventeenth century. These later included adventure seekers, amateur scientists, and botanists, whose tantalizing accounts were intended to encourage European colonialism. The resident foreign community did not reach any size until the nineteenth century, when its major components were Italians and Maltese. Though they tended to recycle anecdotes that were sensationalized as a marketing strategy, they provide detailed observations that supplement information from other sources. The earliest texts are the brief report by Anselme Adorne (1470) and the edited memoirs of the merchant Nicolas Béranger (1684–1706). For the eighteenth century, the major sources are the French botanists Jean-André Peyssonel (in Tunisia in 1724–1725) and René Louiche Desfontaines (1783–1786); the British amateur Orientalist Thomas Shaw (1727); and the consul of Holland, Antoine Nyssen (1788). Later publications include those of bureaucrats such as the American consuls Mordecai Noah (1815) and Amos Perry (1869); a consul of Sardinia named Filippi (1825–1830); the French colonial official E. Pellissier (1853);

and those serving in semiofficial capacities such as the French doctor Louis Frank (1816) and the Piedmontese military instructor Louis Calligaris (1834). Finally, there was an increasing number of leisure travelers such as Charles-Marie de la Condamine (1731); the Scot Thomas MacGill (1808); the British Grenville Temple (1835); the Prussian prince Hermann von Pückler-Muskau (1837); the Irish captain John Clark Kennedy (1845); the Protestant missionary Nathan Davis (1846–1850); the Swiss founder of the Red Cross, Henry Dunant (1857); the Austrian Ernst von Hesse-Wartegg (1882); and the French Charles Lallemand (1889), though there were certainly many others who visited the province.

Throughout the book, readers will encounter a succession of beys, their spouses and children, prominent ministers, and slaves, through various angles of their lives: what they ate, how they dressed, how they presented themselves to the inhabitants of the province or to European diplomats and travelers. A step towards completing a more comprehensive social history of Ottoman Tunisia with emphasis on women and family perhaps raises more questions than one book can address. While it begins to explore provincial elite culture more broadly, palace practices were hardly representative of common family structures, household organization, or culinary practices. The documentary sources used offer but a few insights on the emotional meaning of family, and certainly much more could be said about relations between siblings, spouses, parents, and children. It is hoped that future research will continue to probe questions related to women's experiences both within the palace and beyond, including archeological and visual sources, women's writings, and shari'a court records, to further address the complexity of the family and women's lives.

While concentrating on the ruling family of Tunis, this story locates them in the midst of political and economic changes in the Ottoman Empire and around the Mediterranean, transnational intellectual currents, and migratory movements that lead to and included the onset of European colonial rule in the Middle East and geostrategic shifts that brought Tunisia to the foreground of imperial projects. These transformations altered the meaning of wealth, the ways in which it was utilized, and the ability of the beys and their families to support a paternal and redistributive government. While the details are particular to Tunisia and comparable to other places in the Middle East, the story of the palace women and the political importance of the family is part of European histories, the colonial experience, and the global processes of modernity.

Chapter 1

FAMILY AND THE
POLITICS OF MARRIAGE

This month [October 1702] there were so many marriages
between the courtesans of the bey and the wives and daughters of
the deceased Muhammad Bey that it would be tedious to enumer-
ate them all. I want only to note that of Husayn ibn 'Ali, the bey's
deputy [kahia] with the wife of Ramadan Bey, who was the daugh-
ter of Murad.

NICOLAS BÉRANGER, *LA RÉGENCE DE TUNIS À LA FIN DU XVIIE*
SIÈCLE; MÉMOIRE POUR SERVIR À L'HISTOIRE DE TUNIS DEPUIS
L'ANNÉE 1684

By 1650, the household had become an important feature of Ottoman politics and a key institution in the training and recruitment of bureaucratic personnel. Instruction and patronage within the households of ministers rivaled earlier practices centered in the palace such as military training and *devşirme* (slave recruitment) as they accommodated the increasing specialization of imperial administration.[1] A corresponding process took place on the provincial level that allowed for greater participation of local notables in provincial administration often dominated by a few families and their extended networks. Across the empire in the provinces of Cairo, Damascus, Mosul, Nablus, and Mount Lebanon, influential families received imperial support for their political roles.[2] Their households included blood relatives, mamluks, concubines, servants, employees, and other retainers, incorporating various forms of economic, military, and social clientage that were crucial to social mobility so that the composition of the ruling elite was heterogeneous.

The rise of household politics within Ottoman provincial administration coincided with the period following the conquest of Tunis in 1574, becoming a feature of its government at least until French occupation in 1881. While the Ottoman conquest secured the position of its military by establishing roughly fifteen garrisons in the capital and countryside, it did not guarantee suzerainty over the population. Thus, the extension of imperial rule relied on patronage networks grounded in the household and supplemented by marriage to build connections between families, legitimize government authority, and create political continuity. Over the course of the first century of Ottoman rule, this would allow the governing family to establish ties with the military elite, religious scholars, tribal notables from the capital, and major provincial cities and occasionally to extend their circles to the political class in neighboring Algeria and Tripoli.

The beginning of family hegemony can be traced to Murad Bey (r. 1613–1631), one the most successful governors of the early Ottoman era, though quarrels amongst his descendants towards the end of the seventeenth century weakened their claim to authority. This political infighting directly contributed to the rise of Husayn ibn ʿAli (r. 1705–1735), who stabilized the hereditary nature of the governorship. While traditional narratives often view the reign of ibn ʿAli as constituting a break from a period when imperial interests were prevalent, and inaugurating one marked by local autonomy, this traditional narrative obscures the numerous continuities between the two men as reflected by the persons in their households. In fact, while the centrality of household networks to political affairs became particularly evident during the periods of heightened political conflict from 1675 to 1702, and between 1728 and 1756, when followers were armed and transformed into opposing armies, the networks were also paramount during periods of calm and stability. During both clashes, violence stemmed from succession disputes within the family, even if the 1728–1756 dynastic infighting spiraled into the major political event of the early eighteenth century involving Ottoman governors in Algiers and their soldiers, as well as much of the population in the northwest and around Qayrawan. While these conflicts can be told as a story of military confrontation, political intrigue, and economic calculations, incorporating the mobilization of household networks into the picture underscores the proximity between family and politics.

This chapter begins with an elaboration of the structures of Ottoman provincial government in Tunis and the significance of the household in the seventeenth century, before turning to the role of marriage alliances as a dynastic and imperial strategy and its application in Tunis. It then reframes the civil war through the metaphor of divorce to expand the analytical focus of early eighteenth-century politics to the household, suggest common patterns between Tunis and other Ottoman provinces, delineate the social and political prominence of the family, and demonstrate how political traditions were inherited through women.

Why a similar pattern of local autonomy and hereditary governing developed in Tunis relates to the broader geopolitical context of the sixteenth and early seventeenth century. By the sixteenth century, the Hafsid dynasty that had ruled parts of northern Africa from Tunis since 1229 was considerably weakened by internal disputes and economic problems. The region briefly became the site of competition between the Ottoman Empire and the Spanish Habsburgs, both acting through the intermediary of local proxies. A number of these strongmen owed their power to success in corsairing in the western Mediterranean where the business of captives was lucrative. The activities of the merchant marines flourished in coastal regions and were supported by Tunis, Algiers, Tripoli, the Italian city-states, and even Atlantic powers such as the Dutch and the English. Corsairing was officially sanctioned by the English, which blurred the line between privateering and plunder, and overlapped with the trans-Atlantic slave trade as captives were sold at slave markets in Spain, France, and across the Italian peninsula. The exchange of captives was a routine part of diplomacy between the Ottoman Empire and powers on the African coast and with Europe.[3] In northern Africa, some captives were ransomed to the church, and a number of others (derogatorily referred to as renegades) converted to Islam, made careers for themselves at sea, and utilized their wealth and military acumen to make bids for power.[4]

Khayr al-Din, an enterprising privateer with a base in Algiers, offered gifts to the sultan requesting Ottoman recognition to sanction his political claim over the city. Ottoman forces had recently defeated the Mamluk Sultanate based in Cairo and were engaged in disputes over the provinces of Baghdad and Basra with the Safavids. The alliance with Khayr al-Din contributed to strengthening the Mediterranean fleet and offered strategic outposts from which to attack the merchant marines of its European foes.[5] Thus, Selim I (1512–1520) granted Khayr al-Din the Ottoman rank of *beylerbeyi* (corresponding to a provincial governor, or a governor-general, though not all *beylerbeyi* held an equivalent rank), and Khayr al-Din subsequently extended his dominions to Tunis, where he ruled from 1529 to 1534. After briefly returning to nominal Hafsid rule (supported by the Spanish king), Tunis was reconquered between 1569 and 1572 by a second corsair named 'Ilij 'Ali, who had Ottoman backing. Finally, in 1574 Sultan Selim II (1566–1574) sent troops under the command of his Grand Vizir Sinan Pasha, seconded by 'Ilij 'Ali and further supported by soldiers from Qayrawan and Tripoli, securing its conquest.[6] More than a local power struggle, these events stemmed from broader imperial competition and were viewed by contemporary and later scholars as preserving the Muslim character of the region from the threat of Spanish Christianity.[7]

Though the Ottomans were intent on stalling Spanish expansion and protecting trade, the center of imperial attention soon shifted towards Europe, which was a rational consideration, given the costs and material constraints of early modern warfare. Since the majority of military activities consisted of border skirmishes and not imperial campaigns, Tunis receded in terms of priority after 1574.[8] Immediate suzerainty over the three western provinces of Algiers, Tunis, and Tripoli was delegated to 'Ilij 'Ali with the rank of *kapudan pasha* (*qubtan pasha* in Arabic), or commander of the Ottoman fleet. He was senior to the governors of Tunis and Tripoli and served as the intermediary between the provinces and Istanbul. In Tunis, a pasha was appointed by the sultan for one-year terms to govern with the assistance of a council of military officers and civilian notables known as the *diwan*. By the late sixteenth century, the sultan granted special status to Tunis as *eyalat-i mumtaze*, or privileged province.[9] Among other particularities, this meant that local troops selected their own officers and the province organized its own fleet. This arrangement recognized and built upon the strength of the North African corsairs whose marines contributed to imperial campaigns, disrupted trade, took captives, or attacked the ships of Ottoman rivals. For instance, the Tunisian fleet participated in a joint expedition with the Algerian forces against Venice in the early seventeenth century and participated in the Ottoman war against Crete in the 1640s.[10] In exchange, they were exempted from paying annual tributes. While the three provinces were expected to adhere to the contours of imperial agreements with foreign powers, the governors could sign separate treaties. For instance, the pasha and the *diwan* of Tunis signed treaties with France, Holland, and England in the seventeenth century that corresponded to the Capitulations agreements between these states and the sultan. This established the formal structures of autonomy from the imperial center, which coexisted with the expectation of allegiance and military support.

Only a small portion of the troops sent from Istanbul in 1574 were imperial janissaries (the salaried/professional military corps). Instead, the majority were *sekban*, or irregular troops composed of Muslims from Anatolia employed specifically for the period of the campaign.[11] The prevalence of irregular troops was in stark contrast to the situation in Algiers, where there was a larger proportion of imperial janissaries and frequent recruitment from Istanbul. This concentration of forces was concomitant with its status as the empire's western frontier. The ruling class in Algeria intentionally distinguished members of the military from the local population by discouraging marriage with the local population and excluding the latter's descendants from inheriting the military positions of their fathers.[12] In Tunis, not only were janissaries less influential than in Algiers, but marriages with local families were encouraged or tacitly accepted by the *diwan*, and their sons were salaried soldiers.

The irregular troops also came to play a more prominent role in government by the turn of the seventeenth century. Organized into units of one hundred men under a grade of officer known as a *dey* (from the Turkish for "maternal uncle"), they protested in 1591 against their subordination to janissary officers. As a result, they succeeded in earning recognition for one of the approximately thirty deys to be elected to the *diwan*. Thus, the differing composition of the two militaries constituted the basis of structural differences in provincial organization between Tunis and Algiers. The greater military presence, and the janissaries in particular, in Algiers, which served as the base for the *qubtan pasha*, also explains the tendency of Algiers-based officials to intervene in the affairs of Tunis. These officials in the capital supplemented the administration of the interior that was run by local notables in place since the Hafsid era.[13]

In practice, political authority was dependent on individual initiative and popular support, which was maintained through household networks. Though the pasha held the highest rank, minor officials with the titles of bey and dey dominated the political scene for much of the seventeenth century. At this time, the bey was a military commander assigned to new territories in the empire with fiscal and administrative responsibilities. In Tunis, the bey was responsible for leading the *mahalla*, the biannual tax-collecting missions in the interior (a practice that dated to the Hafsid era, if not earlier). The first figure of note was ʿUthman Dey (1598–1610), who was closely allied with the troops and civilian authorities, becoming a prominent government official who maintained a household of some fifty dependents and followers.[14] He was succeeded by Yusuf Dey (1610–1635), an officer in the military whose loyalty to ʿUthman Dey was compensated by marriage to his patron's daughter, cementing his designation as heir. The smooth transition of power provided continuity that led to greater political stability. Though the position of dey declined in importance because of consistent bickering amongst the deys for supremacy, ʿUthman Dey's household maintained enough clout over the next century that his female descendants often married men in the ruling class.

Subsequently, economic and political power was consolidated in the hands of the bey, particularly under Ramadan Bey (c. 1613). A soldier sent from Istanbul who contributed to consolidating central authority over the interior, he held the title of bey until his death around 1613.[15] Murad, a renegade who was part of the household of Ramadan Bey, used this position to gain loyalty of troops, pacify the countryside, and accumulate enough wealth to own slaves. He eventually married the daughter of his patron, and in 1631 he bought recognition from the sultan to award him the rank of pasha. In fact, Moalla suggests that the sultan viewed the bey as akin to the loyal palace mamluks and preferred relying on his authority to that of the unpredictable dey, whose military power base was reminiscent of the janissaries.[16] With enough income to pay the military, and enjoying official support from Istanbul, Murad was primarily responsible for elevating the position of bey to the principal authority in the province. His descendants were able to maintain this political role for the next three generations—his son Hammuda (1631–1666); grandson Murad (1666–1675); and two of his great-grandsons, 'Ali (1675–1686) and Muhammad (1686–1696)—before escalating disputes within the family led to their loss of power. Their monopoly on government is referred to as the Muradite dynasty. The first period of political stability following the establishment of Ottoman rule was attained through seamless transitions of authority between 'Uthman Dey and his son-in-law Yusuf Dey, and between Ramadan Bey and his son-in-law Murad, so that household alliances confirmed political power.

PROVINCIAL STRUCTURES IN THE SEVENTEENTH CENTURY

Despite the provisional autonomy, numerous features of provincial government bore a close resemblance to Ottoman models. For instance, the structure of the military was a condensed version of that in Istanbul in terms of the organization of soldiers into distinct divisions, titles, responsibilities, and hierarchy of its officers.[17] Much the same can be said of the administration, the treasury, the rates of taxation, and the fiscal system in general, which "conformed to the same principles and practices as in the rest of the Empire."[18] The fiscal system was marked by a dual approach, whereby a large gold coin—in Tunis, called a *sultani* or *mahbub*—was used to facilitate long-distance trade. The largest coin in circulation in Tunis was the piaster, which was minted in the province but bore the name of the sultan. There was a mint within the palace where smaller denominations were also produced, though imperial prerogatives did not extend to silver or copper coins.[19] These coins were used in situations that evoked the broader Ottoman context such as the payment of soldiers and as gifts to imperial officials visiting the province.[20]

Though titles did not determine the arrangement of power, they were used to secure, bolster, and confirm such authority as approved by the sultan. In the earlier period of Ottoman rule, a number of beys requested the title of pasha from the sultan by sending gifts; this was the case with Khayr al-Din, Murad, and two of his descendants. It was also current practice in Algeria to purchase official titles, as demonstrated by Salah Bey of Constantine (1771-1792), who became one of the most influential governors of the city.[21] By the eighteenth century, it was standard for each bey to formally petition the sultan for his title, which was confirmed by an imperial decree (or *firman*) of investiture and a *qaftan* (or cloak). Both items maintained political relevance and were utilized by ʿAli Bey in 1777 to confirm his choice of successor when he requested that the sultan confer them on his son Hammuda (1777-1814). Once Hammuda formally received the title pasha, ʿAli Bey took an early retirement.[22] The imperial *firman* and *qaftan* were delivered by the *qubtan pasha*, or one of his envoys (the *shawash*), in a symbolic manifestation of Ottoman ties. They were presented in a military ceremony attended by the *diwan*, and each member present received money.

The province was required "to offer gifts to the Sublime Porte when a new sultan took the throne of the empire, to demonstrate and proclaim obedience to him, and similarly, on the accession of a pasha in Tunis, when his reign was secured, and he had received the accord of the people, he is to send gifts to the state and request a *firman* and the blessed sash, to make clear his announcement [of obedience]."[23] These gifts required extensive preparation, as they were sent by the boatload and were destined not only to the sultan but to various members of the imperial household, including the sultan's mother, sisters, and principal counselors. They included jewels, decorated swords, tissues and embroidery, and articles of local manufacture such as perfume, and on one occasion, the bey sent 257 dozen *shashia* to Istanbul.[24] While ties to Istanbul were often symbolic, the frequent preparation of gifts gave them an additional materiality that recognized the political relevance of the sultan's household.

In dealing with Istanbul, the bey combined official petitions of recognition with requests for the sultan's approval of diplomatic or military actions and commercial matters in the capital. The regularity of such exchanges fluctuated in relation to regional and international politics and the whims of particular governors. High-ranking officials and confidants were sent to the sultan's court, returning with a *firman*, troops, or slaves. There was a consistent flow of messengers from Istanbul bearing official news and orders on average of once every two to three years. The majority of correspondence with the central government was carried out through senior palace officials such as the *kapiji pasha* (Arabized as *qabiji*). The *kapiji*s were janissaries who guarded the main gate to the sultan's palace and were also sent to deliver the sultan's orders to provincial governors. In addition to recognizing the bey as governor, or confirming his investiture, they announced the accession of a new sultan and brought news of the birth of children to the sultan (an occasion when cannons were sounded); orders regarding trade, taxation, and foreign policy; and the imperial *firman* confirming the nomination of the bey. When the *kapiji*s and *qubtan pasha* stayed in the capital, the bey provided extensive provisions throughout their sojourn, including stocking their ships with grains, oil, spices, livestock, and hundreds or thousands of loaves of bread, for the return voyage.[25]

From 1756 to 1807, the governors of Tunis paid tribute to their superiors in Algiers as well, making regular offerings of olive oil, gunpowder, and hundreds of *shashia*.[26] On occasion, the dey of Algiers sought to claim the privilege of presenting imperial orders to the governors of Tunis in deference to their status as intermediaries with the sultan, hoping to intervene in matters of succession, promote their clients, and distribute the official *qaftan* of investiture on behalf of the sultan. At different times, officials in Tunis similarly interfered with the selection of governors in Tripoli; sought alliances with powerful patrons in Istanbul against aggressive Algerian governors; and took refuge in Algiers, expanding local conflicts into the neighboring province. This bickering reached the point that the sultan instructed the provinces to achieve peace with each other.[27]

There were significant shifts in power during the first century and a half of Ottoman rule, the first of which altered the chain of command among the troops and allowed their officers to establish political authority. Almost at the same time, the minor imperial denomination of "bey" was transformed from something akin to a district governor, to a military commander responsible for collecting taxes, and finally to the supreme authority within the province often operating in the name of the sultan as pasha. The sultan sanctioned this order and sent regular envoys; the beys consistently provided gifts in return, requested the renewal of their position, and followed the parameters of imperial foreign policy. Prominent figures in the government owed their authority to a variety of factors, including the allegiance of the military, imperial recognition, and the support or quiescence of Algiers. Seemingly disparate constituencies, household networks served to create ties between the military and the civilian political elite, between the capital and the hinterland, demonstrating that family was one element of political power.

MARRIAGE ALLIANCES AND POLITICAL TRANSITION: IMPERIAL PRECEDENT AND LOCAL PATTERNS

From the first generations of Ottoman rulers, marriage and reproduction were treated as matters of political significance. In the fourteenth and fifteenth centuries, they relied on interdynastic marriages with the daughters of regional potentates (both Christian and Muslim) to establish their authority in Anatolia and incorporate smaller polities as they expanded territorially.[28] The political significance of interdynastic marriages was evident by the absence of offspring and lack of a reproductive function. This stemmed from the concern that their political advantages would be offset by intrigue if the resulting children were coopted by ambitious in-laws to act against the ruling family. Once the Ottomans had secured their status, exogamy was more of a liability than an asset, especially when neighboring rulers were no longer seen as their peers. Instead, female slave concubines fulfilled the dynasty's reproductive needs, while the marriages between royal women and the slave elite wrapped the government's inner circle more tightly together.[29] These various approaches to selecting spouses reflect the initial Ottoman ascension above the Anatolian ruling class, the consolidation of the household during the initial phase of imperial expansion, and the reliance on the loyalty of the slave elite.

In a number of early modern empires, the intersection of family and government meant that marriage formed a component of dynastic policy. China's Qing emperors, who were culturally and ethnically distinct from much of their subject population, married Manchu and Mongol notables to secure elite support and incorporated them into their multiethnic empire, though marriages between cousins were common. This pattern helped accord women a greater political role, as did alliances between senior women and their in-laws, while imperial daughters were considered an integral part of the natal family, who brought the husbands into the palace instead of having the daughters leave after marriage.[30] India's Mughal dynasts also relied on marriage to cement political alliances, especially as they transformed themselves from peripatetic to sedentary sovereigns.[31] In Europe as well, marriages between courts constituted a habitual feature of foreign relations. France's Bourbon monarchs practiced a form of royal endogamy, marrying exclusively with other European noble lineages in conjunction with political alliances, for instance, with Spain in the late sixteenth and early seventeenth century.

Even without a royal pedigree, provincial governors utilized marriage as a central institution for building household networks and creating ties to local notables. Marriage alliances confirmed the authority of Yusuf Dey and Murad Bey and established a clear line of succession. In the case of Murad Bey, who extended his authority over much of the province, he built further connections through a number of strategic collaborations with prominent families. Hammuda married the daughter of a local chief, ʿAli al-Hannashi, and also the daughter of an important renegade.[32] Though Murad was a Corsican, a slave, and a convert to Islam, his upbringing in the house of Ramadan Bey, his marriage to the latter's daughter, and his ties with prominent government families firmly incorporated him into the household networks of the provincial elite.

Marriages with distinguished families continued under his descendants: Hammuda Pasha married his sons to the daughter of a pasha, the daughter of one of the deys, and the granddaughter of ʿUthman Dey. Murad ibn Hammuda's son Ahmad married the daughter of ʿUthman Dey, the pasha of Tripoli—indicating that the family considered itself the social equals of the governing class in other provinces as they expanded their networks beyond the immediate vicinity.[33] While the bey consolidated his rule, he often attempted to influence the selection of the dey to earn his gratitude or subservience. Thus, in the second half of the seventeenth century, there were also marriage alliances between the family of the bey and men who served as dey. For instance, Hammuda ibn Murad suggested Mustafa Laz as dey and then offered him a slave to marry, a common gesture of patronage and affinity.[34] Hajj Hammuda Usta Murad, a notable in the capital and descendant of a man who served as dey from 1637 to 1640, was married to the sister of Fatma bint ʿUthman Dey (Husayn ibn ʿAli's wife).[35] These alliances between households and among the ruling elite facilitated the consolidation of political power amongst a few families and their connection to the ruling elite of neighboring provinces.

Trouble within the family led to their downfall but not to their extinction. In the 1680s and 1690s, disagreements over succession between potential heirs (ʿAli and Muhammad, sons of Murad ibn Hammuda Bey) contributed to a period of political instability. They alternated in taking refuge in Algiers, where recourse to support from its military encouraged its deys to become involved in the affairs of Tunis and attempt to place their own clients in power. The ensuing violence inflicted by various members of the family upon each other and continuing military confrontation involving both Algiers and Tripoli led the sultan to intervene by dispatching a military commander to the province, Ibrahim al-Sharif. Hoping to stave off prolonged warfare, Sharif killed the bey's male relations and most of his military entourage, assuming power in May 1702.[36] The sultan confirmed his position shortly thereafter and granted him the title of pasha.[37] While Sharif's political career was short-lived (he was taken prisoner in Algiers in 1705 and executed returning to Tunis later that year), he too attempted to establish authority by building alliances with the principal households in the province. He spared the women in the Muradite family, marrying the widow of the last Muradite in power, Mabruka, the daughter of a shaykh from western Tunisia, who had been married to the two previous beys.[38]

Ibn ʿAli's rise to preeminence was similarly dependent on connections with the Muradite family and its networks. These were initiated by his father, ʿAli al-Turki, a mamluk from the island of Crete, who became a military commander in Tunis. Most sources concur that he was married at least twice, once to a woman from the Arab tribe of the Shenifa in the west near the Algerian border and then to a woman named Hafsia from the Sharin, a Berber tribe near Qayrawan. Political support from the former was important since the Shenifa often avoided central authority by migrating between the provinces of Tunis and Algeria. Moalla goes so far as to speculate that each tribal constituency was affiliated with the extended networks of different potential successors in the Muradite family and were on opposing sides in the struggle for power. As a janissary with political aspirations, ʿAli al-Turki strategically placed members of his family in both camps, hoping to emerge from their conflicts unscathed.[39]

As he established his military career, ibn ʿAli relied upon two strategic unions that strengthened his household networks.[40] He married his cousin Fatma Ghazalia of the Sharin, cementing ties to his mother's side of the family and increasing his standing with the Sharin and their tribal affiliates. The daughter of the Shaykh Muhammad al-Ghazali, she came from a wealthy family and owned extensive residential and commercial properties.[41] He drew close enough to his wife's family and his maternal relatives that he entrusted his uncle to lead a military contingent on his behalf against a potential challenger. At the same time, he married Fatma bint ʿUthman Dey, who was the widow of one of the Muradite contenders. She was a descendant of the former dey and part of the Muradite inner circle, and so their union positioned Husayn ibn ʿAli as the legitimate successor to the previous governing dynasty. In addition, he inherited at least one mamluk from the deceased governors, another confirmation of his place as heir that reconfirmed ties between ibn 'Ali and the Muradites. A French merchant who spent about twenty years in Tunis recorded that following the assassination of the Muradite men in 1702, their wives and daughters married other members of the extensive family entourage, of which ibn 'Ali was the most memorable example.[42] Ibn 'Ali supplemented connections to the established political class with a firm grounding in the province via tribal populations so that his marriages expanded his basis of support beyond the military.

After he secured the position of bey in 1705, ibn 'Ali continued to develop family networks. For instance, he initiated the union between his nephew 'Ali (1735-1756), his brother Muhammad's son, and Kebira Mamia.[43] Kebira was the granddaughter of Mahmud ibn Mami, a well-known legal scholar from the region of Beja and the daughter of Muhammad ibn Mami, also a respected scholar, jurisconsult, and poet. Mahmud ibn Mami's daughter Fatma was also the wife of the Imam Yusuf Burteghiz, who was ibn 'Ali's most respected advisor (as was his son) and intimate friend. This served to reaffirm his reliance on Burteghiz, who was his confidant. Burteghiz may have initiated the union, as he was known to have been very close with his wife, and their respective marriages with Mami women brought the two men even closer together.[44]

Ibn 'Ali's children were critical in the formation of household networks. He had at least three daughters who survived beyond childhood, though the exact number is difficult to ascertain since sources do not consistently refer to them by name. These three were Hafsia (b. 1702), Fatma (1713-1793), and Khadija (d. 1757), each of whom married important men from within the family entourage and among the governing elite.[45] One of these daughters married the mamluk Suleiman Kahia, a man who ibn 'Ali had inherited from the entourage of Muhammad ibn Murad Bey. He was freed, left Tunis to undertake the pilgrimage, and then reintegrated into government service as the *kahia dar al-pasha*, the head deputy responsible for paying the troops. He was a close confidant of ibn 'Ali, and he worked as a messenger and informer.[46]

Fatma married the mamluk Ahmad Shelebi, a loyal retainer who was responsible for the education of ibn 'Ali's children and later served his son Muhammad al-Rashid (1759-1759). Following his death around 1728, the widowed Fatma married the prominent mamluk Rejeb Khaznadar, who was particularly close with her brothers.[47] He accompanied the family during its exile in Algeria, became treasurer, and commanded the tax-collecting missions. When he died in the early 1790s, he was buried in the family mausoleum of Sidi Qasem al-Sbabti.[48] In 1714, Hafsia married her cousin ʿAli, her father's close confidant who held important political and military positions. At the time, ʿAli was poised as heir since the bey's three sons were still quite young and political succession was not limited to direct descent. Though it may have been rare for elite women to be part of polygamous households, the fact that ʿAli did not divorce his first wife reinforces the political exigency of their union. These marriages wove the web around the political elite and the family even tighter.

Though not much is known about the bey's wives and the married lives of the daughters, it is plausible that they were engaged in politics alongside their husbands and contributed to the business of matchmaking. While marriages were influenced by family considerations, they were not without emotion and attachment. Women counseled their husbands offering valued advice, as ʿAli Pasha followed Kebira Mamia's suggestions of who to place in influential positions. When ibn ʿAli did not have any sons, it was his wife Fatma bint ʿUthman who proposed that he take a concubine to ensure the birth of a male heir. In at least one rendition, she personally selected a Genoese slave known as Jannat from the harem, dressed her, and brought her to the bey's apartments. By positioning herself as the benefactor of the Genoese woman and an intermediary between her husband and his new concubine, she asserted her control over a potential rival and protected her position as the most senior wife.[49] Finally, some of these marriages were known to include love and affection, implying that others were primarily political. For one, ibn Yusuf contrasts ʿAli Pasha's love for Kebira Mamia with his relation to his cousin Hafsia. Kebira Mamia was the mother of his sons; he may not have been intimate with Hafsia.[50] Similarly, ibn Yusuf says little about ibn ʿAli's wife Fatma Ghazalia, while noting the bey's appreciation of Fatma bint ʿUthman. This suggests that women were respected confidants and appreciated by their husbands.

It was common for upper-class women to own property, and their wealth and managerial skills were crucial during times of instability. The sisters Hafsia, Fatma, and Khadija were commercially active; they bought and sold property and later endowed them as inheritance to their female descendants. Each of the sisters owned agricultural estates; farms growing olives, grapes, and figs; and residential and commercial properties, including coffee houses, a mill, and a bakery. One of Fatma's endowments to a woman named Hajja Jannat included land with over fifteen hundred olive trees, a press for its pits, and an oil press, suggesting her involvement in producing olive oil.[51] Inheriting from their father and husbands, these women were engaged in a range of economic activities that contributed to the wealth and social standing of their family.

Women also loaned money to their husbands and utilized their assets to protect their families as they benefited from relative immunity. Ibn 'Ali borrowed money from his wife Fatma bint 'Uthman to send Burteghiz as his delegate on the pilgrimage.[52] Kebira Mamia was entrusted with valuables when her husband fled, and she went into hiding with their two younger sons, indicating that he trusted her to manage their affairs. Though she eventually turned to her husband's rival for protection, ibn Yusuf explained that a wife was not responsible for her husband's behavior: "After all, what do I have to fear? I am only a woman, and women do not mount horses or ride off into the night, and I am not one who would unsheathe a sword and use it to kill."[53] This gendered vision of warfare and political disputes allowed women to preserve the family financial resources.

Ibn 'Ali's respect for Fatma bint 'Uthman and her skill in orchestrating family affairs suggest political acumen and savvy. Much of this can be credited to her transition from the household of Ramadan Bey to that of ibn 'Ali, providing stability to what was otherwise a turbulent period around the turn of the seventeenth century. The same can be said for Mabruka, the widow of Muhammad Bey and Murad Bey, who was briefly married to Ibrahim al-Sharif. As Hathaway details in the case of the Qazdaglis in eighteenth-century Egypt, widow remarriage within the political elite or the practice of heritable wives was one that conferred the authority of the patron onto prominent political figures from within their entourage. From the woman's vantage point, these remarriages were a way to maintain status and authority.[54]

Qazdagli women acted as their husband's financial agents, securing the wealth of the household and becoming the "guardians of household property," as they were considered external to political disputes.[55] Upper-class women in Cairo put their wealth towards productive economic activities, such as engaging in long-distance trade.[56] In Aleppo as well, by owning property, elite women were able to offer their families or husbands a degree of security during periods of political and economic uncertainty. Particularly in the smaller urban centers of the provinces, women were often acquainted with members of their husbands' families before marriage, as was presumably the case in Tunis.[57] Marital alliances were important in consolidating family wealth and creating political power, whether to top ministers and retainers, prominent local families, or relatives, and most early modern ruling families practiced some form of intraelite endogamy. Without functioning as an offshoot of imperial policy, the strategic approach to marriage in Tunis corresponded to patterns across the empire particularly during the ascendancy of the household in provincial politics.

FAMILY, MARRIAGE, AND DIVORCE

Just as marriage could affirm political ties and improve social relations, networks based in the family were deployed as part of political rivalries. Disputes over succession were at the heart of the wars from 1728 to 1756 that pitted ibn 'Ali against his nephew 'Ali Pasha. The latter was among the most visible figures in government during the 1710s, became the bey's son-in-law, and seemed prime for succession. Yet with four surviving boys by the following decade, Muhammad al-Rashid (c. 1710), 'Ali (b. 1712), Mahmud (b. 1714), and Mustafa (c. 1716), ibn 'Ali sought to displace his nephew in favor of his eldest son. The major narrative source for the early eighteenth century is Muhammad al-Saghir ibn Yusuf's *Al-Mashr'a al-mulki fi saltanat awlad 'Ali al-Turki* [The Path of Kings in the State of 'Ali al-Turki's Sons]. A well-to-do landowner and a minor scholar, he constructed his manuscript as both an eyewitness report of "what I saw with my eyes or my ears heard" and historical treatise. Ibn Yusuf made frequent note of family affairs, which he posits as integral to the detailing of official activities and battles.[58]

Initially attempting a diplomatic guarantee of his son's triumph without alienating his nephew, Husayn ibn 'Ali turned to his ministers for advice. One of them suggested:

> You must promote both of them, send [a messenger] to Istanbul with wondrous gifts for the Grand Vizir, if he accepts, then he shall ask Sultan Ahmad for the *qaftan* and *firman* of honorable obedience for your nephew, and thus send to you the office of pasha for your nephew.[59]

The successful delegation to Istanbul returned in 1725 with gifts from the sultan and the imperial *firman*. While holding an honorable rank, the pasha could boast only minor responsibilities in the capital where this officer often resided, and the granting of this office to 'Ali signaled a departure from the family home in Bardo. This demotion allowed ibn 'Ali's eldest son Muhammad al-Rashid to replace his cousin as commander of the *mahalla*, an implicit statement of his claim to the beyship.

As ibn Yusuf recounts it, 'Ali Pasha responded by carefully planning a clandestine escape, arranging with members of his entourage to leave Tunis without raising suspicions and reconnoiter in the mountainous region near the border of Algeria, where they could gather an army against his uncle. As part of the ruse, he feigned an argument with Hafsia, creating a premise to send her back to her father's home.[60] He subsequently left the capital for the mountains and armed his supporters. Ibn ʿAli sent a delegation of religious notables to encourage ʿAli to return, hoping "to spare the bloodshed of this community and reconcile the nephew and his uncle,"[61] though he was unable to repair the rift within the family. Under different circumstances, a spousal disagreement or visit to her father would have been unremarkable, yet in the context of his rebellion, returning Hafsia to her father signaled the termination of their marriage and the severing of ties with his uncle.

Not only did family relations permeate the debut of the conflict, but wartime opportunism led to new household alliances. ʿAli Pasha's first supporters were from the western parts of the province, particularly the tribe of the Awlad ʿAmar and the Hanansha. Their two leaders, Muhammad Saghir and his brother Sultan, wrote to ʿAli Pasha, asking that he demonstrate his trust by sending his eldest son, Yunus, to stay with them.[62] Alongside political claims, the militarization of extended households and networks and the general escalation of violence benefited from local enmities, weak harvests, and depressed economic conditions.[63]

This phase of the conflict quickly ended with ʿAli's defeat and flight to Algiers, where he bid his time as a guest and prisoner of the dey (detained at his uncle's expense). Yet he returned to the capital with support from Algerian troops to achieve a temporary victory in 1735, forcing ibn ʿAli and his sons to retreat to Qayrawan in the interior and inaugurating a five-year period of armed conflict that culminated in ʿAli Pasha's assassination of ibn ʿAli, whose family took refuge in Algiers. He sealed his triumph by reconnecting with the Awlad ʿAmar, marrying the daughter of the shaykh Muhammad Saghir, and his son Yunus married one of the women from the allied tribe of Bu ʿAziz.[64]

As the conflict intensified, ibn ʿAli arranged a number of additional marriages between his immediate descendants and prominent social groups in the province. From their base in Qayrawan, ibn ʿAli's oldest son, Muhammad al-Rashid, married the daughter of Jamal al-Din, the qaʾid (a district or town governor) of Sousse, a large provincial city along the coast. Muhammad al-Rashid also married a woman from the Ghazali lineage, who continued to be close with the family until at least Muhammad al-Rashid's death in 1759.[65] His son ʿAli married a woman from the

Hanansha tribe, who was the granddaughter of Bou 'Aziz (who was related to 'Ali Pasha's branch of the family as well).[66] A third son, Mahmud, was married to a woman referred to as Trakiya, the daughter of Si Yusuf Dey, in an additional alliance with the descendants of 'Uthman Dey.[67] While this perpetuated their ties with the political elite, the preference during the war was for strengthening ties to notables outside the capital.

Since ibn Yusuf was a partisan of ibn 'Ali and his sons, he sought to reduce 'Ali Pasha's marital politics to a question of shallow materialism. After taking the capital in 1735 and settling into the palace, 'Ali Pasha doted on his new wife and encouraged her to invite her father, Muhammad Saghir, to be their guest. He regaled his father-in-law with gifts, treated him to a decadent meal, and offered him beautiful clothes and a concubine, gestures that appeared to value their family ties. Instead, 'Ali Pasha was motivated by wartime calculations. Ibn Yusuf has him reveal to his father-in-law:

> I sought an alliance with you and to marry your daughter only so that I could count on your support in case of difficulties and to be sure that your tribe would fight to defend me. If the bey Husayn knew that you [and your brother] were both my supporters, he would be at a great loss and would never dream of returning to the Hanansha lands.[68]

In this telling, Muhammad Saghir was flattered by such praise; departed with additional gifts of gold, silver, jewels, clothing, and provisions; and convinced his brother Sultan to accept another offer to visit the palace. While the pasha welcomed them with rich presents and treated them with respect, the entire affair was a sinister ruse; at nightfall, the two men were strangled and all of the troops that had accompanied them were imprisoned. This again signaled a divorce between 'Ali Pasha and the extended networks of his erstwhile in-laws, and the rest of the Hanansha fled to Algeria.

The end of the conflict was reached by invoking imperial politics and through marriage alliances, the twin themes of this chapter. On the one hand, both men attempted to secure their claims to power by drawing support from the Ottoman ruling class. The backing of the governor of Algiers was a decisive element of 'Ali Pasha's victorious return in 1735, and his ultimate failure in 1756, when Hassan Bey of Constantine and his military backed Muhammad al-Rashid and 'Ali ibn Husayn's bid to reclaim the beyship from their cousin. Istanbul appeared to make only occasional efforts to promote its clients, preferring to sanction those who proved effective by awarding them the requisite symbols of investiture and creating space for Algiers to assert its privileged status in the Maghrib. On the other hand, while the pasha's grown sons were sent to Algeria to remain under the watchful eye of the dey, his wives and young children resided at Bardo alongside their extended family, where they were financially provided for from 1756 until 1828, when the last of his descendants passed away.[69] This reincorporated them into the ruling household, albeit in a subordinate and dependent position. Muhammad al-Rashid Bey further reconciled the family, uniting its disparate branches through the marriage of 'Ali Pasha's daughter Trakiya to his younger brother, 'Ali ibn Husayn. Just as the period of hostility was opened by divorce, so was it closed by marriage.

As Ottoman rule extended from military control of the capital and its garrison to include much of the province, there were a number of changes to administrative organization. At the outset, the top-ranking authority was the imperially appointed pasha (under the admiralty of the *qubtan pasha*), whose decisions were implemented by a governing council composed of officers and local notables. The first major change resulted in greater representation for rank-and-file soldiers via the dey, at a time when the three westernmost Ottoman provinces were exempt from taxation in kind but paid in service via military contributions. The second change was the rise of the bey from a district or town governor to a major military commander who controlled significant revenues.

While increasingly devoid of power, the rank of pasha continued to be valuable and was requested by at least three of Murad's descendants and by Husayn ibn 'Ali for his nephew, before it became a secondary title of the bey who stood as the predominant authority in the province. Despite the shift towards local decision-making, the ceremonials surrounding the meeting of the *diwan*, the reading of imperial edicts, and the dressing of the bey in the official *qaftan* placed the bey within the Ottoman military-administrative hierarchy, indicating how imperial structures were respected in military and administrative organization, fiscal policy, and foreign relations. The eventual establishment of a hereditary governorship did not pose a direct challenge to the sultan's authority, nor did it constitute a significant departure from the organization of provincial politics, as the examples of Egypt or Tripoli illustrate.

The governing elite in Tunis acted similarly to the ruling classes in Cairo, Aleppo, Mosul, Mount Lebanon, or Jerusalem in other ways as well, namely, in the overlap of family and politics so that the basis of political authority resided in the household. From the first years of Ottoman rule, marriage between a client and his patron's daughter or widow contributed to political continuity and the rise of household politics. The presence of slaves as household retainers further underscored the importance of patronage to the first beys. Other alliances allowed the political class in Tunis to create ties to religious notables, the governors of Tripoli, and Arab and Berber tribes such as the Shenifa and the Sharin. Family relations facilitated the rise of a European-born outsider such as Murad Bey, who was able to assimilate into the ruling class enough to earn the sultan's recognition and the authority to pass this position along to his sons.

Around the end of the seventeenth century, similar structures contributed to ibn 'Ali's ascension through the ranks of the military and attachment to the Muradite household as a soldier. This status was confirmed by his marriage to his patron's widow, because women transmitted political authority, experience, and wealth. Ibn 'Ali aligned with prominent tribes and families in the interior, expanding his networks through his wives, sons, daughters, and nephew. Yet just as marriage could broaden the political reach of a household, and smooth succession could perpetuate family authority, so divorce or competition among heirs could tear the family apart. In the last quarter of the seventeenth century, violent disputes among Murad's descendants provoked the sultan's intervention and the annihilation of the male members of the family by the hand of Sharif. In the early eighteenth century, 'Ali Pasha's challenge to his uncle ibn 'Ali, and the mobilization of their household networks into open combat, led to the reassertion of Algerian suzerainty over the province as privileged intermediaries of the sultan.

The importance of familial connections made for an overlap of the administrative state and the palace family beginning in the seventeenth century. Though this facilitated the localization of politics over the next two centuries, both the rise of the household and the increase of provincial autonomy were prevalent across the Ottoman Empire. By thus accepting the political agency of the household, we must consider how ibn 'Ali inherited authority from the Muradites and mobilized his household network against his nephew as integral to the narrative of political contestation during this period. Ibn Yusuf's text blends anecdotes on family and personal relations with an event-based narration of the period and the unfolding of the civil war, indicating that he considered questions of marriage relevant to the discussion of politics, power, and the state. In this respect, his references to social networks, marriage alliances, and the opposing factions of the war are an insightful contribution to the centrality of family to politics. The issue of succession did not pose a problem again until 1814, and over the intervening generations, the ruling families further consolidated their power and authority as a family and as provincial rulers. It is the material and discursive traces of this process that are the focus of the next section.

FAMILY AND PROVINCIAL GOVERNMENT, 1756–1840

Part II

When ʿAbd al-Basit ibn Halil, an Egyptian merchant and literati, visited Tunis in 1462, he dined at the Hafsid palace of Raʾs al-Tabia. Aside from the pleasant company, beautiful gardens, three-story palace, and marble fountain, his travel account (or *rihla*) carefully described one of the dishes called *mujabban*, "which is an Andalusian cheese bread."[1] If "kings and grandees in al-Andalus and the Maghrib" appreciated some of the same delicacies, according to a recipe for fowl in the *Kanz al-fawaʾid fi tanwiʿ al-maʾid*, and there were two styles of *mujabban* in Ibn Razin's thirteenth-century collection, the dishes were certainly known east of Tunis.[2] *Mujabban* was included in a thirteenth-century manuscript that circulated between Aleppo, Cairo, Damascus, and later Istanbul; other culinary works of the Abbasid era included additional recipes of North African inspiration, couscous in particular, and referenced specific North African varieties of herbs.[3] During Grenville Temple's tour of the province in 1835, he offered the following comments on a meal with a provincial notable:

> At one o'clock our own dinner was announced when to our astonishment we found the table laid out with knives and forks, and wine; and the dishes, which amounted in number to at least forty, were excellent, but all cooked according to the principles laid down by the cookery books of Europe, excepting, however, the Moorish cooscussu and the Turkish pillaw.[4]

As these two anecdotes suggest, the significance of sharing a meal transcended its nutritive functions, with particular dishes evoking status and cultural identity.

Temple's comments point towards the way in which power could be demonstrated in the number of courses served at a meal, seating arrangements, table settings, and personnel. At one banquet in 1696, the Safavid Shahs offered 150 entrees and an additional 150 plates of sweets; they carefully orchestrated the placement of guests, dishware, and the manner of serving and were so deeply invested in the symbols of hosting that it

informed palace architectural design.[5] If Ottoman sultans did not promote an empire-wide culinary regime, they appreciated haute cuisine,
collected writings on the medicinal benefits of food, and were attentive
to etiquette. They had a specialized kitchen of officers, clerks, and butlers
who waited on the sultan; an official who washed his hands before meals;
servants who poured water; a fruit server; a pickle server; tray carriers; a
taster; a sweet-maker; and a chief syrup-maker. They too calculated the
quantity and variety of dishes appropriate for particular occasions such
as feasts on the hunt or official receptions.[6] Palace personnel contributed
to images of imperial grandeur, though whether they were the personal
guard of black soldiers surrounding Morocco's Alawite sultans, the vast
imperial household department of the Qing dynasty, or the sizeable staff
of richly adorned aristocrats serving at the courts of Vienna and Versailles
was determined by local politics of value.[7]

As Sidney Mintz elaborated in the case of seventeenth-century Europe,
a seemingly innocuous comestible such as sugar could become a luxury
good and a poignant symbol of power.[8] In fact, sugar continued to contribute to royal spectacles, demonstrations of class, and national identity
until the end of the nineteenth century.[9] If the particular meaning of luxury differed from one place to the next, since distant origins often represented the ruler's global reach, food continued to hold a prevalent place in
the panoply of elite symbolism as courtly vogues connected consumption
"to the demonstration of political power."[10]

The collection of luxury goods extended beyond the table and had real
economic ramifications. The early eighteenth-century mania for tulips,
which led to garden cultivation, outdoor parties, and new clothing patterns
and decorative motifs, offers a poignant example of how elites in Istanbul utilized conspicuous consumption in their contest for influence. The
eponymous Tulip Era (1718–1730) was one of cultural flourishing, innovation, and decadence at the Ottoman center. Central Asian bulbs were used
to stake political claims and exhibit social status in ways that challenged
standards of behavior, and tested social boundaries. In Europe as well, a
fascination with tulips was only one manifestation of the huge expansion
in consumption in the eighteenth century, where Enlightenment-inspired
philosophers in France and England became luxury apologists encouraging consumerism for its artistic and cultural benefits.[11] More than a symbol of imperial refinement, the tulip and its connection to transregional
networks of trade offer an example of the Ottoman contribution to early
modern consumer culture.[12]

How did the dishes served to travelers in Tunis allude to its position within material circuits of trade and early modern consumerism? One of the epithets for the ruling household was Bardo *al-m'amura*, meaning "the inhabited" or "prosperous" palace. This epithet equated vast resources with the population they sustained as a tangible sign of wealth similar to clothing and dietary habits. A minor economic hub, Tunisia stood at the crossroads of Mediterranean, trans-Saharan, North African, and intra-Ottoman circuits of commodities, people, and ideas, with the palace a central market for goods and services since at least the middle of the eighteenth century. While the beys of Tunis did not claim Sherifian ancestry nor the titles of sultan or shah, they did utilize material objects to distinguish themselves from the local population.

Yet even when the beys imported marble from Pisa and glazed tiles from Anatolia and Spain, the bulk of construction material, such as limestone, plaster, sandstone, iron, and copper, was locally mined.[13] Thus, elite consumption frequently relied on local resources. It could both protect and support domestic industry while forging ties between the palace, merchants, artisans, and farmers. As the governing families mediated between global courtly practices and the local market, consumption created a nexus for the production of social relations. The dependents—including hundreds of slaves, male and female servants, eunuchs, and notables, remarkable for their numbers—performed a combination of household and administrative functions consistent with the overlap between family and early modern state.

Part II focuses on consumption in terms of household networks and elite social practices (Chapter 2), interior design and domestic production (Chapter 3), and local networks of distribution (Chapter 4). It encompasses a period of general political and economic stability following the assassination of ʿAli Pasha in 1756 until roughly 1830, the French conquest of Algiers. It relies on a set of accounting registers from 1770 to the 1830s, after which accelerated reforms and increasing financial constraints transformed the provincial economy (Chapter 5, in Part III).[14] This locates the beylical court in a nexus of regional and local goods, people, practices, and values.

This chapter begins with a discussion of palace personnel and household organization to demonstrate the overlap of administrative and domestic functions within Bardo, as the diverse staff formed an inestimable component of prestige and the desire to portray wealth. By belonging to the palace households, elites and laborers contributed to a common political project. Using account registers as a source for social history, the second section of the chapter continues the discussion of palace meals, their ingredients, and the use of food in demarcating status and demonstrating patronage that complemented notions of patriarchal benevolence and economic privilege. These items are in turn compared with the provincial diets in the countryside and among notables to suggest the similarities among the latter and further to reinforce the role of food as a mark of status. Finally, I briefly suggest how changing consumer habits in the nineteenth century increasingly reflected an awareness of European tastes and appreciation for colonial products. The particular blending of Andalusian architectural styles, Arabic calligraphy, Venetian glass chandeliers, and Persian rugs were indicative of Bardo's location at the crossroads of different cultural currents.

THE PALACE POPULATION

The ability to maintain a sizeable retinue required financial resources. At most courts, such personnel combined domestic and political tasks concomitant with the overlapping patriarchal model of the family and state. For instance, at Istanbul's Topkapi, there were at least forty personnel to manage the sultan's clothing: this included men who carried the sultan's boots and slippers when he went riding; officials in charge of cleaning, storing, and purchasing turbans; and a separate unit devoted to laundering. Similarly, there were 1,100 to 1,700 people (mostly men) in the inner-household services of France's Bourbon kings, while that of the queen mother, the queen, and the wife of the heir apparent each numbered between 400 and 650. Aside from the thousands of guards, the staff at Versailles in the eighteenth century ranged from 3,000 to 5,100.[15] Even in Egypt, there were approximately 500 mamluks in the personal service of Egypt's Muhammad 'Ali at the beginning of the nineteenth century and over 1,600 in the court as a whole, approximately five times those in Tunis.[16]

By global standards, the Bardo retinue was remarkably basic, though as it grew, the small court adopted global status symbols alongside its local elements. When the sons of Husayn ibn 'Ali returned from Algiers to claim the position of bey from their cousin 'Ali Pasha in 1756, with a relatively modest entourage, their extended family was small enough to fit into two carriages.[17] Their wives and dependents moved into Bardo, forming small households in separate apartments. The end of the extended period of warfare brought stability to the family, facilitating its almost doubling in size by the end of the century from seven households in 1759 to twelve in 1800, growing to at least eighteen in 1841. Each of these households was formed around the wife, concubine, or widow of one of the beys or adult women such as sisters, cousins, and aunts. In 1800, the palace family consisted of the main house of the ruling bey Hammuda Pasha (probably inhabited by his mother Mahbuba), his second house (that of his wife, the daughter of the *mufti* [a religious scholar and jurisconsult] Muhammad ibn Husayn al-Barudi), at least five *juar*, and the households of his brother ʿUthman's three wives, a *jaria*, and four sons, his sister Khaduja, his sister Jannat, his cousin Ismail, his cousin Mahmud's mother (a wife of his deceased uncle Muhammad al-Rashid), a second wife of his deceased uncle Muhammad al-Rashid (the mother of his daughters), the two *juar* of his late brother Muhammad al-Mimun and his two children, the third wife of his uncle Muhammad al-Rashid named Mna Ghazalia or Ghazali's daughter, and the wife of the late Hammuda Shelebi (Fatma bint Husayn's son from her first marriage to Ahmad Shelebi).[18] The men in the family were generally polygamous, and as far as it is possible to ascertain, they complied with the stipulations of Islamic law by providing separate housing for each wife. The palace was organized around these numerous households, referred to as *diyar* (sing. *dar*, the house), which served as the basic unit of palace accounting.

The number of personnel at Bardo fluctuated, growing from the hundreds to possibly the thousands to accommodate its economic, governmental, and military functions; the complex contained a tribunal, a mosque, a chapel, a library, a bakery, a kitchen, a sizeable bathhouse, two treasuries, stables, and a garage for the bey's carriages. The grounds included a prison and a marketplace of boutiques, with the 1840 addition of a foundry, a school, a dormitory for students and instructors, and a mint. Family networks and loyalty to the bey stood as the two main unifying factors within this mini-metropolis. As the supreme patriarch over the palace and its occupants, the bey was financially responsible for their sustenance, the distribution of food, clothing, and the provision of at least minimal health services. In return, the reigning bey was addressed as *Sidna*, meaning "our master" or "our lord." The bey's female relatives were identified by their relation to him. Once the position of governor became hereditary, the title "bey" served as a patronymic for men in the ruling family, marking their potential for rule and their direct familial ties to the sovereign. When archives include the names of servants and employees, many of them combined proper names, titles, and references to kinship that were indicative of connections to the ruling family.

There was a military base at Bardo and troops stationed in the palace. Units of Arab and Turkish *subahiya* (sing. *subahi*) stood at the first and second gates respectively. The name derives from the Ottoman "cavalry," the *sipahi*, and these soldiers doubled as couriers between the palace and the *diwan*. A second interior gate was guarded by the *hawanib* (sing. *hanba*), an elite unit of soldiers. In both name and responsibility, they were akin to the Turkish *canbaz*, the personal guard of provincial governors across the empire serving as a sort of noble guard comparable to the *muteferri-kas* of the sultan's household. The soldiers attached to the palace and the personal suite of the bey were organized in a manner that resembled that of other provincial governors, which were modeled on the palaces of the sultan and his chief ministers, with the number of *subahiya* and *hawanib* increasing from about 250 in 1790 to 500 in 1825. They too were organized according to a household model grouped into units of 25 soldiers that were referred to as *diyar*.[19]

A central component of the palace population was the slaves who were delegated administrative, military, and domestic tasks. These slaves often arrived in the province via trans-Saharan caravan routes that passed through Algeria, bringing bath attendants (sing. *ra'is-hammam*) who served in each household, from Warqla.[20] After an extensive and exhausting voyage by foot, the slaves were sold directly in the homes of the well-to-do or were purchased at the slave market, the *suq al-birka*, for an average of 350 piasters.[21] Around the end of the eighteenth century, there were servants and valets in the harem, such as the *bash agha*, who stood guard at the door of the harem, and there was a separate unit of guards formed of black slaves.[22] European women visiting the harem in the nineteenth century mentioned the "great number of black and white female slaves," which they guessed "certainly exceeded a thousand." As he watched the funeral procession of Husayn Bey in 1835, Pückler-Muskau postulated that it included around 600 black women and 200 black men who were freed slaves (called *khadem* [pl. *khedam*]).[23] Exact figures of *khedam* are difficult to come by, though they probably numbered in the hundreds.[24]

The immediate entourage of the ruling family was composed primarily of white male slaves, or mamluks, who were attached to the bey and the younger men in the family. In the eighteenth century, there were mamluks from the Italian peninsula, Sardinia, Malta, France, and Spain, though their numbers declined along with the activities of corsairs, and more of the mamluks were Georgian, Circassian, Greek, or Moldavian.[25] Though the organization of the mamluk corps shifted along with their numbers, they were generally divided into two groups: those who stood as guards at the entranceway (the *mamluks al-sqifa*) and those serving in the interior (the *mamluks al-bit* or *mamluks al-saray*). The latter corresponded roughly to the young pages attached to the bey, who were sometimes referred to as *mamluks al-saghir*. Between 1775 and 1785, the bey owned 31 to 37 *mamluks al-bit* and a comparable number of *mamluks al-saghir*, with the total number of mamluks hovering from 100 to 150 over the second half of the eighteenth century. The mamluk corps reached a peak of 270 in the 1820s before its size steadily diminished after the 1840s.[26] More than servants, the mamluks were raised alongside men in the ruling family; the beys developed close relationships with mamluks they had fraternized with as children and appointed them as their principal advisors. These ties were framed by kinship terms by which certain mamluks were revered as "our father," and in turn they addressed the younger beys as sons. More than polite formalities, this gestured towards the profound respect that existed between prominent mamluks and the ruling family and the emotional bonds between them.[27]

Scions of the provincial elite also owned mamluks, raising them in their homes, and at times offering them to the beys to sow the seeds of future alliances. Successful examples of this practice are seen in the case of the Jallulis, one of the wealthiest families in Tunis. Notables in the city of Sfax, they had served in various governmental positions throughout much of the Ottoman era.[28] Though they never married with the palace families, they were closely associated with Bardo through two powerful mamluks. Bekkar Jalluli, a coffee merchant, purchased a slave in Istanbul whom he trained and eventually offered to Hammuda Pasha. This mamluk, Yusuf Sahib al-Taba'a, ascended to positions of considerable authority, married the bey's sister Khaduja, and became one of the most influential and wealthy men in government. He accumulated a fortune from business associations with Jalluli and other merchants in Sfax, and the mamluk played a critical role in Jalluli's own social ascension.[29] Bekkar's son, Mahmud Jalluli, purchased another slave for the palace: Mustafa Sahib al-Taba'a served in a series of prominent positions throughout the nineteenth century in the entourage of Hammuda Pasha, Mahmud Bey, Mustafa Bey, and Ahmad Bey. He married Mustafa Bey's daughter, Mahbuba, and throughout maintained close relations with Jalluli.[30]

Women in the palace were served by a female staff. This included a bath attendant (a *ra'is-hammam*), a servant responsible for supervising food preparation called the *kamanja*, nannies, governesses, wet nurses as necessary, and a number of slaves.[31] In addition to *khedam*, the women's households counted up to ten *'alaji* (sing. *'aljia*). In the palace, an *'aljia* was a white, female slave, though the term had been deployed for a non-Muslim man (*'alj*) in the sixteenth century.[32] Similar to the *juar* (sing.

jaria), who were white slaves who sang, performed in the palace, or were the personal servants and sometimes concubines of the bey, these women were from the Christian populations of the Ottoman East. These female slaves received a minimal education and were taught skills such as music or embroidery. They were few in number due to the prohibitive cost of bringing them from Istanbul. In the eighteenth century, prices ranged from about 800 to 1,200 piasters; this was before the doubling or tripling of prices with the subsequent waning of the official slave trade, and so in the 1830s, a slave might have cost between 2,450 and 4,650 piasters, with one female slave reaching 9,150 piasters.[33] Similar to mamluks, female slaves were incorporated into the palace's patriarchal structures in a way that reiterated their dependent, though familial, relationship.

Juar were treated as daughters in economic and, possibly, emotional terms; the bey paid for their trousseaus and arranged their marriages to men at court. This was common in the early eighteenth century; for example, ibn ʿAli gave a slave to Burteghiz following his wife's death and ʿAli Pasha gave one of his female slaves to his father-in-law, Muhammad Saghir, along with clothing and jewelry.[34] According to ibn Yusuf, the slave who killed ʿAli Pasha's co-conspirator Ahmad ibn Methisha was told he would be emancipated and married to one of the women in ibn ʿAli's service as a reward.[35] The *jaria* who married Muhammad al-Rashid in 1757 was furnished with a trousseau comparable to those of the palace women, which included 2,750 piasters in cash, and Khadija, an *ʿaljia* belonging to one of ʿAli Bey's sisters, married a man in the palace service in the 1770s.[36] Ibn Dhiaf describes the *jaria* who married Husayn Bey's son Hammuda Bey in 1826 as "raised by his grandfather Mahmud Bey."[37] With decades of service in the scribal bureaucracy, ibn Dhiaf himself received at least two concubines from the palace.[38] Thanks to the proximity of slave women to the ruling family, the periodic offering of concubines to men in the inner circle of government strengthened familial ties between the palace and local elites.

Another component of the bey's entourage were the *qazqat* (sing. *qazaq*), who functioned as guards similar to the mamluks near the palace entrance, with the notable difference that the *qazqat* were practicing Christians.[39] Presumably captives of the merchant marine who had chosen to remain at the Tunisian court, they did not convert to Islam or adopt Arabic names. They were provided meals during the month of Ramadan when the remainder of the palace would have been fasting; instead, they appear to have abstained from meat during Lent, which the palace replaced with extra quantities of beans, lentils, and chickpeas for "their holiday."[40] The head of the *qazqat* (or *bash qazaq*) in 1776 was named Antoine and a later successor, Nicolo, was in the palace from around 1813 to 1832.[41] At least in the final decades of the eighteenth century, they ranged from thirty-five to fifty-five in number, with an average of around forty-seven *qazqat*.[42] A cohort of Sicilian Christians, called *warda roba* (from the Italian for wardrobe), was responsible for the personal affairs of the bey and his mamluks.[43] It is plausible that they replicated and combined the functions of the sultan's head valet (the *baş çokadar*) and the *kahya hoftanci*, who were responsible for all matters related to the sultan's clothing.[44]

The Bardo retinue counted any number of Europeans, whether they were on brief commission or became long-term residents with families. As early as 1754, there were two to five Christian doctors serving the bey, many of whom remained at court long enough (up to twenty years in some cases) to establish roots in the province, while often doubling as informed consular liaisons.[45] From the 1830s onward, there were additional European Christians temporarily employed training the troops, working on industrial projects or at cloth factories, or building ships.[46] Those who did prolong their sojourn in Tunis assimilated into the palace households; a skilled mechanic and watchmaker captured by the merchant marine named Gian Battista was given to ʿAli Bey to maintain the palace clocks in the 1770s. He soon settled at Bardo and married a French woman. Not only did his son Giuseppe (or Joseph) Raffo become one of the most visible ministers and an active intermediary between the palace and foreign consuls in the mid-nineteenth century, but one of his daughters, Elena-Grazia, converted to Islam and married Mustafa Bey.[47] While Giuseppe Raffo's upbringing in the palace bears resemblance to the trajectory of mamluks, he was a practicing Catholic, traveled to Italy, and formed part of the capital's "creole" community of Europeans who had integrated the household networks of power.[48]

If household structures facilitated the incorporation of slaves and dependents, who traveled great distances before arriving in Tunis, they offered avenues of social mobility for the subject population as well. Local women were hired as wet nurses and midwives, and there was a range of options for men to enter palace service.[49] Semiskilled laborers such as gardeners, barbers, painters, and construction workers, and religious officials such as instructors for the palace children, the imam, and the two muezzins were recruited from within the province. This brought educated men from respected families, as well as those with modest origins, into the palace.[50] Other personnel in the financial administration were drawn from Tunisia's Jewish community, as were artisans, jewelers, and occasionally cooks.[51] The palace families patronized local crafts in the procurement of *shashia*, slippers, clothing, and saddles. These forms of temporary employment iterate the economic importance of court consumption and its role in sustaining and protecting local industry.

Clothing was at once a demonstration of wealth and a sign of belonging; when the designation of sultanic authority was conferred on the bey, his incorporation into the imperial sartorial order was accompanied by the granting of a *qaftan*.[52] The bey, *'alaji*, *khedam*, and mamluks were given new clothing twice each year, as were the palace families.[53] A second tier of palace personnel such as the *qazqat*, the Jewish employees at the mint (the *taba'aji*), and the palace doctors were regularly accorded shoes or articles of clothing.[54] While the gesture blurred the lines between servitude and filial responsibility, the luxury of their dress clearly distinguished the servants from the served; in 1776, each *'aljia* was given a *qaftan* worth 14½ piasters, while the clothes for women in the ruling family were priced at 450 piasters each.[55]

While the diversity of palace personnel was indicative of Tunisia's connection to wider economic and cultural networks, the patronage of artisans, accountants, household staff, and religious personnel bespoke of its reliance on the province's subjects. The household model transcended the political and military functions of the palace. It allowed for the incorporation of diverse individuals in their common service to the ruling bey and was a place where slaves, servants, and other domestic staff shared a common dependence on the bey, as did his extended family.

HOUSEHOLD DIET AND THE PALACE KITCHEN

The table was a central feature of the Bardo households, and the business of provisioning and food distribution occupied a conspicuous place in its monthly accounting. Each household, or unit of soldiers, was allocated a fixed quantity of monthly staples, the composition of which was elaborated on the opening pages of the annual expense registers placing family and food—at least figuratively—at the forefront of palace spending. The palace definition of basic necessities diverged from that of the general population; for starters, those in the palace had access to a greater variety of products. These were not distributed in equal amounts, and the quantity of foodstuffs distinguished varying degrees of status within the palace.

The total of monthly provisions in 1777 for the largest house in the palace, that of 'Ali Bey and his wife Trakiya bint 'Ali Pasha, suggests the overall composition of the palace diet. It consisted of the following: 12 *qafiz*s of wheat; 12 *metar*s of olive oil; 12 *qila*s of clarified butter; 100 *ratl*s of rice; 30 *ratl*s of sugar; 12 *wiba*s of salt; 20 *ratl*s of honey; 10 *ratl*s of cheese; 10 *ratl*s of olives; 30 piasters worth of vegetables; 210 chickens; 60 pairs of pigeons; 2,200 eggs; 62 piasters worth of fruit and another 68 piasters worth of fruit for storage; 1½ *ratl*s of pepper; ½ *ratl* of cinnamon; and small amounts of saffron, ginger, and cloves. Aside from the supplementary ingredients for making sweets and particular holiday dishes, the household was allocated one *qintar* and 10 *ratl*s of meat (presumably mutton) each day.[56]

At the imperial level, a standard package of goods was provided per household for each of the sultan's daughters, with half and quarter quotas to the unmarried princesses who still lived in the harem. While this typically consisted of similar items such as bread and meat (again, primarily mutton), supplemented by poultry, spices, and beans, the prevalence of yogurt and cheeses at the imperial center was not matched in Tunis.[57] The reliance of both courts on the household as the basic unit of calculation, and not on the individual, did not necessarily result from a conscious act of emulation on the part of the bey of Tunis; it may be more indicative of the centrality of the household to palace structures at Topkapi and Bardo.

The staples filling the palace pantry drew heavily on the province's abundant grain supply and its prevalent olive trees and date palms. While these products were common to the most basic rural, subsistence diet, they were consumed in such considerable quantities at the palace to warrant separate accounting. There was an attendant responsible for the monthly transportation of 72 *qafiz*s of wheat to Bardo in 1790, and he kept his own records, inserting only the occasional receipt or total into annual balance sheets.[58] Along similar lines, there are few references in the main account books to the household distribution of mutton, though one set of records from the late eighteenth century offers some details (see Table 2.1). While the regular access to meat of any sort was a privilege for the vast majority of working people, mutton was a main ingredient in the palace kitchen.

It may be possible to extrapolate from these totals the size of each household. First, it is probable that the ruling families consumed greater portions than the holiday ration provided at the soup kitchens in Tunis of about 160 grams.[59] Artan presumes that members of the royal retinue ate more than the 160 to 190 grams that were served to the average janissary; she estimated that at the smaller palaces of the princesses in Istan-

TABLE 2.1. DAILY MEAT CONSUMPTION CIRCA 1775,
REGISTER III

Household	Ratls of Meat	Est. # of Persons
Sidna's ['Ali Bey's] house	110	220
Hammuda Pasha	70	140
Hammuda Pasha's new house	30	60
Hammuda Pasha's *jaria*	10	20
Mahmud Bey	30	60
'Uthman's house	20	40
'Uthman's second house	30	60
'Uthman's new house	20	40
'Uthman's house on the square	30	60
Sidna's first daughter	30	60
Ismail Bey	30	60
Ismail's new house	30	60
Om al-bnat	20	40
Ghazalia	20	40
The late Sidna's fourth house	20	40
The deceased's first daughter	20	40
Late Sidi Mahmud, bint Yusuf Dey	10	20
'Ali Pasha's dependents	20	40

bul, the daily ration of mutton was about 250 grams per person.[60] Second, if roughly the same portion can be applied to Tunis, based on the total amount of mutton, it is possible to calculate that most households contained twenty, forty, or sixty dependents, while the principal entourage of the bey was closer to two hundred. While table 2.1 for the palace households accounts for 5 *qintars* and 50 *ratls* of meat consumption, a record from 1769 places the total daily meat supply for Bardo and all its dependents at 9 *qintars* and 55 *ratls*, enough to feed nearly two thousand people.[61]

Monthly distributions of vegetables, eggs, chickens, and pigeons to each household were clearly recorded in the late eighteenth century, roughly corresponding to the size and hierarchy of each household (Table 2.2). Aside from the generic notation of vegetables (*khodra*), the detailed tallying of pairs of pigeons and numbers of eggs is indicative of the minimal value of these items, which mark the first tier of nonstaple foods. While 210 chickens for the largest house would portion out to about one

TABLE 2.2. MONTHLY DISTRIBUTION OF VEGETABLES, CHICKEN, AND EGGS IN 1200 (1785/6), REGISTER 243

Name	Vegetables (in piasters)	Chickens	Eggs	Pairs of Pigeons
Sidna's [Hammuda Pasha] mother	43″06	180	900	
Sidna's house	22″ ½	210	2250	16
Sidna's new house [bint al-Barudi]	15	90	600	
Sidna's three *juar*	22″ ½			
Mahmud's house	15	60	600	30
Two *juar* of the late Muhammad	30			
'Uthman's two houses	30	60	600	
['Uthman's] *jaria*	15	60	450	
['Uthman's] second *jaria*	7″ ½	30	225	
Sidna's first sister	15	60	600	30
Sidna's second sister	15	60	600	30
Ismail's mother	15	60	600	30
[Ismail's] house	15	60	450	
House of the deceased [bey Muhammad al-Rashid] Om al-bnat	10			
[Muhammad al-Rashid's] house, bint al-Ghazali	10			
[Muhammad al-Rashid's] first daughter	15			
[Muhammad al-Rashid's] second daughter	15			
Sidna's aunt [Fatma bint Husayn]	22″ ½	150		
Hammuda Shelebi		60	620	30
Descendants of 'Ali Pasha	15			

a month for each person, their use in stews would add another 250-gram serving of meat almost once a week for each individual.[62] According to a 1790 tally, based on household size, a household received between three and six *haml*s of vegetables.[63] The supply varied according to season, as it was drawn primarily from local production, though again, the palace accountants did not take the time to identify individual items. As various travelers mentioned, the urban markets sold a considerable variety of crops such as okra, cauliflower, endive, and eggplant. The U.S. consul Mordechai Noah reported on "cabbages, cauliflowers, turnips, onions, garlic, salad, lettuce, cellery, leeks, beans, peas, lentiles, raddishes, carrots, asparagus, spinnage, artichokes, cucumbers, peppers, &c. and these in great abundance. Potatoes have also been planted, and have succeeded well with some attention."[64] By the end of the eighteenth century, vegetables, eggs, chickens, and pigeons were still tallied together, though only the composite sum per household was included in account books, ranging from 10 piasters to slightly over 100 for Hammuda Pasha. The principal house of the reigning bey consistently received the largest quantities, followed by other adult men in the family and the senior women, then the younger generations, and finally the concubines, with the total for these four items reaching nearly 900 piasters.

The variety of fruits was similar to that of vegetables, though again, aside from the occasional reference to sweet limes, oranges, or melons, the accounting shorthand lists only totals spent on fruits (*ghilla*). These arrived in large quantities in the summer so that a portion could be made into jams and preserves. According again to Noah,

> Fruits, are choice and abundant, such as figs, pomegranates, plums, nectarines, apples, pears, peaches, red and white mulberries, some strawberries, raised with care, lemons, limes, oranges, citrons, dates, cherries, apricots, prickly pear, melons of every description, quinces, and several kinds of rich grape.[65]

Tomatoes had been grown since at least the early eighteenth century if not earlier, thanks to the prominent Andalusian community and the spread of new world crops from the west to the east of the Muslim world.[66] This supports the conclusion that by the medieval era, Tunis had been acclimatized to a range of previously foreign crops such as rice, spinach, and eggplant, all of which were featured in medieval recipes.[67]

Celebration of the major Muslim holidays—the two ʿid, Mawlid and ʿAshura'—included the preparation of special dishes. For instance, throughout the month of Ramadan, culinary treats for the palace households included sweets made of sesame or almonds and *zlabia*, a fried dough dipped in honey (see Table 2.3).[68] The standard ration was six *ratl*s of sweets per day, with half portions to the *juar* and larger ones for the senior households.[69] A dish called *mruzia* was regularly served at ʿid al-Fitr and resembled the medieval recipe for *mawruziya*, a stewed meat featuring vinegar, and prunes (or cherries in one variation), with raisins, nuts, and saffron.[70] The Bardo iteration included 10 *ratl*s of honey; 10 *ratl*s of raisins; 5 *ratl*s of almonds; 5 *ratl*s of cornstarch; and small amounts of pepper, gin-

House	Zlabia	Sweets
Sidna [Hammuda Pasha]'s big house	4	8
Sidna [Hammuda Pasha]'s new house	2	4
[Hammuda Pasha] six *juar*	6	12
House of Sidi Mahmud	2	4
House of Sidna's first sister	2	4
House of his second sister	2	4
House of his third sister	2	4
'Uthman's first house	2	4
['Uthman's] second house	2	4
['Uthman's] house on square	2	4
House of Si Ismail	2	4
[Ismail's] mother's house	2	4
House of late Mimun	2	4
[Mimun's] *jaria*	1	2
'Uthman's *jaria*	1	2
House of the deceased [bey Muhammad al-Rashid] Om al-bnat	2	4
[Muhammad al-Rashid's] wife bint al-Ghazali	2	4
for *kummania* of sweets	4	7.5
House of 'Ali Pasha	1.5	3
House of Hajj Ahmed Bash Hanba	1	2
Sons of Si Hammuda Shelebi	1	2
Aghas at Bardo houses	1	2

ger, saffron, rose water, cinnamon, and cloves. For 'Ashura' in 1825, an extra 2 *qintar*s of almonds, 2 *qintar*s of pistachios, 2 *qintar*s of hazelnuts, a *qintar* of raisins, and 5,000 walnuts were delivered to the palace.[71] On 'id al-Idha in 1780, nearly 200 lambs were slaughtered at Bardo and distributed to each household according to its number of dependents and position within the palace hierarchy (see Table 2.4). Such stratification favored adult and widowed women, such as the governor's sister Fatma bint Husayn and his wives.[72]

The basic diet altered when the bey toured the countryside on the *mahalla*, transporting dried goods such as beans, lentils, and chickpeas and provisioning in perishables along the way.[73] The bey, his aides, and their provincial associates hunted for deer, rabbits, partridge, larks, and

TABLE 2.4. LAMBS FOR ‘ID AL-IDHA CIRCA 1775, REGISTER III

Name	Number of Lambs
Sidna's ['Ali Bey] big house [Trakiya]	20
Hammuda Pasha's house [his mother Mahbuba]	20
[Hammuda's] new house [his wife, bint al-Barudi]	10
[Hammuda's] *jaria*	5
Mahmud's house [Amina bint 'Ali Bey]	10
'Uthman's house	10
['Uthman's] second house	10
['Uthman's] third house	10
Sidna's first daughter	10
Sidna's second daughter	10
Ismail's house	10
Om al-bnat	5
Ghazalia	5
[Muhammad al-Rashid's] fourth house	8
[Muhammad al-Rashid's] first daughter [Khaduja]	10
[Muhammad al-Rashid's] second daughter [Hafsia]	10
Sidna's sister [Fatma bint Husayn]	30
['Ali] Pasha's family	5

other game to cook as well.[74] Intermittent notes suggest that the palace kitchen stocked orzo and pasta, beans, parsley, raisins for making sweet drinks (*shurbat*), and an array of spices and aromatics. The last two included black pepper, saffron, ginger, dried roses, cinnamon, musk, and cloves.[75] Almonds, walnuts, pistachios, and hazelnuts were regularly consumed and locally harvested for use in stews and sweets. One of the more common one was *halwat*, which included ½ *qafiz* of wheat; 3 *metar*s of olive oil; 3 *qila*s of butterfat; 50 *ratl*s of almonds; 50 *ratl*s of honey; 50 *ratl*s of dates; 6 *ratl*s of cornstarch; 50 eggs; 45 *ratl*s of sugar; and small quantities of pepper, ginger, cinnamon, cloves, saffron, mastic, and rose water.[76]

One of the primary imported foods was coffee, thanks to an active Tunisian merchant community in Cairo in the eighteenth century, and the palace consumed a significant portion.[77] Though cafés may have appeared around the seventeenth century, it remained an urban, luxury commodity into the nineteenth century.[78] It was routinely served at the palace and during social occasions, where even the harem contained an alcove for preparing coffee (see Figure 2.1).[79] The mid-eighteenth century introduction of the less expensive bean, referred to as *qahwa suri* from Martinique and imported by French merchants, displaced the costlier Yemeni bean or Mokka, brought via Cairo.[80] Coffee was the single commodity that could boast a specialized staff, with a *qahwaji* responsible for all coffee affairs from procuring supplies, to storage, the preparation of coffee, and purchasing cups and saucers; the bey had a *qahwaji*, as did junior palace men. There was a *qahwaji* serving guests, and another accompanied the *mahalla*.[81] Guests at the palace consistently reported drinking coffee, and Davis described a café tent that was pitched whenever the *mahalla* halted, serving both coffee and hot chocolate.[82] For the two-month *mahalla* in the summer of 1780, the *qahwaji* was responsible for 35 *ratl*s of coffee, 25 *ratl*s of powdered sugar, 4 containers of tea, 200 cups, and 8 pots.[83]

The governing family owned agricultural land across the province, with grapevines, date trees, and gardens near Bardo and in Sukra, wheat in Manuba and vast terrains with olives. A number of the family's suburban palaces included orange groves and lemon trees, and they had farmlands in Binzart, Beja, Khenis, Ghar al-Milh, Mater, Moknine, Rades, Suleiman, Sousse, Teburba, Tebursuq, and Zaghwan. One of the endowments

FIGURE 2.1.   *An alcove for preparing coffee in the palace at Bardo, with some coffee accessories. Bardo Museum, Tunisia, photo by the author.*

made by ʿAli Bey in 1773 lists over 5,000 olive trees, and an 1855 inventory dividing up Muhammad Bey's inheritance following his death lists nearly 130,000 trees.[84] There are a number of references in the expense registers to costs for harvesting the estates or for the transportation of wheat, as opposed to its sale, indicating that a portion of what was consumed in the palace was produced on family property.[85]

Was all the food delivered to Bardo consumed by its inhabitants? At least certain individuals purchased additional foods with their monthly stipends and independent incomes.[86] Moreover, while the numbers are staggering, in the 1820s and 1830s, expenses related to provisioning the palace and its guest houses occupied less than 5 percent of annual expenditures.[87] Some of the food may have left the palace, since it was common in early modern courts for the kitchen to redistribute food to the public.

The budgets, stipends, salaries, and allocations that were channeled through the household emphasize how the household constituted a prominent organizational feature of the palace. This model allowed the bey to combine his role as head of the province and the palace, fulfilling the masculine responsibility of economic support by feeding his immediate kin, extended family, slaves, servants, and other dependents. Special dishes formed a component of holidays and celebrations, just as the centralized distribution of food was essential to legitimizing the palace's patriarchal order and sustaining family hierarchies.

QUANTITY, VARIETY, AND STATUS

Fragments of the Abbasid passion for food that was extolled in poetry, elaborated in cookbooks, explained in medical treatises, and performed in cooking competitions trickled down to the early modern Muslim world.[88] The names of medieval dishes, such as *buran*, *bahar*, *ma'muniya*, and *muhallibi*, appear in lists of dishes served at imperial banquets, even if Ottomans were also influenced by central Asian and Persian cuisine.[89] The beys of Tunis inherited Arab and Andalusian culinary traditions (such as *zlabia* and *mruzia*) and were also fond of Ottoman pastries, *baklawa* (the Turkish baklava) in particular.[90] Yet aside from the rare imported goods of sugar, coffee, tea, and chocolate, the vast majority of what was served at the palace was available across the province, especially in its towns. Bardo's courtly customs distinguished them from those of the subject population by quantity and consistency.

If an ordinary day in the countryside began with a meal of bread and olives, those with more means dipped their bread in honey and butter.[91] All these were included in morning meals at the palace, which consisted of bread, olives, butter, honey, and cheese.[92] Honey was a cheaper sweetener than sugar, though more expensive than dates. The price of honey fluctuated throughout the year; for instance, between August 1792 and August 1793, it ranged from thirty-five to sixty piasters per *qintar*.[93] That honey was a valued commodity was suggested by its distribution to members of the *diwan* on holidays.

Thanks to an abundant olive crop, olive oil was an affordable source of fat, as opposed to butterfat (*samn*), which was at least fifty percent more expensive.[94] Though *samn* was the preferred ingredient for stewing meats and preparing pastries across the Middle East, Tunisia was one of the few regions with olive oil production substantial enough for it to be more than a luxury commodity.[95] Olive oil was nonetheless appreciated in the palace and consumed in amounts almost equal to *samn*.

Just as bread held the central place in the morning meal, couscous was the main component of the midday meal. Couscous was a staple for people of all classes in the eighteenth and nineteenth centuries, particularly in rural areas.[96] The basic preparation consisted of vegetables and spices with any additional ingredients indicating privilege. Served enough couscous during his voyage to conclude that it was the "national dish of Northern Africa," Kennedy explained that the simple version, with only "pepper, spices and vegetables," was altered "according to taste and means," for instance, by adding mutton or stewed gazelle.[97] Regular provisions for a country gentleman, which might be added to a couscous, included beef, mutton, and lamb.[98] Though fish was plentiful along the coasts, mutton was the cheapest meat, with the price of sheep as low as a few piasters, whereas a chicken cost one piaster; with daily wages calculated in *nasri*s reaching one-quarter or one-half piaster, however, these represented considerable sums for the laboring population.[99] In contrast, meat supplies in the palace were plentiful and varied with items including roasted chicken and pigeons, various grilled kebabs, stewed mutton, and beef wrapped in grape leaves.[100]

The basic diet of soldiers confirms the distinctions between those inside and outside the palace, though soldiers fared better than the lower echelons of society. Even if rank-and-file troops were given rations of "barley, bread, and olives," as Temple claimed, they also received mutton twice a week and small amounts of coffee and tobacco.[101] The military elite, the *hawanib* and mamluks, ate in a separate palace kitchen where meat was served on a daily basis, with items such as chickpeas, eggs, vegetables, and rice. They received honey, butterfat, and seasonings such as pepper, garlic, and saffron.[102] Saffron was expensive enough to be calculated in a small denomination, the *waqa*, at about two and one-half piasters per *waqa*.[103] While rice was only served twice each week, it was a veritable luxury, costing approximately six times more than wheat, and constituted a bonus for a select set of palace personnel, such as the doctors and skilled artisans.[104] Any variation was a sign of privilege as the diet of rural populations, especially nomadic ones, was rather monotonous. European travelers who departed from the capital and consular circles complained that the majority of the population subsisted on "couscous, fruit, and coffee," and even in villages provisions were limited to "coffee without sugar, eggs, milk, bad butter [. . . and] fowls."[105]

Kennedy's 1845 tour of Tunisia offers further insight on the dining habits of the upper class as he described a dinner hosted for his party by the Jalluli family in Sfax, "the wealthiest man in the Regency."[106] Though he details only the dishes that struck him as noteworthy, these included

> pigeons roasted, and stuffed with a pudding composed of almonds, pistachio-nuts, raisins, pepper, spices, herbs, and crumbs of bread, mixed with butter, and slightly flavoured with saffron; lamb cutlets stewed in a rich sauce, with sweet almonds; small triangular pieces of light pastry, containing a spoonful of forcemeat and fried in oil; mutton stuffed with pistachio nuts; and greens boiled in oil to the consistence of porridge. Besides all these we had the usual Moorish dishes, soups, hashes, sweetmeats, &c., finishing with couscousoo.[107]

Kennedy later explained that the "usual Moorish dishes" consisted of "thick soup, with vermicelli, stewed meat and vegetables [. . .] and couscousoo, more highly spiced and peppered than among the Arabs." His party was regularly served "the sweet cakes, crusted with sugar, for which the Tunisian confectioners are celebrated."[108] Recall that both abundance and variety were emphasized by Temple, who boasted that in Sousse, he was served an array of at least forty dishes.[109]

Wealthy families, including those at Bardo, also regularly served sweets, either after a meal or with coffee. These contained expensive items such as nuts, honey, and rose water. Pistachios and almonds cost eighty-five and ninety piasters per *qintar* respectively in 1835.[110] *Zlabia* were less expensive than the sesame and almond *halwa*, though still considered an indulgence.[111] Fruits were candied or made into lozenges, which ibn Yusuf describes as "confections that facilitate digestion."[112] While such expenses may have meant that sweets were primarily reserved for holidays, celebrations, and social visits, they feature in palace records more than any other repast. Other sweets at the palace included *milbis*, made from wheat, clarified butter, sugar, eggs, almonds, and spices, which was routinely included in palace accounts, as was a second variety of *halwa* based on equal amounts of dates, honey, and almonds with cornstarch and eggs.[113]

The hierarchy between palace households associated seniority and status with the number of dependents, connecting the food that was served to the people serving it. The homes of urban notables often included servants' quarters, an architectural sign of status, as they owned any number of slaves. This practice was common among rural landowners too until the mid-nineteenth century.[114] Muhammad al-ʿAziz Bu ʿAttur, a senior government official under Muhammad al-Sadoq Bey (1859-1882) and the French protectorate, maintained a staff of approximately twenty servants of guards, coachmen, grooms, gardeners, women to cook and do laundry, another woman to run errands, and the occasional wet nurse. This retinue did not include those compensated with room and board, seasonal employees hired to prepare annual provisions, or temporary staff to assist with wedding preparations.[115] Similar to the personnel at Bardo, female domestics were organized hierarchically underneath the authority of the woman of the house.[116]

The elite of the capital, whether merchants or *ʿulamaʾ* (learned scholars), owned estates within a hundred kilometers of Tunis, with olives, grains, and livestock for household consumption.[117] Grains, spices, dried meat and fish, olives, honey, salt, and pepper were stored in specific rooms (the *makhzen* or *bit al-muna*) destined for this purpose, making it unnecessary to purchase any of these goods.[118] As the average family may have had only a few small shelves for staples such as couscous, grains, chickpeas, and olive oil, the size of the pantry was an indication of comfort.[119] These reserves offered food security and were closely tied to the prestige of owning land, which protected the family from reliance on the market. In addition to these items, the palace *kummania* contained significant quantities of fruit preserves and sweets, permitting residents access to plentiful and varied meals throughout the year.

As mentioned above, Temple was treated to a lavish and "excellent" meal in a provincial town that included European dishes as well as couscous and rice pilaf.[120] Temple here hints at an intriguing paradox: while European travelers were attentive to local particularities, elite fashion was never completely provincial nor insular. Ahmad Bey employed at least two French chefs in the 1840s: Philippe Beranger and his brother-in-law Francois Pascal.[121] Ahmad Bey's interest in European cuisine was demonstrated in the preparations for his 1846 voyage to France. Whereas 'Ali Bey's 1777 envoy had included a *qahwaji* and chef to slaughter and cook his meat, Ahmad Bey requested a religious opinion (or *fatwa*) clarifying that it was permissible to consume foods prepared by Christians.[122] Unfortunately, aside from knowing that he sampled the soldier's soup and tested the bread of another regiment, we know little about the details of the bey's magnificent lunch at Versailles or dinner with military officers.[123] Ibn Dhiaf was presumably less impressed by their host's cooking than he was by the Tuilieries, Versailles, and the theater, as he makes no mention of what they ate.[124] In the end, Ahmad Bey apparently preferred Tunisian cooking (*couscous*, *brik*, and a porridge called *'assida*), which he requested from the kitchens of urban notables.[125]

The adoption of French- or Italian-style dishes was accompanied by European forms of table etiquette, as evidenced by Temple's surprise at seeing "the table laid out with knives and forks." European-style furniture was similarly popular; Pückler-Muskau said that chairs were brought in for the European guests when they met with the bey in 1835, and their coffee was served in "large cups of French china."[126] When Davis accompanied the *mahalla* in 1856, he noted that while the floor of his private tent was covered with a thick Jerban carpet, it was furnished with "several chairs, a table, [and] a capital bed."[127]

The fad among the notability for imported furniture could have begun before the palace picked it up, as the wealthy also traveled abroad and maintained contacts with European merchants. By the time of his premature death in 1826, the merchant Bekkar Jalluli had already acquired a number of luxury imports; these included dishware, an imported iron-framed bed, two gold-enameled chairs, and a glass chandelier.[128] Muhammad ibn Qasim al-Mahrizi, a religious notable who died in 1819, owned chairs, whereas the *'alim* Muhammad al-Tahir ibn Ashur left behind an estate that included sofas, easy chairs, dressers, a dressing table with mirrors, and crystal chandeliers.[129] Visiting the mansion of Khayr al-Din, another traveler noted that "Madame Kereddin uses knife and fork like all other grand ladies in Tunis, but orthodox ladies and those of the middle classes eat with their fingers."[130]

If the beys appreciated Italian baroque decorations, much the same could be said for the capital's urban society, as by the end of the nineteenth century, even modest homes included crude replications of Italian art.[131] Manors in Qayrawan and Sfax also manifested clear Italian (and Genoese) influences.[132] Such trends were increasingly identified by Europeans. In 1844, one visitor remarked upon the "European sofas and chairs, chandeliers and lamps" that she noticed at the palace. She concluded that in "most of the respectable Moorish houses as also at the Bardo, European furniture is now fashionable."[133] Hesse-Wartegg described the bey's palace as being "furnished with some furniture of the time of Louis XVI"; for instance, the bedroom contained "European style" pieces such as a chest of drawers, a looking glass, and easy chairs. As Khayr al-Din's palace contained "carpets, mirrors, and bronze ornaments in the style of Louis XVI," he similarly concluded "the Orientals have adopted Parisian furniture."[134]

Though the vogue for baroque architectural styles did not become widespread until the nineteenth century, Italian influences had already been apparent in interior décor even under the Hafsids. When he only briefly passed through Tunis in 1731, Charles-Marie de la Condamine noticed that the gallery of one of the palace courtyards was adorned with "large and handsome Venetian mirrors" that were evidently custom made.[135] He also noted English clocks, which were among the earlier imports. For instance, they figured among the gifts that Louis XVI sent to Tunis with the envoy Suleiman Agha following his 1777 voyage.[136]

Similar interests in European-inspired culinary experimentation and imported furnishings were apparent in Istanbul at roughly the same time. Sultan Mahmud II (1808–1839) not only preferred to eat with a fork and knife in the European manner, he also sent one of the cooks from the imperial kitchen to study European cuisine in Vienna. European fashions and furnishings coexisted with imperial customs, and European dishes were often served in addition to staples of the Ottoman table.[137] In Istanbul, imported clocks, watches, trays, and chairs were fashionable in the eighteenth century, and the most popular Western goods were watches.[138] In Beirut as well, by the end of the nineteenth century, the increasing quantity of European imports included pieces of furniture noted in Tunisian homes such as chairs and metal bedsteads.[139]

These lengthy trajectories of interest in European goods are indicative of an awareness, and appreciation, of European arts and culture. The chairs and silverware provided to European guests and the furnishing of the Dar al-Bey "entirely in European style" for royal visitors underscored the local attentiveness to European etiquette.[140] As a number of scholars have noted for the late nineteenth and early twentieth centuries, when Western goods were more widely available, they were selectively adapted into the local repertoire. This process of incorporation highlights how the transition to a modern consumerist economy and the cultivation of increasingly global tastes cannot be reduced to an uncritical westernization.[141] For the elites of Tunis, such goods were integral to class identities, without apparently challenging the notion of self. To return to Temple's comment, there was a coexistence of diverse influences, where the "Moorish" couscous, and "Turkish pilaf" were served alongside European dishes.

The basic staples of the culinary regime in Tunis were comparable to those in other Ottoman urban centers. The main component of the average Damascene diet was bread, supplemented by beans, seasonal produce, jams, dried fruits, and pickles. Both clarified butter and olive oil were also consumed (olive oil being the cheaper alternative); the difference in diet between the upper classes and the rest of the population was that the upper classes could afford to eat meat (usually mutton), and pastries, once again, were a sign of privilege.[142] In Anatolia as well, bread and the occasional vermicelli soup were prominent in the basic diet, and though sausage and dried meat were relatively more accessible than mutton and lamb, which were less expensive than poultry, large portions of the population could not afford meat on a regular basis. In addition to fruit preserves, sweet drinks based on fruit juices, various types of sweet breads and baklava, there were an array of sweets referred to simply as *helva*. These included one with honey and almonds and a second with sesame, which may have been comparable to the Ramadan sweets in Tunis; "both fruit and sweets were characteristic of Ottoman cuisine."[143] Yet there were also significant differences between these locales, as yogurt and cream certainly did not appear in the Bardo pantries to the extent that they appeared in Istanbul, and the Ottomans did not demonstrate the desire to spread a uniform culinary culture across their empire. What resemblances that existed between Damascus, Tunis, or Istanbul were seen in the hierarchies of food, and either quality (in the case of bread) or quantity (in the case of meat, pastries, and provisions) served to distinguish between social strata.

The beys of Tunis envisioned themselves as part of an early modern elite culture that emphasized abundance, which they reinforced by serving sweets and coffee to guests; provisioning travelers; and consuming pigeons, pistachios, and other delicacies that much of the population could not afford with any regularity. They ate baklava and drank coffee, added tomatoes (*tamatim*) to their stews, and received regular supplies of pasta (*maqruna*). The range of ingredients in their pantry suggested the combined influences of Ottoman elite habits, Iberian immigration, and Italian commerce. Instead of condensing this potlatch into a Tunisian recipe book of national cuisine or hastily drawing a rice-couscous boundary separating the Arab East from the West, the beys may have considered dinnertime a manifestation of class identity.[144]

It mattered not only what one ate but how one ate, including how often and how much. When ʿAli Pasha brought an artisan from Istanbul to design his glassware, he distinguished his table from those adorned with local products and proclaimed his affinity with imperial styles. Similarly, when Temple's hosts set his place with knives and forks, they signaled to their guests their comfort with European manners. When attentive to these broader cultural currents, meals at Bardo demonstrated how early modern courts shared an appreciation of culinary sophistication and spectacle that often transgressed religious or national boundaries. They also suggested the intermediary position of the ruling families in Tunis and the importance of their myriad ties to the established elite, even as the bey aspired to resemble the ruling classes of other provincial capitals.

Networks of consumption indicate the importance of the household as an organizational feature of the palace. They constituted the core of material life, where budgets, stipends, salaries, and allocations were grouped by household. As head of the province and the palace, the bey fulfilled the masculine responsibility of economic support by providing cash, clothes, and a variety of food for his immediate kin, extended family, slaves, servants, and other dependents. Foods were essential to holidays, celebrations, and social life, its amount and variety corresponding to the hierarchical order within the palace, between the subhouseholds of the ruling family, and even between divisions of soldiers. These vertical relationships were reiterated in naming conventions that specified proximity to the bey and incorporated individuals into the palace family. On the one hand, the relative political stability of the eighteenth and early nineteenth centuries allowed for state consolidation and a bureaucratic development that placed family at the center of the government. On the other, the shifting trends of elite consumption hinted at an interest in regional culture and a desire for change.

The bey [Husayn] has five wives, among whom Lady Fatma,
who died two years ago, was the most powerful.

FILIPPI, IN MONCHICOURT, *DOCUMENTS HISTORIQUE*

The palace at Bardo was under constant renovations, particularly in the eighteenth and nineteenth centuries when it functioned as the political center. Built in the early fifteenth century, it was one of the Hafsid's sub-urban retreats, with the Dar al-Bey in the center of Tunis serving official purposes. Slightly southwest of the capital, the Bardo's expansive gardens, pavilions, and decorative fountains evoked Almohad and Andalusian pala-tial models, though the entire complex was surrounded by fortified walls and five towers.[1] The Bardo was confiscated by the Ottoman imperial troops who conquered Tunis in the sixteenth century and purchased from the *diwan* by Hammuda Pasha in 1643, becoming the primary residence of the Muradite family a generation later. In the early eighteenth century, both Husayn ibn 'Ali and 'Ali Pasha expanded and renovated the original three buildings and vast gardens, with the former adding a mosque and a *hammam*, or bath house.[2] 'Ali Pasha turned his attention to the tribunal, or throne room, which was used for official ceremonies, and he covered the walls with marble, faience, and calligraphy in sculpted plaster with the in-tention of creating an edifice as magnificent as the mosques of Andalusia.[3]

Renovations continued under subsequent generations, becoming ex-tensive enough to merit a separate branch of the administration that regularly tallied thousands of piasters a month (see Figure 3.1).[4] When Muhammad al-Rashid and 'Ali returned from their Algerian exile in 1756, they were accompanied by a relatively small entourage; at least two of their sisters were still living, though only Fatma, who was married to their advisor, settled in Bardo. As the family expanded, benefitting from the improved political stability of the late eighteenth century, more of their sisters, wives, and daughters appear in the palace records. With their increasing prosperity, the beys built summer homes along the coast in

79

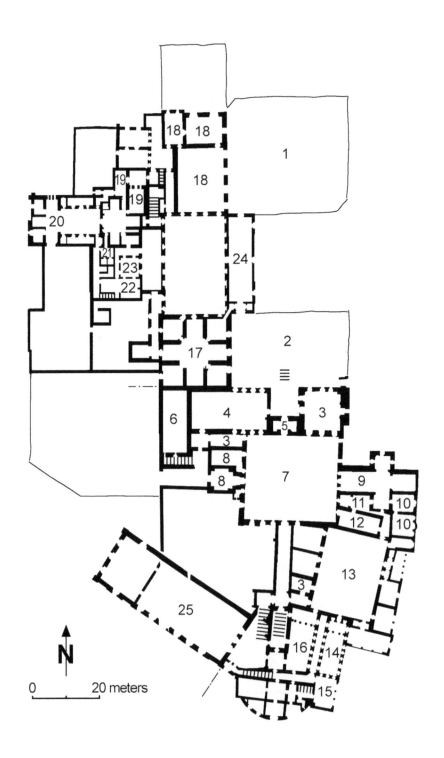

Marsa and Sidi bou Said, and they often wintered near the hot springs in Hammam-Lif.

In the mid-nineteenth century, Ahmad Bey began the process of investing considerable sums outside Bardo, preferring to expand the palace known as Muhammadiya. Instead of reserving it for a seasonal retreat, he transferred the court there permanently between 1846 and 1852, before spending his final years in Halq al-Wad. These palaces were intermittently used by junior beys and their brother-in-laws, so that by the end of the nineteenth century, not only had Bardo been transformed by the addition of a room of mirrors (the *bit al-bellar*), a music room, and a dining room to match the changing tastes of the era, but the family was no longer concentrated in one location that doubled as the official residence.[5]

The palaces in Tunis were dynamic spaces that were reconfigured in relation to Arab dynastic traditions, Ottoman ceremonials, local exigencies, and the predilections of each sovereign. Amidst these renovations, the

---

FIGURE 3.1. (OPPOSITE) *The main structures of the Bardo palace and some of its gardens in the late nineteenth century, after Jacques Revault,* Palais et résidences d'été de la région de Tunis, XVIe-XIXe siècles. *Paris: Editions du Centre national de la recherche scientifique, 1974. Numbers 1–16 represent the ground floor; 17–25, the upper level. The larger courtyards were surrounded by columns and often two stories in height. The ground-level storage spaces and cistern are not shown.*

KEY:

Ground Floor
1. courtyard
2. second courtyard with the lion staircase
3. guard rooms
4. tribunal, hall of justice
5. *sqifa*, antechamber
6. gallery looking onto gardens
7. interior courtyard
8. *bit al-mshaikh*
9. *bit al-basha*
10. *masjid*, prayer room for palace staff
11. small interior courtyard
12. *khazna*, archives and treasury
13. interior courtyard

14. *bit al-billar*, room of mirrors
15. terrace and sitting room
16. courtyard

Upper Floor
17. *dar al-harim*, or *byut al-ʿalaji*, women's apartments
18. *suraya*, reception rooms
19. private rooms
20. apartment
21. *hammam*, baths
22. kitchen
23. courtyard
24. music room
25. throne room

FIGURE 3.2. *A courtyard in the section of the harem renovated by Husayn Bey, Bardo Museum, Tunisia, photo by the author.*

palace consistently contained two distinct spaces: those for official business and the residential areas, or the harem. The exterior doorway opened onto a long road lined with shops before leading to the main building with its sequential gates and courtyards, with passage between its administrative and domestic wings controlled by a series of palace attendants. While harem refers to a range of institutions of considerable geographic and temporal variety from the early Islamic caliphates through the modern era, it was a key component of palace social organization, the heterogeneous nature of which defied modern spatial binaries between public and private.[6]

By the early nineteenth century, the Bardo harem contained numerous multiroom apartments, at least two private courtyards, a garden, and reception rooms. Paved with marble, the walls covered with decorative tiles in floral motifs and vases, its rich ornamentation included vaulted ceilings and elaborately carved wood friezes. Each courtyard contained a marble fountain and was surrounded with white marble columns that formed a gallery in front of the arched doorways leading to different apartments (see Figure 3.2). The windows were filled with complex stuccowork, and a grilled bay window allowed the women to observe activities in the entrance halls below. Private corridors led from the harem to the *hammam* and the servants' quarters.[7] When such spaces were used for entertaining, they were richly adorned. European women described sitting in a long rectangular salon off the main courtyard that held tapestries and red velvet cloth with gold stitching that decorated its surfaces. On these occasions, the entranceway was covered with brightly colored silk curtains; gilt birdcages hung from the ceiling; and collections of clocks, weapons, and mother-of-pearl boxes were displayed throughout the room.[8] The use of expensive materials, such as marble, combined with architectural details and artisanal flourish, allowed the harem to reiterate the image of abundance, luxury, and privilege that was apparent in the range of administrative staff and quantities of food.

Ruling-class ideology and palace structures located the harem in a semiotics of power; these were infused with local values characteristic of provincial household organization. The palace families were acutely aware of the almost contradictory tensions this produced between the prerogative of distinction and the need to belong. Under the guise of social activities, the harem created an ideal setting for the elaboration of local dynastic customs to high-society women and distinguished foreign guests. Yet for all their public activities, the sources on the wives, sisters, and mothers of the beys, let alone the junior women in the ruling family, or the female staff composed mainly of slaves, are fragmentary. This chapter assembles these disparate traces to sketch the internal functioning of the harem as an institution and present a general picture of women's lives. These women provided an indispensable link between the palace and urban society, connections that were evident in marriage alliances and that fostered common cultural practices. Turning to a discussion of prominent women in each generation, the chapter demonstrates how women's political and diplomatic activities intersected with the familial model of government. Finally, it offers a close reading of palace socializing to examine the interaction of the palace families with local notables and foreign diplomats by comparing the visits by the shaykh Muhammad Saghir during the rule of ʿAli Pasha and those of European women in the 1830s. Oscillating between imperial repertoires and local dynamics, this chapter fleshes out the intermediary position of the ruling families in Tunis. The size of the palace suggests that the beys aspired to membership in the class of early modern rulers, an ideal complemented by the activities of palace women who strove to establish a local base of support so that the construction, production, and presentation of political power were a family affair.

The harem was primarily a residential space containing the apartments of the extended family, often under the authority of a wife, concubine, widow, or female relative of the bey. The senior women bore the ultimate responsibility for the logistics of managing a sizeable household. Whether they performed such tasks themselves or monitored their execution, the majority of its inhabitants spent their time "engaged in various occupations."[9] This included gold and silver embroidery; the decoration of clothing, tablecloths, curtains, and other linens; the stuffing of mattresses and pillows; and the storage and preparation of the impressive quantities of food regularly delivered to the palace (see Figure 3.3).[10] Approximately half of the seasonal fruit supply was candied and preserved for the winter months, and the pickled olives required a constant supply of vinegar. The women made pastries and pressed their own rose water.[11] Wheat was ground at the palace mills, and both bread and couscous were domestically produced throughout this period.[12] At least one visitor to the harem noted that the women "employ a portion of the day in making pastries and couscous and other dainty dishes."[13] The labor of these women substituted for an extensive kitchen staff; even for occasions such as wedding banquets, few butchers and cooks were required.

The wives and concubines of the beys were expected to meet the reproductive needs of hereditary rule. Despite the palace families benefiting from a relatively balanced diet, regular access to water, and the constant presence of doctors, infant and child mortality was a feature of palace life, and death in childbirth was not uncommon; in 1827, Husayn Bey's wife Fatma died from an illness she had contracted during labor.[14] While there were only three small, unmarked tombs built in the main family mausoleum, in the late eighteenth century at least one child was lost approximately every five years. Certain children appear only once in the records: a daughter of Mahmud ibn Muhammad al-Rashid, 'Ali ibn Husayn's son Suleiman, and Yusuf, the son of Mahmud ibn Husayn.[15] Funerals were held for others who were buried in the family mausoleum, including one of the daughters of Mna Ghazalia and Muhammad al-Rashid in 1760; Trakiya, the young daughter of 'Ali Bey in 1772; and the sons of 'Uthman Bey and Hammuda Pasha, who died in 1793 and 1800 before either had reached the age of ten, a loss that profoundly disheartened Hammuda Pasha.[16]

Infertility may have further complicated the task in certain situations; though Hammuda Pasha had many concubines, he had only one son, and

FIGURE 3.3. *"Tunisian women unwinding silk," from Charles Lallemand,* Tunis et ses environs, *Paris, Maison Quantin, 1890.*

similarly neither Ahmad Bey nor Muhammad al-Sadoq Bey had any surviving children. The number of children varied from one household to the next, though generally the men with more wives or concubines had larger families. Husayn ibn ʿAli had at least eight children, as did his son ʿAli, and Husayn ibn Mahmud Bey had fifteen surviving children. The average number of children per family within the palace can only be estimated, since the data are partial. The number of male children is often easier to establish than that of female, and the number of wives and children is easier to verify for those men who eventually governed than those who did not. Table 3.1 summarizes the available information, grouped by generation. This indicates that polygamous men and those with multiple concubines fathered more children, though the average number of surviving children per woman was less than two.

The data on the family size of most of the bey's daughters who married are even scantier for the period prior to 1850. In the case of Hafsia, whose marriage with her cousin ʿAli Pasha ended in divorce, and that of Trakiya with her cousin, the political importance of these alliances outweighed their role in childbearing; though both men had children with other wives, they may have practiced abstinence with their cousins. Similarly, there is no indication that Khaduja bint ʿAli Bey had children with either of her husbands (Mustafa Khoja or later Yusuf Sahib al-Tabaʿa, as

TABLE 3.I. NUMBER OF CHILDREN PER PALACE MALE

Male head of house	Number of known wives and concubines	Number of known surviving children	Number of children per woman
Husayn ibn 'Ali	3	8	2.7
Muhammad ibn 'Ali	1	4	4.0
'Ali Pasha	4	6	1.5
Muhammad al-Rashid	5	6	1.2
'Ali ibn Husayn	4	8	2.0
Yunus ibn 'Ali Pasha	2	4	2.0
Muhammad ibn 'Ali Pasha	1	3	3.0
Suleiman ibn 'Ali Pasha	1	2	2.0
Mahmud ibn Muhammad al-Rashid	2	3	1.5
Ismail ibn Muhammad al-Rashid	2	?	0.0
Hammuda ibn 'Ali	8	0	0.0
'Uthman ibn 'Ali	3	5	1.7
Muhammad al-Mimun ibn 'Ali	1	1	1.0
Husayn ibn Mahmud	5	15	3.0
Mustafa ibn Mahmud	3	7	2.3

most sources concur that the latter was executed before the marriage was consummated). An undated inheritance document states that 'Ali Bey's daughter Jannat also died without offspring.[17] None of the other women appear to have had extraordinarily large families; Fatma bint Husayn may have had two children, Amina bint 'Ali Bey had four, her sister 'Aisha had two or three, and Amina's daughter 'Aziza had four.

Each birth was an occasion for celebrations, feasts, and gifts. When a woman went into labor, she was given new clothes, while outfits were prepared for the infant.[18] An array of rich food was prepared that included nuts, sweets, eggs, and mutton.[19] Especially in the late eighteenth century when the bey often traveled outside the capital on the *mahalla*, he distributed a reward to whoever announced the good news of a birth at Bardo, whether soldiers, guards, or doctors. On one occasion in 1757, an otherwise unidentifiable woman was gifted forty piasters.[20] The wives, or *juar*, increased in status with motherhood, as indicated by the moniker of one of Muhammad al-Rashid Bey's wives, *Om al-bnat*, "the mother of his daughters."[21]

Children were raised under the supervision of their mothers, wet nurses, nannies, and tutors. Both girls and boys received at least a minimal Qur'anic education and were encouraged to memorize its passages.[22] Even in the late eighteenth century, teachers employed by the palace included local women, such as the female instructor named Khadija, as well as foreigners, such as the tutor Fatma the Genoese.[23] Europeans were more visible in the early nineteenth century, at least to their compatriots, as travelers remarked upon a palace interpreter rumored to be a Christian from Tuscany and French nursemaids.[24] Around mid-century, Muhammad al-Sadoq Bey requested that French missionaries then resident in Tunis send instructors to the palace for the education of his children.[25] While these references were scattered, coinciding with a vogue for hiring European women as governesses at the provincial court in Cairo, the majority of the female personnel consisted of slaves.

Bardo was continually expanding so that it could easily accommodate additional apartments for each marital couple. As they began their new lives, brides in the family received a cash dowry and considerable quantities of valuable clothing and household items. In 1774, Muhammad al-Rashid's daughter was given 1,000 piasters, and the items in her trousseau (*jihaz*) totaled twice that amount. By the 1850s, the bey was rumored to give each bride 30,000 piasters, while the expenses on the trousseau reached over 110,000 piasters.[26] Upon marriage, a woman became entitled to the package of subsidies that included foods, Ramadan sweets, lambs at 'id al-Idha, new summer and winter uniforms each year, and clothing for slaves in her service. This entitlement applied when men in the family took new wives or when their sisters and daughters married, though concubines received approximately half of the provisions package.

Dress and provisions constituted material signs of hierarchies within the harem, where women with adult children commanded more respect and deference than those with younger children. These distinctions were marked discursively and structurally in accounting records that refer to a senior woman as constituting *al-dar al-kebira*, the primary or main household, of her son or husband. Other wives and concubines were differentiated in the order of their marriages as *al-dar al-ula*, *al-dar al-thaniya* for the first or second house, or *al-dar al-jedida* for newlyweds. Tables 3.2 and 3.3 reproduce the complete salary lists for 1758 and 1783 to illustrate how

TABLE 3.2. HOUSEHOLD SALARIES, REGISTER 99 (1171/1758)

Name	Salary (piasters per month)
Sidna's [Muhammad al-Rashid Bey] big house	20
Sidna's first house	15
Sidna's second house	15
Sidna's house that came from Algeria	20
Sidna's *juar*	15
'Ali Bey's first house	15
Sidna's sister [Fatma]	50
Sidna's sister's daughter	15

nominal distinctions corresponded to material ones. These stipends were destined to support the wives and dependents of men in the ruling family (as adult men received personal salaries after 1783). In 1758 the largest sum went to Fatma bint Husayn, whereas in 1783 'Ali Bey's wife Trakiya bint 'Ali Pasha and Hammuda Pasha's mother each received fifty piasters per month, almost double the mean allocation for junior women. Amounts of the monthly stipends depended upon the hierarchical organization of the palace's female residents presided over by the mother of the reigning bey, his wives, and an older generation of women and then the younger women such as married daughters or nieces. Girls who were not yet married were included in the households of their mothers. These gradations were reiterated in staple foods, holiday bonuses, clothing, and the number of slaves in each household.

Whether married, divorced, or widowed, women had a continued right to financial support throughout their lives. After Muhammad al-Rashid died in 1759, his wife Mna Ghazalia received enough maintenance to sustain at least a small entourage of female slaves until her death sometime around 1810.[27] Ismail's wife also received foods and money through 1836, though her husband had never been governor and had died twenty years earlier. For mature adult women who resided in separate households, the death of a spouse was not detrimental to their position within the family, since they depended on the bey as the ultimate family patriarch.

The first names of women in the family were not included in salary registers, and they were instead identified by their relation to the ruling

TABLE 3.3. HOUSEHOLD SALARIES, REGISTER 229 (1197/1783)

Name	Salary (piasters per month)
Mahmud	350.0
Muhammad al-Mimun	300.0
'Uthman	300.0
Ismail	350.0
Sidna's first house [bint al-Barudi]	30.0
Sidna's mother [Mahbuba]	50.0
His four *juar* (20 each)	80.0
House of late Sidna ['Ali, Trakiya bint 'Ali Pasha]	50.0
'Uthman's three houses	65.0
'Uthman's house	20.0
'Uthman's *jaria*	10.0
Mahmud's house	30.0
Sidna's first sister [Amina]	30.0
Sidna's second sister [Jannat]	30.0
Sidna's little sister [Khaduja]	30.0
Muhammad al-Mimun's house	20.0
Ismail's mother	15.0
Ismail's *jaria*	20.0
House of the deceased [Muhammad al-Rashid], Om al-bnat	10.0
House of bint al-Ghazali [Mna]	10.0
[Muhammad al-Rashid's] two daughters	10.0
Sidna's aunt [Fatma]	50.0
House of [Fatma's son] Hammuda Shelebi	7.5

bey. For instance, Fatma, the daughter of Husayn ibn 'Ali, was first mentioned as *dar okht Sidna*, or "the house of our lord's sister" during the government of her brothers Muhammad al-Rashid and 'Ali, and later as *dar 'amt Sidna*, or "our lord's paternal aunt" when her nephew Hammuda was bey.[28] When the palace women married mamluks, they maintained a certain degree of seniority since they had neither co-wives nor female in-laws in their immediate households. Their husbands' names and titles could be added, as in the case of Kebura, the daughter of Husayn Bey, who was referred to as "Sidna's third daughter the wife of Husayn Khoja."[29] These records do not offer any evidence that palace women lived in polygamous households, which was probably a sign of their status.

Though they were considered ineligible for the beyship, the children of the bey's female relatives could receive support from the general treasury. Only one of Husayn ibn ʿAli's daughters lived in the palace after 1756: Fatma, the full sister of Muhammad al-Rashid and ʿAli and one of the prominent palace women from the 1760s through 1780s.[30] A son from her first marriage, Hammuda Shelebi, seems to have lived in the palace, and his wife was supported after his death.[31] A series of receipts for the bey's niece beginning with a 1756 wedding were presumably for Fatma's daughter, who was given twenty-four diamonds and gold-embroidered clothing. It is possible that the wedding was celebrated alongside the nuptials of the reigning bey Muhammad al-Rashid and his cousin Mna Ghazalia the same year.[32] Immediately thereafter, this niece was added to salary lists at the current rate for junior women.[33] When Fatma's daughter had a baby in 1759, special foods were prepared in celebration, and there were further festivities when her grandson was circumcised in 1766, with money given to guests who brought sweets and considerable amounts of charities distributed on the same day.[34] Fatma died in February 1793, and her burial was coordinated by a respected urban official, the shaykh al-Medina. She was commemorated in the days following her death and the fortieth day afterwards.[35] In the early decades of the nineteenth century, ʿAziza bint Mahmud Bey's four children were included in the ruling family and appear to have been raised in the palace. Marriages through the maternal line retied family connections.[36]

The archival construction of household organization, with its categories and implicit hierarchies, reiterated on a smaller scale the structural privileging of seniority prevalent in Istanbul.[37] It also presents the family as a rigid institution operating according to reproductive necessity and labor requirements, obscuring the profoundly human aspects of love and affection that colored the life of the family. As will be detailed below, the beys were often fond of their sisters, consulted their mothers, and heeded the advice of their wives. Local notables considered the palace women more secluded than their own wives and daughters, but this did not preclude the fostering of numerous commonalities between Bardo and the elites of the capital, which were sustained by women.[38]

PALACE PRACTICES IN LOCAL AND REGIONAL CONTEXTS

Marriage constituted a significant transition in the life of the palace households, one that involved both the vast output of labor and extensive festivities. This continued to be a significant way to confirm and solidify alliances. On the one hand, even though the beys may have kept concubines, they were formally married to their freed slaves, a practice that was also common among urban notables.[39] On the other hand, into the nineteenth century, men and women in the palace continued to marry with prominent provincial families. A few of these (Ahmad Bey to Menana bint Shelebi, Fatma bint Husayn Bey to Muhammad al-Murabit, Zeniha bint Husayn Bey to Ahmad Zarruq) confirmed the proximity of these families to the political center, while others created alliances with prominent commercial and religious lineages (Mahmud Bey to the daughter of ʿAli ibn Mustafa al-Andalusi, Muhammad al-Sadoq Bey to the daughter of Muhammad al-Arusi, Hammuda Pasha to the daughter of the mufti Muhammad ibn Husayn al-Barudi, and Muhammad ibn Husayn Bey to the daughter of shaykh Muhammad Bayram). Later in the nineteenth century, mamluks whose fortunes originated in the palace and who married palace women, such as Mustafa Bash Agha and Mustafa Khaznadar, transitioned into urban society, founding lineages and integrating with business and religious circles to the point of marrying with them.[40] Wealthy merchants collaborated with the bey in the export of *shashia*s, respected *ʿulama* were in constant contact with the palace, and whether as scribes, notaries, or in-laws, these constant and intimate engagements between Bardo and the local notability meant that by the early nineteenth century, the beys were closely tied to the established lineages of the capital.[41]

As many wealthy families combined domestic space with business activities, the structure of their homes demarcated these spheres in ways comparable to Bardo. Each contained multiple vestibules or antechambers (the *sqifa* or *driba*) for receiving visitors who had business with the head of the household so that social requirements did not disturb the functioning of the household. At the same time, such passageways distanced their homes from the street, creating an atmosphere of privacy and seclusion within a densely populated urban setting. As a wealthy family acquired new properties, its members transformed the homes of commoners into vast residential complexes suited to their status by the addition of a *driba*, upper floor, and stables.[42] Other families adopted the term *saraya* to denote the space containing the private apartments of the family. Most included rooms to lodge guests, housed domestic servants and slaves, and had considerable space for the storage of provisions such as grains and olives brought from their agricultural estates, called the *bit al-muna*, *kummania*, or *ʿulaʾ al-khazin*, depending on the region.[43]

Many of these homes were polygamous, adopting an internal organization that was described using terminology similar to that found in the palace. For instance, when the officer 'Abd al-Wahhab ibn Yusuf al-Sharni took a second wife, she was provided with a recently purchased neighboring house annexed to his own known as *al-dar al-saghira*, whereas his first wife remained in the primary residence, *al-dar al-kebira*.[44] At least in the eighteenth century and the first half of the nineteenth, a number of prominent urban men, both merchants and *'ulama'*, were married more than once, such as Muhammad ibn 'Ashur, Yusuf Jait, Hasan Haddad, Hammuda Muhsin, as well as men in the al-Asram, Nayffar, Mestiri, and Sharif families. Over the course of the nineteenth century, financial difficulties and changing mores meant that monogamous marriages were more widespread among the elites of the capital, with an increasing association between polygamy and rural or peasant practices.[45] One sample from the middle class suggested that by the late nineteenth century, less than 9 percent of families were polygamous.[46] In the palace, polygamy was relatively universal for the bey and his male descendants through the mid-nineteenth century, and its waning by the turn of the twentieth century can be partially attributed to financial constraints.

Blili's study of family life during the French colonial era indicated that the average family in Tunis had 3.4 surviving children. Polygamous households contained more children (4.5) than monogamous ones (about 3).[47] One of the factors mitigating against large families was the relatively high rate of infant and child mortality, to which Bardo was not immune. Combined with periodic epidemics, this was high enough in the countryside so that the rate of population growth was quite slow. Even in urban areas, Christian missionaries claimed that infant and child mortality remained considerable throughout the nineteenth century.[48] These figures allow for the tentative conclusion that the number of children in Bardo's households was quite comparable with the average number of surviving children in the general population.

While the organization of domestic space around an interior courtyard was amenable to joint-family households, the composition varied from one family to the next and over the course of the life cycle. In the choicest neighborhoods of the capital, those near the main *suq* and the Zaytuna mosque, homeowners resorted to purchasing adjacent properties or owned multiple houses in one vicinity, due to the constraints of urban space. Even in homes that were made into *awqaf*, multiple-family households were not the norm.[49] Among other sectors of the population, there was even greater variety; at one point, the Shili residence included four generations, whereas single-story homes may have consisted of only two sisters or a divorced woman and her aunt.[50] The only discernible commonalities were the departure of young women upon marriage, their return as widows or divorcees, and the rarity of nuclear families. That the family home did not include married daughters was articulated in a number of endowment records specifying single, divorced, and widowed women.[51]

The ruling family diverged from these patterns, as Bardo was constantly a multigenerational home that incorporated married women who established independent households within the palace. As the bey's daughters married exclusively with men raised in the palace, whether mamluks or members of their extended family, Bardo functioned as their natal home and that of their husbands. Its location a few kilometers from the capital facilitated additions and expansions.

While by the mid-eighteenth century, marriage alliances were less a question of military tactic, they remained central to social relations. In terms of cultural norms, the households at Bardo were comparable to upper-class families in the capital. For instance, in a study of twenty elite families spanning the late nineteenth and much of the twentieth century, Sophie Ferchiou found that that the predominant pattern was for two families or sets of families to contract repeat marriages between their children. This was more frequent than marriage between cousins, which occurred about 9 percent of the time (including paternal and maternal cousins).[52] While in some families there was not a single instance of cousin marriage, in others it was as frequent as 14 to 17 percent.[53] The 'ulama' did not demonstrate any marked corporate endogamy, and even if there was a preference for repeat marriages between families, intrafamily marriages were rare by the second half of the nineteenth century.[54]

We can observe a similar pattern at Bardo, as there were four documented cousin-marriages between 1750 and 1850, first between paternal cousins, and then maternal cousins.[55] These were Trakiya bint 'Ali Pasha and 'Ali ibn Husayn Bey (around 1756) and Amina bint 'Ali Bey with her cousin Mahmud ibn Muhammad al-Rashid (in 1776); Fatma Mestiri's son Muhammad al-Sadoq married her brother's daughter Henana (in 1835), and Zeneiha bint Husayn married her maternal cousin 'Ali around the same time (he was the son of Husayn's sister 'Aziza and Suleiman Kahia).[56] The third example demonstrates the proclivity for unions with the Mestiri family, which also included 'Aziza's daughter Zubeida, who married her uncle Ahmad Mestiri. There were also multiple marriages with the descendants of 'Uthman Dey and the Shelebi family (wives of Husayn ibn Mahmud and Ahmad ibn Mustafa). The dominant preference within the palace was for marriages with female slaves and mamluks, and those between cousins accounted for slightly over 10 percent of the reasonably well documented unions.

Even if women's role in negotiating marriage alliances was conspicuous when one of the spouses was a maternal relative, palace women presumably participated in the process on a much more regular basis. In the population at large, women's opinions were predominant in marital arrangements, and social conventions permitted older women a greater range of activities within their families.[57] This suggests women's weight in the management of household affairs because marriage was a considerable family investment, especially among the scions of the elite who viewed themselves as part of a lineage. The celebration of marriages consumed vast resources. While expectations varied according to regional differences, the parents of both the bride and the groom contributed materially to the establishment of the new household. Dowries included gold, pearls, and clothing, and the bride's parents provided dozens of tunics, larger quantities of scarves, and long lists of jewelry in the form of a trousseau. The newlyweds were also furnished with curtains, pillows, blankets, and bedroom furniture (see Figure 3.4), and when they had the means, parents might also provide the couple with a slave.[58] Though families were patriarchal in composition, this did not preclude women from exercising authority within the average home, where the senior patriarch often shared his power with other elders in the family, notably the women.

Affluent families often relied upon the services of domestics and slaves, though wives and daughters still contributed to household labor. Particularly among merchants who preferred to live in close proximity to the main *suq*, a spacious home and its courtyards became an extension of their businesses. For instance, the wives of perfume merchants distilled flowers and prepared ointments and incenses to be sold in the market.[59] There existed a hierarchy of labor within such homes, with domestics and slaves responsible for doing the wash or preparing couscous, with wives and mothers supervising the activities of their kitchens and contributing to prestigious activities such as baking pastries for celebrations as opposed to engaging in routine chores.[60] A considerable amount of time and energy, particularly during the summer, was devoted to stocking provisions for the winter to fill the multiple rooms reserved for this function. Ideally, wheat, produce, and livestock were brought from family estates so that little was purchased from the market, and everything from couscous and olive oil to dried tomatoes, pickled vegetables, sausage (or *mer-*

FIGURE 3.4. *"Wedding gifts," from Charles Lallemand,* Tunis et ses environs, *Paris, Maison Quantin, 1890.*

gez), and dried mutton (called *qadid*) was prepared at home. Even anecdotal evidence indicates that the kitchen operations of the notability were extensive, reiterating how the amount of food a family could afford, and the number of people it fed, projected the image of household wealth and status.[61]

The ruling families benefited from a spacious extraurban palace that could expand to accommodate married daughters, the presence of multiple generations, agnatic kin, and polygamous households. While marriages with mamluks and *juar* were frequent, the beys affirmed and anticipated alliances with the notable families of Tunis. In addition, the beys deferred to the *ʿulamaʾ* and were careful to cultivate relations with them;

the bey was as liable to observe an erudite scholar teaching as he was to attend the funeral of an imam.[62] Any royal pretensions thus coexisted with demonstrations of respect for the established families of the province with whom they exchanged slaves and dependents and celebrated family events.

WOMEN AND PALACE FACTIONS

Whether through their mamluk spouses or by virtue of their proximity to the bey, the activities of palace women shaped court politics in the period between 1750 and 1850. They could arrange marriages between their daughters or nieces and promising mamluks, thus bringing them into the family as son-in-laws. Such machinations may have been at play in the brief rivalry between Ismail Kahia and Mustafa Khoja around 1780. As the two men vied for influence over the bey, each was associated with a different party at court. Ismail Kahia was supported by his wife ʿAisha, the bey's eldest daughter, and Mustafa Khoja relied on the intercession of the bey's wife Trakiya bint ʿAli Pasha, who facilitated his marriage to the bey's daughter Khaduja.[63] As was true during the early eighteenth century, when women such as Kebira Mamia and Fatma bint ʿUthman acted as advisors to their husbands, palace women continued to weigh in on decisions for promotion and favoritism among government servants. For instance, Ahmad Bey's mother was credited with the vertiginous ascent of Mustafa Khaznadar and his tenacious hold on power, as she was particularly fond of him and treated him like a grandson.[64] Women's authority was closely tied to that of mamluks, because they both benefited from the familial structures of government and a political culture that was heavily personal.

While much of women's strategizing occurred behind the scenes, their involvement became more apparent during periods of political instability, when greater attention was drawn to palace affairs. There were smooth transitions of rule after 1756, first from elder to younger brother and then from father to son, without adhering to any established pattern. When Hammuda Pasha died without an heir in 1814, the two candidates for succession were his older cousin Mahmud and younger brother ʿUthman. While the choice of the former would privilege seniority, the latter would prioritize one branch of the family; either option had implications for women and ramifications for their children, depending on their proximity to the two contenders. In fact, after ʿUthman was nominated by the men at court, he took concrete steps to ensure the succession of his sons to the detriment of the family at large, namely, Mahmud and his descendants. In December 1814, Mahmud and his sons Husayn and Mustafa led an insurrection against 'Uthman, killing him and his older sons Salah and 'Ali, though they spared their wives and younger children.[65] Mahmud was assisted by about one hundred palace personnel and supported by the military, and his investiture was sanctioned by the majority of the ministers, advisors, and notables.[66] Though reminiscent of the eighteenth century wars that spiraled from an identical problem, this was contained within the palace.

According to ibn Dhiaf, Mahmud's wife Amina was a strong advocate for her husband and sons. The daughter of 'Ali Bey and his wife Mahbuba, Amina's three children (Husayn, Mustafa and 'Aziza) stood to benefit from potential access to the beyship versus further marginalization within the palace, just as she had been a close confidant of her brother Hammuda before 'Uthman distanced her. Her sons were not given important positions in 'Uthman's government but were passed over for his own partisans.[67] This had material ramifications, since 'Uthman's preparations for the succession of his son Salah included doubling the young man's monthly stipend.[68] These measures indicated his preference for primogeniture, which would have invalidated the claims of Amina's husband and sons.

Ibn Dhiaf retrospectively justifies the assassination by emphasizing succession by age and focusing on family relationships and emotional ties. Hammuda's attachment to Amina and his affection for her sons stood in contrast to 'Uthman's disrespect for her and disengagement with her sons. This was particularly pronounced when 'Uthman decided to remove Amina from their father's apartment in Bardo, downgrading her to smaller accommodations elsewhere in the palace. Considered an affront to both Amina and Mahmud, Mahmud chastised his cousin for having "disregarded us, and treated me as one would treat the younger ones in the household," in a blatant breach of seniority.[69] Even if Amina served as a vector for relations between the two men, and Amina stood to gain from the changing order of succession, ibn Dhiaf does not explicitly indicate that she was an active conspirator in Mahmud's ousting of 'Uthman.

Emotional relationships between siblings or lack thereof had concrete political ramifications in ibn Dhiaf's narrative. While these center around Amina, who earned the affection of her brother Hammuda, the confidence of her husband, and the deference of her sons, ibn Dhiaf frames the relationships within her adherence to the hierarchical order of the family and respect for gender roles. On the evening following Mahmud's investiture, Amina summoned her sons Husayn and Mustafa to swear loyalty to each other and respect the role of seniority in succession. The pact between the brothers was posited as foundational, symbolizing Amina's authority over her sons and the goodwill that predominated between the two brothers. Through this pledge, her intercession guaranteed fraternal harmony and was able to prevent further discord within the family.[70]

Amina presumably had a hand in arranging marriages over the course of the following year between four mamluks from Hammuda Pasha's innermost circle and women in the family. These were the unions of her daughter 'Aziza to Suleiman Kahia, her younger sister Khaduja to Yusuf Sahib al-Taba'a, and her sister 'Aisha's two daughters Halima and Fatma to Khayr al-Din Kahia and Yusuf Kahia Dar al-Basha respectively.[71] As was typical for such occasions, the nuptial celebrations entailed considerable expenses from the bakers and butchers preparing the feast to weavers and tailors making rugs and gold-embroidered clothing for the brides.[72] Affiliating Hammuda Pasha's advisors to Mahmud's family ensured their support and demonstrated continuity between the two beys. The festivities allowed Mahmud to host the local elites at the palace, offer charities, and act as the family patriarch, benevolently doting on the younger generation of women in various branches of the family.

The new pattern of succession was beneficial to Mahmud, Amina, their children, and their daughter-in-law, Fatma Mestiri, who hailed from a prominent family in the capital. Fatma's brother Muhammad Mestiri was an influential local notable and successful merchant specializing in the *shashia* business, and ibn Dhiaf says she was a descendant of 'Uthman Dey.[73] Fatma was also a close confidant of her husband and had much to gain by the transfer of power to her father-in-law. She solidified her position within the palace through additional marriages, as it is highly likely that she inspired at least two other unions: that of her son 'Allala (from her first marriage) and Husayn's daughter Hafsia (in 1821), and one between her son Muhammad al-Sadoq and her brother Ahmad Mestiri's daughter Henana (in 1826).[74] These successive alliances tightened the ties to these paragons of provincial commerce who were an integral component of local society.

By all accounts, Fatma Mestiri was a powerful woman. Ibn Dhiaf praised and commended her as a wife who brought good fortune to her husband. Reflecting on her death in 1827, when Husayn and a number of men at court wore mourning attire for a full year, he wrote that she was worthy of this level of respect because of her generosity "and for the way she knew how to make people love her husband." He not only stressed how such qualities were those of a virtuous wife, he also appreciated her maternal sentimentality: "She pitied the humble, tended to orphans, and helped those who suffered from misfortune." She was proper and respectful, and her death following childbirth only reinforced the image of her as a virtuous mother dedicated to her family.[75]

In sharp contrast to this picture, European observers condoned her influence as a threat. Upon her death, the French consul Constantin Guys observed, "The bey appears to be profoundly affected by the loss of a woman that he was very attached to," but he chastised the way she "had acquired so much influence over his moods that she governed more than he did."[76] As indicated in the epigraph to this chapter, Fatma was recognized as "the most powerful" of Husayn's wives, and Temple referred to her ominously as "the famous Fatma."[77] Luigi Calligaris, a native of Piedmont who served briefly as the vice-consul of Sardinia, was her most virulent critic. He arrived in 1834, seven years after Fatma's death, and his writing reflects hearsay and the rumors in circulation about palace women. He accused her of bribery, corruption, and selfish materialism, claiming that she used her money to buy the loyalty of palace personnel, was rewarded by marriage to Husayn, and loved jewels to such a degree that Husayn depleted the treasury to please her.[78] While these comments evoke the European stereotype of female consumerism as harmful, they brand women's authority as illegitimate and imply an otherwise unsubstantiated role in the plot against 'Uthman.

Whether Amina goaded her sons in their attack against 'Uthman, as Calligaris claims, or was merely an opinionated woman who was respected by her sons is difficult to discern. However speculative, these tales about women's devious schemes to manipulate rival factions at court provide an indication of their authority and substantiates how the question of succession directly impacted them. For the supporters who praised their influence as ensuring harmony at court, and the opponents who criticized them for sowing the seeds of destruction, both accolade and criticism framed these arguments on a common understanding of gender roles and women's commitment to their families.

HAREM VISITS

Women held their own court in the harem when they hosted guests. Social calls offered an occasion to deploy their culinary talents, parade sizeable entourages, and dress in the finest clothes. Europeans were intrigued by the harem and carefully noted details relating to food, clothing, and decoration, some finding signs of bourgeois domesticity, while others identified models of liberation or were fixated with the trope of imprisonment. Although a number of European men were received at the different palaces of Tunis, they were able to enter the harem only when it was empty. Few Tunisians seem to have written in detail about experiences at palace events. Instead, earlier writings about the harem are often secondhand and authored by men. Nevertheless, they offer a glimpse of palace socializing and hint at its political purposes.

Ibn Yusuf sheds light on the palace interior in the eighteenth century, and as a member of the military, he would have been familiar with Bardo, though his writing undoubtedly reflected his literary interests as well. He provides a lengthy description of the reception of Muhammad Saghir, a central figure of the powerful Awlad 'Amar tribe who was considered a key ally by both contenders in the dispute over succession. Recall that around 1735, after 'Ali Pasha's marriage to Muhammad Saghir's daughter, he encouraged his bride to invite her father to the palace. Presented with gifts and treated to a fine meal, he was escorted by the head eunuch to his daughter's residence in the harem, which was "such a paradise, and he was amazed at the luxury of this apartment." There he was greeted by "white slaves, concubines, servants, old women, and all of the harem personnel," and then by the "white slaves and odalisques in his daughter's suite, who were overjoyed to see him." Muhammad Saghir's reaction can be partially attributed to ibn Yusuf's portrayal of the Awlad 'Amar as uncultivated. Still, he was given royal treatment that included a private bath, a massage, plush towels, and "clothing more rich than he had ever imagined."[79]

Transcending the gender divide of the palace, Muhammad Saghir's stay in the harem was arranged so that the luxury and comfort of the harem were matched by impressive demonstrations of the pasha's power. He was offered numerous gifts and invited to observe the pasha rendering justice. He was accompanied by an array of palace personnel, from the head eunuch to bath attendants, the servants and slaves in the harem, those attached to his daughter, and finally the slaves in the suite of the concubine, whom the pasha gave to him. It is not clear to what extent his daughter was complicit in the pasha's plan to entrap Muhammad Saghir and her uncle Sultan or how much of the story is apocryphal. Either way, it communicates how the material comforts of the palace, from the splendid harem apartments and its exquisite decoration to the fine food and jewel-encrusted clothing, could create an enticing and irresistible image deployed to meet political needs, in this case, 'Ali Pasha's desire to eliminate two potential traitors.

The 1816 visit of the Princess of Wales (the future Queen Caroline) set the stage for the stream of diplomatic wives and bourgeois tourists who later frequented the palace and similarly highlights the overlap of palace socializing with diplomacy. In honor of her royal status, Mahmud Bey furnished the princess' lodging in the Dar al-Bey palace in Tunis in European style, and his sons Husayn and Mustafa sponsored spectacular festivities on at least three or four evenings of her eight-day sojourn. She was respectfully welcomed with visits by the bey's minister of the navy, the head interpreter, the treasurer, and the French consul. Her arrival in Tunis coincided with the docking of an English squadron in its harbor. After bombarding Algiers, it was set to undertake a similar operation in Tunis to enforce an antipiracy treaty. In light of these circumstances, the bey and his ministers presented their case to the princess, encouraging her to intercede with the British government on their behalf, and successfully toned down the belligerence of the mission.[80] While not an official envoy, the princess' visit had clear political implications.

Most palace socializing was not set in the dramatic contexts of assassination and bombardment. Diplomats, scholars, and travelers often met with the bey, sat in the audience of the palace courtroom, and attended banquets where they enjoyed "sumptuous refreshments."[81] The first references to European women visiting the harem date to the 1830s. These quickly became popular enough that after Pückler-Muskau's 1835 trip, he remarked that "the European women are allowed free entrance to the harems, and the wives of the consuls are often invited to the Bardo by the princesses."[82] Calligaris and Dunant both reported the presence of European guests in the harem for celebrations or social calls.[83] In the latter part of the nineteenth century, the wives of the French and British consuls, such as Camille Roches and Christina Wood, were regulars at Bardo and the family's summer retreats, relationships that were prolonged through correspondence.[84] As it became fashionable to receive Europeans at the palace, elite families throughout the province hosted these visits as well; Temple mentions that the wives of various officials across the province welcomed the party into the female quarters, and Filippi recalled dining with the wives of the qa'id of Gafsa when he toured the interior.[85]

The two most detailed accounts of harem visits in the 1830s are that of Lady Temple and Madame Berner, the Swiss wife of the Danish consul, though neither woman published her own writing. While the first was quoted by her husband, the gentleman tourist Sir Grenville Temple, the second was copied into the travelogue of the Prussian dandy Pückler-

Muskau.[86] The schema of the two visits followed a common pattern: both women were escorted to the harem, accompanied by an interpreter, had coffee and pastries with the palace women, were given a tour, and accorded a brief interview with the bey. These itineraries and other details suggest that the reception of these women was carefully coordinated.

Lady Temple and her party were met at the palace entrance by the minister Giuseppe Raffo, already a prominent figure at court thanks to his Italian origins and connections with the foreign diplomatic community. While this was a sign of privilege, it was also one of control, as Raffo could guide the women through the palace and prevent them from wandering. When he reached the women's quarters, he turned them over to an Italian interpreter, who escorted them to the door of the harem where "Lillah Kebirah," the senior wife of the bey, was waiting. Berner was also chaperoned by "the female interpreter," an otherwise anonymous "Italian lady," who accompanied the guests for the remainder of the visit.[87] While again providing a necessary service, as a palace employee, she was in a position to influence and filter their understanding of the palace.

Berner stated that her party was cordially greeted by the wife of Husayn Bey (presumably the same one whom Temple met), "who rose on our entrance and requested us to take places near her." During their conversation, the bey's wife continued to dote on her and "often took my hand, and had me constantly pressed to eat," and she personally escorted them to additional reception rooms.[88] Temple too notes that her hostess "took me by the hand" into the courtyard and then "led me by the hand through the *patio*" into a long room with a low, silk-covered table laid with desserts, to which she responded with Victorian self-restraint.[89] Berner, for her part, was impressed by the variety of dishes they were offered: "All sorts of sweetmeats and confectioneries which the country can produce, mingled with many delicacies from Europe," including "bon-bons and warm cakes" and jellied fruits that she describes as "*compotes.*"[90] The comportment of the bey's wife and her demonstration of proper etiquette certainly impressed Berner and Temple, who found her "agreeable and good humoured" and "most gracious."[91] The recording of small details of how the senior woman of the harem doted on them, asking about Temple's children and later entreating Temple to visit again, demonstrate the ability of the bey's wife to make the women feel that each was the center of attention.

As Berner sat next to the beya, she gazed into "several other rooms" where she noticed "a great number of black and white female slaves" that she estimated "certainly exceeded a thousand."[92] Temple also noted the presence of slaves as the beya escorted her through the courtyard. Berner's vantage point in particular suggests that the ability to catch a glimpse of the harem retinue was not accidental but a staged demonstration of the extensive palace entourage. Similarly, the bey's wife gave the women "a tour through the whole harem," where Berner noticed "a little sleeping-room of the bey's where the walls were adorned from top to bottom with small watches."[93] The tour was a standard component of bourgeois sociability and may have impressed upon the guests the complexity and size of the women's apartments, while suggesting the women's familiarity with European conventions.

As quoted at the beginning of this chapter, Temple recorded a number of details related to architecture and interior design. She noticed the marble floors, fluted pillars, glazed tiles, an interior garden, the vaulted ceiling, stucco work, and mother-of-pearl boxes, and she described the harem as "delightful" and "enchanting."[94] She was particularly loquacious about the reception room, where the wall was decorated with a "splendid" collection of the bey's arms: "yataghans covered with stones, pistols, swords, and every kind of weapon; but the most beautiful one was called a *topuz*, the whole of which was of fretted gold, completely studded (especially the globe at the end of the handle) with diamonds, emeralds and rubies: it was the most magnificent thing in the way of arms I ever beheld."[95]

Since Berner was present for the wedding of the bey's daughter ʿAisha with Shakir Sahib al-Tabaʿa, she had additional opportunities to appreciate the lavishness of the occasion. The event took place "in the beautiful marble court of the harem," which was decorated with a red awning, lit with painted wax lights and colored lamps. Carefully observing the bride, she noted, "The bride was brought in by her brothers, seated on a cushion of gold brocade [. . .] and placed on an antique and very costly arm-chair in the middle of the court. She was dressed heavily, but with wonderful magnificence. I especially admired a diadem glittering with jewels, and dazzling foot-clasps and armlets." A slave standing by her side collected "presents of gold, jewels, and other valuables. [. . .] Two decanters set with large diamonds, and several packets of wrought gold, appeared to be the most considerable."[96]

Both women admired the prevalence of jewels and the ornamentation of women's clothing. Each summer and winter, considerable sums of money were spent on clothing, surpassing the total for monthly food expenses. On average, new clothing for each man cost 725 piasters, whereas that for their wives and daughters was 450 piasters, and attire for their *juar* was 300 piasters per woman, compared to the *qaftan* of the slaves, which averaged ten piasters.[97] Temple devoted considerable time to describing the beya and Ahmed Bey's wife Menana, whom she found to be "a handsome woman, with brilliant black eyes."[98] While the attention to detail was a staple of Orientalist travel writing to satiate the curiosity of readers, her description of attire, hair, and jewelry is worth quoting at length, as it hints at the care the palace women devoted to their appearance, especially when the beya was hosting:

> Her dress consisted of crimson silk trousers, loose till reaching the calf of the leg; they were then made to fit tight, down to the ancle, where they were covered with the most beautiful, rich, and tasteful embroidery, in gold lace. The bare feet were thrust into slippers, very richly embroidered with gold, with here and there a precious stone, and just large enough to admit four of the extremities of her feet. [. . .] A jacket made of tissue of silk and gold, reaches down to the waists, with no sleeves; in place of these her highness, however, wore a chemise which being made of gauze were very loose, and long enough to be tied in a knot behind her shoulders. Over all this she had a blue figured gauze blouse, confined only at the neck, without any belt at the waist; her head was dressed with a Tunis silk handkerchief, embroidered in the corners with gold, and which was tied tight round her head.

Temple compared the beya's ensemble to that of the younger bey's wife, adding a description of the senior woman's earrings and "rings of brilliants of enormous size; round her neck were chains in great numbers, to which were suspended all sorts of ornaments in gold and precious stones [. . .] and some rows of pearls on her arms."[99] To substantiate his wife's account, Grenville Temple chimed in to attest that the tailoring of these uniforms was such a laborious task that each was "six to nine months in making."[100] If the dress of everyone at court was intended to present an image of opulence and power, then Temple's attention to fabrics, embroidery, color, accessories, cut, and design suggests that they were on the mark.

To conclude their visits, the guests were served coffee, lemonade, and chocolates, and both women met the bey. Berner found him courteous and praised his skills as a host, sharing with her readers his polite insistence that "we were here in our own house."[101] Temple similarly boasted that towards the end, the "very smiling and affable" bey made a brief appearance with all of his sons to greet the women and exchange pleasantries.[102] The beys were cognizant of the market for travel writing and possibly the reconnaissance function they served for foreign governments. For instance, Husayn Bey asked Pückler-Muskau if he had taken good notes during his travels and suggested he write everything down upon his return. Orchestrating these receptions, ministers and palace staff took European male guests to tour the barracks and observe the troops, whether to demonstrate military strength or the success of modernization projects. At least some copies of these travelogues were available in Tunis, as Pückler-Muskau mentions reading Grenville Temple's (which had just come out) in the library of the English consul, and even the Bedouins mentioned Temple to him.[103]

Finally, the dozens of delicacies were "packed into baskets, equally divided among the ladies present, and sent to our several homes." Both Temple and Pückler-Muskau's source mentioned these gifts, later adding that this was "a custom always observed on these and similar occasions."[104] These reports attest an additional function of feasting that reiterated the connection between the display of luxury items and the importance of patronage in the redistribution of wealth. Just as senior women parceled out material resources to dependents within their households, they incorporated guests into these circuits of social protocols and subtle hierarchies.

The bey of Tunis, the harem women, and the inner circle of government viewed tourists as semiofficial representatives of their host countries and used this to their advantage.[105] During visits to the harem, they subtly communicated their wealth and authority through culinary acumen, precious jewels, and an extensive palace support staff. They not only ensured that the harem was polished in the standards of an aristocratic manor, they also strategically seated their guests where they could admire embroidered velvet tapestries and jewel-encrusted weapons. Both Berner's and Temple's accounts highlight the importance of luxury goods and the image of abundance in demonstrating status. In their search for the exotic, European visitors were as vigilant in providing detailed observations about clothing and interior design as the women at Bardo were about their appearances and that of their apartments, hinting at a common set of bourgeois values.

At Ottoman imperial palaces such as the Topkapi, the sultan's private apartments and later those of his wives and children collectively referred to as the harem were not accessible to the general public or even low-ranking palace personnel. This spatial organization evolved from the reverence expressed towards the sultan and dominant conceptualizations of dynastic power in the fifteenth century, when the Topkapi was built. Despite its location inside Istanbul, the palace was situated behind fortified walls, since royal rhetoric built upon Byzantine and Abbasid practices that equated grandeur with seclusion.[106] Similarly, when India's Mughal emperors constructed their first major palace in the sixteenth century to symbolize their transformation from a nomadic confederation to a settled empire, they included separate residences for women, also called the harem. Privacy and restriction were to communicate the sacred nature of the ruling family. If such seclusion placed limitations on women's mobility, it did not hinder the ability of Ottoman and Mughal women to legitimize dynastic rule through public works, investing in urban infrastructure, and openly demonstrating the depth of their faith.[107] While modern spatial dichotomies would relegate women to the domestic or private spheres, in the early modern era, elite women's segregation was coeval with their participation in official public and dynastic affairs.

The articulation of state power, both material and otherwise, evolved in relation to political, military, and economic conditions. Early modern palaces were places of government, centers of business, and the home of complex multigenerational families, whose structures facilitated the participation of court women. The women at Bardo devoted their time to running the households, organizing and stocking provisions, overseeing their domestics and slaves, and embroidering gold and silver thread onto the velvets and silks to decorate the home. In conversation with their male relatives and ministers, they organized palace factions, influenced political decisions, and arranged succession disputes.

Concomitant with the public and private activities at Bardo, for all their seclusion, women's lives were a symbol of status, a topic of scrutiny, and an element of international relations. The smooth coordination of their personnel, the carefully placed decorations, and their well-groomed appearance were all deployed to present an image of authority and control to their European visitors. While Temple's wife and her sisters were among the first European women vacationing in Tunis, by this time it was fairly common for women to accompany their husbands or male relatives on diplomatic affairs or leisure travel to the Ottoman Empire and Qajar Persia.[108] In fact, Lady Temple's writing reiterated the common focus on body, clothing, etiquette, and extensive description of the surroundings typical of women's description of harems in this period, in many ways indebted to the standards set by Lady Mary Montague's travels to Istanbul in 1716. Over coffee and through letters, palace women in Tunis contributed to the image, status, and foreign relations of the ruling family by hosting these guests, just as embassy wives in the modern era have hosted banquets, dinner parties, and other gala events crucial to the smooth functioning of diplomatic relations.[109] As pointed out by Julia Clancy-Smith more than two decades ago, consular visits to the harem formed a sort of unofficial diplomacy that should draw today's scholarly attention away from the myopic association between politics and men at court.[110]

By the time of 'Uthman's assassination, allegations of female deviance and slanderous rumors had tarnished the reputations of royal women for centuries. Hurrem, the wife of Sultan Suleiman, who inaugurated a century of women's involvement in Ottoman imperial politics, was portrayed by contemporaries as scheming, manipulative, and engaged in sorcery. Her participation in court politics and her vilification by rivals were similar to the experiences of English queens such as Anne Boleyn and Elizabeth I, Catherine de Medici in France, and Mary Queen of Scots.[111] The eighteenth-century example of Marie Antoinette, who was tried in 1793 with a host of moral and political crimes from incest to treason, highlights how powerful women were stigmatized in public opinion.[112] In the nineteenth century, the Qing Empress Dowager Cixi (1835–1908) was another prominent matriarch who influenced the most significant political affairs for over half a century.[113] She was resented, as was Malik Jihan (1805–1873), the mother of Persia's Nasir al-Din Shah (1848–1896). A central figure at court and an ally of the Qajar notables, her reputation was smeared by jealous rivals spreading tales of illicit liaisons and sexual promiscuity.[114] Korea's Queen Min, a savvy politician and head of one of the powerful factions at the Chosŏn court, considered hostile to increasing Japanese influence, was brutally assassinated by a band operating on behalf of the Japanese consul.[115] As these examples attest, accusations of improper behavior, deceit, and transgression often stood as a parable for fears about women's public activities and the threat they posed to securing politics, turning it into a masculine prerogative.

The fragmentary references to women's participation in the formation and dissolution of factions at Bardo complement the activities of royal women in a number of early modern dynasties, just as the rumors of corruption resound with a longer trajectory of disparaging women's political participation. It should give pause that contemporaries such as ibn Dhiaf accepted women's political power by locating it within the ideal family and crediting it to emotional ties between the beys and their mothers, sisters, wives, and children. Acting within the script of family hierarchies, palace women offered motherly advice about matters of state and served as bastions of support and encouragement. In contrast, European sources referred to women's authority as transgressing gender norms, disrupting the social and political order, and muddling the separation between public and private affairs. Their attacks against prominent women at Bardo not only reiterated debates over the petticoat influence of European royal women but also coincided with the increasing fascination with women's condition in the Orient. Harem visits, fleeting glimpses on the street, and the confidential revelations of upper-class women were utilized to affirm that its rulers were politically inept and posit that local culture was inferior to European Christian civilization, all while elaborating on the problems of Muslim family life. Efforts to exclude women from political life within Europe and the modern masculinization of the public sphere contributed to European perceptions of female politicians as problematic and of the family as oppressive.

The representation of power through wealth was meaningful only when these displays reached an attentive audience. The palace tribunal created one space for the presentation of beylical power as accessible instead of remote, where authority was personified by a bey who solved anyone's problem. Even if provincial organization was decentralized with authority delegated to regional administrators, the beys marked their presence outside Bardo by the distribution of favors, the construction of public monuments, and the ubiquity of the palace personnel on the biannual *mahalla*.[1] As goods circulated beyond the palace walls, the governing family engaged the subject population by creating a public presence they hoped would legitimize their rule. Philanthropy was part of their public image and considered a responsibility of the upper classes, a view reinforced in contemporary historical writings and customs across the empire. Patriarchal rule implied obligations towards family and dependents, including a commitment to uphold justice, attempts to fulfill the expectations of ideal government, and charitable acts to earn legitimacy in the eyes of the subject population.[2]

At the imperial center, acts of royal magnanimity included state festivities, the founding of public kitchens, and the distribution of food, all of which had reverberations in the provinces. For instance, major circumcision ceremonies in Istanbul in 1582 and 1720 offered public entertainment through guild processions and substantial feasts. By performing a union with his sons and with Ottoman society, the sultan made this event a "collective performance" of enacting and representing state authority.[3] Patriarchal benevolence toward the family and the population similarly emanated from the sultan's table. Leftovers were passed along to lower officials, excess food was also given to a number of soup kitchens throughout the capital, and even individuals receiving rations took smaller portions and passed some along to their own dependents.[4] Both members of the imperial family and provincial governors sponsored public kitchens that served a range of dishes, some intended for scholars, students, and travelers in addition to the common poor. Here the offering of food built upon "a particular religious language of benevolence (albeit at times formulaic) [that] served to maintain and reinforce connections between the populace and the state," as they allowed governing officials to utilize their patriarchal position to demonstrate generosity and concern for the general welfare.[5]

It is possible that meals served at Bardo made their way to more humble tables. Despite Davis' surprise at the hospitality of his hosts and the number of dishes brought to his tent, his servants were accustomed to eating from the table of their superiors, and after the latter were satiated, their subordinates finished the meal.[6] The custom of feeding dependents and retainers was respected among the notability; though Muhammad ibn Qasim al-Mihrizi was not wealthy as far as the standards of the *'ulama'* and owned no luxury objects, his stock of over one hundred plates suggests that people in need frequently ate from his kitchen.[7] The beys supplied provisions to a constant stream of visitors at the Bardo guesthouses (from olives and bread to rice, coffee, mutton, and chicken), including fodder for their animals.[8] Just as holiday bonuses to palace personnel and gifts to government officials and clients reinforced the ties within this circle, other charitable acts destined to support the needy institutionalized generosity to reinforce relations of dependence by investing wealth into social capital. Though the bey's authority was based on hereditary rights and imperial confirmation, the threat of urban disorder, tribal uprisings, or the withdrawal of the support of the *'ulama'* was enough to encourage beylical attention to public opinion.

By the late eighteenth century, the authority of the ruling family and its monopoly on the position of governor was securely established and accepted among the military, political, and religious elite. Their patriarchal image was carefully cultivated in a range of philanthropic activities, financial remunerations, and cash gifts to secure political alliances, assist the needy, and care for the weak. This allowed family fortunes to be put to productive use, forming ties between the palace and the population. This chapter goes beyond the palace walls and elite social circles to the provincial interior and the urban poor. It surveys the important foundations of the beys, their efforts to alleviate poverty, and their interaction with the population. As men and women in the palace invested their wealth in educational projects, public works, and relief for the poor, they strove to cultivate relations with different sectors of the population and demonstrate their piety, while reinforcing the patriarchal authority of the bey.

MAJOR CHARITIES: *AWQAF*

One of the main forms of elite philanthropy was the *waqf* (pl. *awqaf*), the endowment of properties towards a charitable destination (either immediately or after the death of specified inheritors). The Ottoman elite in particular relied on such foundations in the rebuilding of newly conquered cities, embracing a stratified worldview in which those who had the means were expected to share their wealth.[9] In fact, women had participated in urban renewal, dynastic glorification, and demonstrations of piety since the medieval era through foundations that allowed the ruling elite to encourage commerce, demonstrate respect for erudition, and anchor themselves in the urban environment.[10]

Women in the Ottoman ruling household began investing in provincial towns in the earlier period when they accompanied their sons to these posts. After the concentration of the family in Istanbul in the sixteenth century, they focused on the capital and major urban centers. Around 1518, Hafsa, the mother of Sultan Suleiman, built a mosque complex in Istanbul, including schools and a soup kitchen, and encouraged people to relocate to its surrounding neighborhoods. Suleiman's daughter Mihrimah was involved in supporting schools, hostels for pilgrims, soup kitchens, and an inn for travelers in Mecca, Medina, Jerusalem, and Istanbul.[11] Endowments such as Hurrem's soup kitchen in Jerusalem emphasized the role of the sultan as caliph and the Ottoman dedication to the newly acquired holy cities of Mecca, Medina, and Jerusalem. It manifested the imperial commitment to caring for pilgrims and the poor, feeding an average of four hundred people plus staff and guests.[12] Since these complexes were often known by the names of their founders, producing "one of the most salient symbols of royal power to which women had access," charitable activities were a significant avenue for women's participation in legitimizing family eminence.[13] While mosques exemplified imperial concern for the spiritual welfare of the community, schools, libraries, markets, and inns contributed to learning and commerce, supporting the *'ulama'* and merchants.

Particularly during the era of decentralized rule, when provincial governors increasingly identified with the provinces and spent longer terms there, the construction of mosques, markets, and public facilities was an important way to demonstrate the commitment of Ottoman officials to their local constituencies. Salah Bey of Constantine (1777–1792) established foundations that contributed to neighborhood revival, improved connections to the hinterland, and endorsed local commerce. In a reconstruction of the city's geography that was concomitant with his efforts to plant local roots, he created an enduring relationship with the population.[14] The frequent and sizeable foundations by Ottoman governors in Aleppo and Damascus meant that considerable portions of commercial, residential, and agricultural properties in these cities and the surrounding countryside formed part of various *awqaf*. At the same time, a number of smaller endowments consisting of one house or parcels of land indicated the significance of endowing properties for the middle and upper classes for both sexes, as nearly half of founders were women.[15]

The endowments of the beys in the eighteenth and nineteenth centuries adhered to these parameters while building upon the bases set down by their Muradite predecessors. The most significant constructions date to the era of Hammuda ibn Murad, who built a public hospital in 1662 and a secondary school in Qayrawan, in addition to donating to the local religious brotherhoods. Initially planned to provide medical services for soldiers, his hospice offered medical care and respite for those without family, including bedding, mattresses, covers, medicine, and burial shrouds for those who passed away.[16] His descendants continued to invest across the province: Murad ibn Hammuda built a *zawiya*, school, and dormitories on the island of Jerba and another *zawiya* in Binzart in 1673, and Muhammad ibn Murad built a *zawiya* in the town of Zaghwan for Sidi 'Ali 'Azuz, a contemporary mystic renowned for his spiritual authority.[17] There were important continuities between the buildings of Murad Bey and his descendants and those of Husayn ibn 'Ali, who often repaired and added on to earlier foundations. Ibn 'Ali renovated a number of *madrasa*s and *zawiya*s in Beja, Kef, Gafsa, Sfax, and Jerba that were built by his predecessors but had fallen into disuse; his renovations showed his particular reverence for the brotherhood of Sidi 'Ali 'Azuz, as his *zawiya* was a distribution point for charities.[18]

The scale and design of major architectural edifices such as mosques represented a range of styles such as Islamic or Renaissance motifs, to project an image of stature. Yet the act of building had practical implications and involved employing dozens of local laborers and artisans, and the services provided by these foundations were destined for public use. The charitable intentions of the beys were particularly evident in the foundations of 'Ali Bey. Smaller projects included a school and a *turba*. In the capital he used a *waqf* to renovate the water system with underground pipelines that supplied approximately twenty public fountains. He renovated wells, built water wheels, and expanded irrigation, all of which were critical to improving sanitation by increasing the availability of potable water for personal and agricultural use.[19] Yet his most memorable foundation was a hospice, or *takiya*, that operated as a soup kitchen serving approximately ninety people each day from its opening in 1768. While the repast was a simple soup of bulgur wheat and oil, it served meat twice each week throughout the month of Ramadan and on religious holidays (about thirty *ratl*s per day). His endowment provided the funds to purchase the food, cooking utensils, and serving ware and pay the salaries for two cooks and a general manager. He built another hospice with twenty-one rooms and a kitchen, completed in 1774, and a twelve-room shelter for women. At these, the residents received two meals per day comparable to the diet of a commoner beginning with bread and a small amount of oil (one *waqiya*). The typical supper consisted of couscous with vegetables, though on Mondays and Thursdays during the month of Ramadan, and on other religious holidays, the couscous was served with meat, so that it was known as the "*takiya al-kuskusu.*"[20] The more substantial meals served on Thursdays doubled the normal expenses, and four sheep were slaughtered there for 'id al-Idha (serving about eighty individuals). By the mid-nineteenth century, it housed about seventy people and fed an additional one hundred on a daily basis.[21]

Women from both ruling families contributed to dynastic prestige, royal magnanimity, and public piety via endowments. Perhaps the most notable of these was 'Aziza 'Uthmana, the granddaughter of 'Uthman Dey and wife of one of the Muradite Beys. Born in the early seventeenth century, she was an educated woman who undertook the pilgrimage, earning herself a reputation for piety and virtue. She made multiple endowments of her agricultural and residential property, shops, and baths that generated funds to provide trousseaus for poor girls, to circumcise orphaned boys, and to ransom captives. The most significant *waqf* (based on twenty-three buildings) was a public hospital that was known by her name. It continued to provide public services, thanks to additional endowments on behalf of her granddaughter Fatma, the wife of Husayn ibn 'Ali.[22]

Women at Bardo contributed to prominent buildings and endowed their properties towards pious ends. When Kebira Mamia, the wife of 'Ali Pasha, built her mausoleum, she had it elaborately decorated and then endowed it so that charities could be distributed at its doors during her lifetime and after her death.[23] Khaduja bint Yusuf Darguth, the wife of Suleiman ibn 'Ali Pasha, made a considerable endowment to her daughter 'Aisha (known as 'Aishusha) and her descendants.[24] This included real estate; gold and silver jewelry; agricultural property; livestock; and gardens with apricots, mulberries, pomegranates, lemons, olives, and figs. The executors were to subtract seventy piasters each year from these profits for Qur'anic recitation at her tomb and that of her daughter for each night of the seven *mawasim* (pl. of *mawsim*, religious holidays), with the final destination the *awqaf al-haramayn* (the endowments of the holy cities Mecca and Medina). Another *waqf* benefited the Zaytuna mosque in Tunis, providing funds to support students and religious scholars with modest supplements to their income. In another act, Khaduja left specific instructions regarding the amount destined to pay for the circumcision of young boys at the secondary school founded by her husband (the *medresa Slimaniya*) on the festival of 'Ashura' each year.[25]

Later in the eighteenth century, Mna Ghazalia, the wife of Muhammad al-Rashid, placed her substantial inheritance into endowments. One of her *awqaf* was shared with her three sisters (Halima, Fatma, and Jannat) and their brother 'Amar's two daughters (Jannat and Trakiya). In 1784 she endowed her home, three storages, an upper floor, two additional houses, an oven, and a mill first for her personal use, then for her three sisters, their female relations, and finally to the *haramayn*. She also planned to subtract from this money to pay for the reading of parts of the Qur'an at her tomb and those of her two daughters (Hafsia and Saliha).[26] 'Aisha bint 'Ali Bey and her husband Ismail Kahia endowed their properties, including different tracts of land, olive trees, fruit gardens, a mill, and a house, to their children and the Zaytuna mosque for reading the Qur'an.[27] While *awqaf* were a public demonstration of piety, they were also a way for women to control a portion of their inheritance and pass wealth to their female descendants. The palace women showed a marked preference for the *awqaf al-haramayn*, Qur'anic recitation at their tombs, and naming female relatives as inheritors.

Since most palace women did not build mosques or schools, they were similar to women of local families who regularly made smaller *awqaf*. One popular destination was to the Zaytuna mosque for the reading of prayers. At least this was the purpose of endowments made by women such as Hajja Jannat, Haluma al-Saqli, Saida Mamia, Jannat bint Mustafa the Bulukbashi, 'Aisha bint Ahmad al-Sherif al-Qorshi, Om Hania bint al-Sherif al-Haddad, Hanuna bint Ahmad Zaytun, Yamina bint Jaffer al-Turki, and Hafsia bint al-Hajj Muhammad ibn al-Amine.[28] Among the twenty elite families studied by Sophie Ferchiou, of 328 people making endowments, 97 of them (or about 30 percent) were women.[29] Among these same families, women were more likely to inherit property than to buy it themselves, though once they did own property, it was more common to sell it than to give it as gifts or inheritance.[30]

The sponsoring of *awqaf* allowed the women at Bardo to emulate the practices of the imperial family, but it also demonstrated their anchoring in the local context and mirrored more modest donations of women in provincial families as well. By founding mosques and secondary schools or building markets and bridges, the palace families expanded the urban fabric of the capital, improved transportation and commercial capabilities, and broadened educational opportunities. They provided services to students, merchants, and residents of the capital that were also appreciated by the *'ulama'*, many of whom were salaried administrators of the various foundations.[31]

CHARITY AS RELIEF FOR THE POOR

The palace treasury routinely recorded almsgiving in small but frequent amounts of money and food. These were referred to as *sadaqa* (charities) and *ihsan* (good deeds), often associated with a service performed or rendered, and they served as a sort of bonus. At Bardo, ten or twelve and a half piasters were set aside for *sadaqa* each day and noted on the first line of the day's expenses in the annual account books. Other alms were given out on Fridays, usually to five or six individuals receiving one-half piaster each.[32] While paltry compared with the normative scale of palace expenditures, in the eighteenth century, this was roughly the equivalent to two days of salary for a cook and slightly above the daily wage of soldiers guarding construction sites.[33] Even in the 1860s, the daily salary of a manual laborer was only two to three piasters.[34] Most charities were anonymous, with the registers full of statements indicating only "*sadaqa*, nine piasters," without detailing to whom the money was given or for what reason. The palace also provided services such as burial costs for travelers who died in the province with no family, those who died in prison, and the destitute, by purchasing shrouds and making funeral arrangements for the cost of one to two piasters each.[35]

The palace sustained regular charities at a handful of *zawiya*s. This custom began around 1772, when 'Ali Bey included meals at the *zawiya* of Sidi 'Ali 'Azuz in Zaghwan (the one built by Muhammad ibn Murad) on the salary lists at the cost of eight piasters a month. His son, Hammuda Pasha, expanded this practice after 1802 to include the shrines of Sidi bu Hadid in Zaghwan and Sidi 'Ali ibn Ziyad in Tunis, the shrine-mosque complex

FIGURE 4.1.   *Sidi Mahrez mosque, undated postcard, author's private collection.*

of Sidi Mahrez (considered the patron saint of the capital), and that of Sidi Hassan al-Shadly (see Figure 4.1).[36] The beys distributed additional charities when they traveled through the cities and towns of the interior, visiting shrines along the way. On one excursion to Zaghwan, ʿAli Pasha visited the shrine of Sidi ʿAli ʿAzuz, then took his family to Qayrawan to "visit the shaykh of the city and distribute charity to the poor."[37] On a trip to the village of Manuba (a few miles from Tunis) in 1780, Hammuda Pasha donated 3,000 loaves of bread and another 4,000 when he went to Beja later that year; then he gave 2,000 piasters of charity in Qayrawan in 1782 without any specified explanation.[38] He also patronized the shrine of Sidi bu Said al-Beji, at least once spending over 200 piasters on bread there.[39] Such charities were consonant with the beys' personal patronization of revered saints around the province and with their respect for religious scholars and participation in sufi brotherhoods.[40]

Palace women were particularly fond of the thirteenth-century saint Saida Manubia (1190–1266). A young girl named ʿAisha from a modest family in the village of Manuba, she was generous, performed miracles, was knowledgeable about Islam and Islamic sciences, and was later initiated into Sufism by a respected mystic. She was one of the few women whose spiritual authority was profound enough that her life figures in biographical dictionaries.[41] When Fatma bint Husayn's daughter went into labor around 1758, she donated over 300 piasters worth of bread, fish, pomegranates, quince, spinach, chicken, eggs, cheese, butter, and other provisions to the *zawiya* of Saida Manubia.[42] Hammuda Pasha's mother and his sister regularly visited the shrine, transporting hundreds of piasters worth of food that may have served as offerings.[43]

Beylical attention to these shrines matched popular attachment to local saints. The Saida Manubia *zawiya* was a refuge for poor women; many sought her assistance to solve marital problems, cure infertility, and help them conceive, and she was a favorite saint for many women in Tunisia. Of all the *awqaf* destined for her shrine between 1770 and 1879, nearly half were founded by women, and at least six different women endowed houses to the saint. During the same period, at least two women endowed their properties to the shrine of Sidi Mahrez. Whether from the palace or not, these donations reached people in need, as both the *zawiya* of Saida Manubia and that of Sidi 'Ali 'Azuz provided rooms for those in need of shelter, constituting a veritable "refuge for the poor."[44]

Charities corresponded to particular places, occasions, and events. When Muhammad al-Rashid Bey went to Friday prayers at the Zaytuna mosque, he handed out 31 piasters, and his brother 'Ali Bey gave 1,626 piasters of *sadaqa* there in 1761.[45] Donations were a regular occurrence on religious holidays; on 'Ashura' in 1759, there were *sadaqa* of 500 piasters, an extra 30 piasters for the *zawiya* of Sidi Mahrez, and 105 piasters handed out at the mausoleum of Muhammad al-Rashid Bey.[46] The poor were fed as part of the celebration of Mawlid, and during the month of Ramadan in 1779, almost 28,000 loaves of bread were baked for charities (which cost 1,074 piasters).[47]

Funerals provided an opportunity for charities of various kinds, a moment when generosity was hoped to bring benefits to the afterlife of the deceased. It followed that when the bey's young grandson was buried in 1778, he gave away 1,500 loaves of bread. The manumission of slaves following the death of respected persons was also a pious act. As Frank recounts:

> When one of the wives of the beys passes away, anyone who is anyone precipitates to purchase at least one Negro, whom they immediately manumit. Their total number sometimes reaches as many as two hundred. They all follow the funeral procession, each one holding a long stick, at the end of which is attached a sign upon which their certificate of manumission is presented.[48]

When Fatma, the wife of Muhammad al-Mimun Bey, died in the spring of 1817, the bey bought at least seven slaves whom he freed in her honor.[49]

When Muhammad al-Rashid Bey passed away in 1759, ibn Yusuf says that upon his burial "bags of money were opened and the contents were passed out to the poor."[50]

Weddings were a joyous occasion marked by days of extensive festivities and prolific feasts and often involved members of the diplomatic corps and local notables. Guests at the 1826 marriage of four of Husayn Bey's children, for example, included tribal notables and 'ulama', and gifts were distributed to the population during the weeklong celebration.[51] Circumcisions were also celebrated with fanfare and were the basis of considerable charities. For example, at the 1764 circumcision of 'Ali Bey's two sons Hammuda and Suleiman and his nephews Mahmud and Ismail (whose own father had already passed away), he hosted the circumcision of at least three hundred other boys. Each one received a small monetary gift; hundreds of shirts, vests, caps, and cloaks were prepared for the occasion, with some boys receiving items embroidered with silver, others silk or wool clothing, and presumably one of the 510 pairs of shoes recorded for the event.[52]

Over the course of the year, these small amounts accumulated into considerable sums. In the 1760s and 1770s, annual totals hovered around ten thousand, though the accounts merely record that these were "*sadaqa* to the poor" or "*sadaqa* for poor Muslims."[53] Significant charities were provided in kind. For example, Muhammad al-Rashid Bey spent almost two thousand piasters to prepare and serve a meal that consisted of fifty cows and bread (and payments to the butcher, cooks, and people bringing bread and wheat).[54] In 1826, the palace handed out some ninety pairs of shoes.[55] This may confirm the claim of Hammuda ibn 'Abd al-'Aziz that approximately one thousand infirm and disabled persons received daily charity from the palace, with crowds of beggars reaching up to four thousand on occasions when they could expect to receive bread or money.[56]

The bey also provided financial support as damages and compensation to plaintiffs appearing before the Bardo's tribunal. For example, in 1766, 'Ali Bey gave two piasters to "the woman who complained about her husband."[57] Poor people could thus claim dire need and receive small monetary awards that themselves indicated the modest circumstances of some male and female plaintiffs. Another woman was awarded the relatively impressive sum of ten piasters for her pains and compensation in 1775, when she complained that her foot had been run over by the bey's carriage.[58]

While people went to the palace with their grievances or in the hopes of receiving alms, not everyone had the means to travel to Bardo. Nonetheless, they had the occasion to interact with the palace during the *mahalla*, the expansive military contingent that toured the province twice each year to collect taxes. This mobile spectacle served myriad purposes, including legitimizing the governor by demonstrating his control of hundreds of troops, articulating the territorial extent of central authority, and providing an occasional escort for Europeans interested in visiting the interior. The military camp included contingents from the *hanba*, up to a thousand *subahiya*, and greater numbers of irregular troops called *zawawa*, all of them supported by "throngs of servants in charge of numberless cattle for food, and beasts of burthen, such as mules, donkeys and camels, loaded down with baggage."[59] In the eighteenth century, the bey often led the *mahalla*, in continuity with earlier responsibilities associated with the title. Husayn ibn ʿAli set a precedent for including the palace households in the voyage, one that was followed by his son ʿAli Bey, who traveled with his sister and her household in 1772.[60] Similarly, Hammuda Pasha undertook what was remembered as the *mahalla* of the five houses, since he was accompanied by his two brothers ʿUthman and Muhammad al-Mimun, his two cousins Mahmud and Ismail, and his own mother.[61] By the nineteenth century, the bey tended to remain in the capital, appointing a top-ranking mamluk or one of the senior men in the family in his place. It retained its significance as a site of political experience, as the bey of the *mahalla* came to be associated with the title of heir apparent.

While an economically motivated venture and a military parade, the *mahalla*'s circuitous route allowed the palace to distribute justice, interact with the population, and hand out charities. Bringing a considerable palace retinue demonstrated the governor's control of force, and it showcased his paternal concerns and the personal nature of political power by making the sovereign (or ministers) accessible to much of the population. As the camp lingered throughout the countryside, people were encouraged to visit the bey and lay their problems before him.[62] A number of those who greeted the palace contingent brought gifts of local produce and animals that they had caught hunting or fishing. For instance, during one summer near the border of Algeria, two people from Mount Waslat brought cactus fruits, and one from Qlibia offered melons. Others from the suburbs of the capital in Marsa arrived with apples, pears, and figs, and one individual from Hammam Lif brought fish.[63] Each one was compensated with a few piasters.

These acts of giving created debts by implying reciprocity; bringing okra or fava beans to the bey allowed the common people to place the sovereign in a position of obligation towards them, reinforcing the importance of personal relations with the palace. What stands out in these situations is the inexpensive nature of the gifts; far from the luxury items that were consumed at the palace, these represented the average diet. Their modesty and local provenance were a marked contrast with the expensive and costly presents that foreign consuls were required to bring to the bey and his court.[64] Records dating from 1756 to 1777 attest the distributive nature of the *mahalla* and how patronage was sustained through periodic *ihsan* in each and every stop of the tour. The majority of these went to minor officials, notables, tribal shaykhs, and their families, representing an outer circle of government functionaries who doubled as local auxiliaries. The dozens of annual entries in villages across the province, totaling hundreds or thousands of piasters, supplemented their income and reinforced the importance of patronage networks originating in the palace.

An array of additional services were provided as emergency measures intended to benefit fragile sectors of the population in times of crisis and economic hardship. ʿAli Bey provided blankets when it was cold, and his *takiya* was built during the 1776 drought. The subsequent poor harvests may help to explain a reference to *sadaqa* consisting of 10,500 loaves of bread and thirty-three cows in 1778.[65] The beys subsidized grains when the harvest was poor or distributed them free, and during another rough cycle beginning in 1816, the regular Friday charities were increased to include over thirty individuals.[66]

Other acts of charity hinted at the basis of a broad welfare system. When the spring of 1829 began with a dry start, it lead to a shortage of grain. To prevent famine, Husayn Bey imported grain and sold it below market value, an initiative that ibn Dhiaf lauded as "one of his greatest deeds" and one where his only gain was "in god's graces."[67] In the spring of 1854, famine again threatened the province's inhabitants, and Ahmad Bey responded by giving over 1,000 *qafiz*s of wheat to the poor. About half of these were distributed to the different neighborhoods of the capital, including 125 *qafiz*s to the Jewish community with specific instructions that these were to be given to the elderly, infirm, and those with large families. In addition, another 6 *qafiz*s of wheat were baked as bread in portions of one-half *ratl* per loaf, to be distributed at the Qasba, two per person to those in dire circumstances.[68] Faced with increasing economic difficulties in the second half of the nineteenth century, when the effects of poor harvests were multiplied due to rural emigration, increasing urban congestion, and periodically burdensome taxation, the governors supplemented regular charities with additional *sadaqa*, food distribution, and subsidized staples such as grains.[69]

Charities were often funneled under the aegis of religious figures or institutions, handed out at the mosque after Friday prayer, or administered at one of the many sufi shrines throughout the province that doubled as hostels. Governors built mosques, funded schools, and patronized *zawiyas*.[70] While detailed records illustrate how these projects created employment opportunities and set aside funds for students and staff in their daily operations, many of the recipients of palace charities were unnamed. For those among the ranks of the anonymous poor, receiving coins directly from the palace treasury constituted a personal relationship with the palace. By providing customary new clothing, offering gifts, and circumcising local boys with his sons and nephews, the bey made all the children in the province part of his family, equating his personal authority within the palace with his public and political function as sovereign. These charities emphasized the public role of the bey as father of the inhabitants of the province in an extension of his position as the head of the palace households, portraying the governor as a patriarchal ruler responsible for the well-being of all.

The family model of government and its patriarchal structures were acted out through charities that materially demonstrated the bey's financial responsibility and transformed family fortunes into public welfare, albeit on an irregular basis. Even when the income from Hammuda ibn Murad's initial endowment was not enough to sustain the hospital, it continued to function until the 1860s (when the municipal government planned to replace it).[71] The same was true for the *takiya* founded by 'Ali Bey, which operated until 1875, thanks to additional endowments by later beys and elites in the capital.[72] The bey's generosity was part of a contract to rule that depended on people requesting his intervention in the tribunal, at the doors of Bardo, or at the *mahalla* as it crossed the province. That ordinary people sought to implicate themselves in networks of power through the intermediary of the bey suggests a modicum of interaction between the court and the population and the relevance of popular recognition of the bey's authority.

Just as women participated in the hierarchical structures of household organization, as demonstrated in the circulation of goods within the palace, paying for Qur'anic recitation at their tombs or donating meals at the *zawiya* of Saida Manubia contributed to the political identity of the ruling family. Establishing pious foundations and provisioning soup kitchens allowed men and women at Bardo to invest in a redistributive system that functioned as a contract to govern by demonstrating their commitment to the population of the province. Celebrating family events such as weddings and circumcisions or religious holidays, the palace families utilized their wealth to legitimize paternal models of benevolent rule. Periodic handouts did not eradicate poverty any more than they promoted an equitable distribution of resources, just as popular interaction with the bey did not challenge the hierarchical social order. These acts reinforced the dependent nature of the bey's authority and its reliance on personal relationships. Endowments and charities created ties to the *'ulama'*, showed palace patronage of local saints, and provided services to various neighborhood communities.

The family mode of government that predominated from the early eighteenth century (if not the mid-seventeenth) depended on subordination to the bey and personal relations with the sovereign and his family. This system relied heavily on slaves: the accumulation of slaves suggested the wealth of the family, their loyal services to the government reduced the need for salaried bureaucrats, their labor filled the ovens and covered the palace tables when feasts were provided for guests, and their marriages to palace women and notable men anchored Bardo in elite social circles. These features created continuity in government and palace relations to the province, though the period between 1750 and 1830 was not stagnant. There were moments of political turmoil, epochs of economic hardship, and the ruling families increased in size, but throughout this period the authority of the beylical family and the patriarchal mode of government were not seriously put into question.

From this respect, the mid-eighteenth century to early nineteenth century was a period marked by the consolidation of authority, political stability, and limited prosperity, creating a stark contrast with the remainder of the nineteenth century and its economic dislocations, military threats, and transformation of the basic understanding of government. The family model allowed women to intervene through their sons, husbands, and in-laws; to collaborate with diplomatic wives; and to engage in economic and political activities. This personal nature of government was challenged by intellectual reform of the nineteenth century. As the slave trade dwindled, wealth was less associated with conspicuous consumption and stigmatized instead of valued as part of a redistributive system.

NINETEENTH-CENTURY
TRANSFORMATIONS

Part III

THE CONSTITUTION, FINANCIAL
REFORM, AND THE MODERN FAMILY

Chapter 5

Beauty is to be clean from the stain of all debts.

IBN DHIAF, *ITHAF AHL AL-ZAMAN*, VOL. 3

*Nothing can be more irregular and confused than the mode of col-
lecting the revenues, unless we except the mode of spending them.*

AMOS PERRY, *CARTHAGE AND TUNIS*

Though he had already reduced the number of troops because of difficulties paying their salaries, in 1853 Ahmad Bey decided to send a fleet
to assist the sultan in the Crimean War (1853-1856). To fund the contingent, he dipped into his private treasury, handing his jewelry over to his
agent in Europe to sell. His powerful mamluk minister, Mustafa Khaznadar, followed suit, including the jewelry of his wife, Kalthum (Ahmed
Bey's sister).[1] This event, where a sovereign would sell precious luxury
goods to finance an army, captures the shifting dynamics of representing
state power and the reorientation of government resources that accompanied the process of modernization. The broader military context, in
which Tunisian and Ottoman forces faced belligerent European powers,
was indicative of the nineteenth-century resurgence of European imperial projects.

The bey of Tunis had been involved in a series of diplomatic confron-
tations with the Great Powers since the turn of the nineteenth century. To
begin with, while the Porte did not request military action from the bey
in the conflict ensuing from Napoleon's invasion of Egypt (1798-1802),
the province was officially at war with France. As a result, the bey detained French merchants and closed their shops, much to the prolonged
consternation of their consul.[2] Provincial soldiers were later more directly involved in Ottoman efforts to suppress the Greek rebellion that
began in 1821 because Husayn Bey equipped and outfitted a warship that
he sent to Navarino.[3] Despite the Ottoman ability to quell the revolt, the

success was overturned by combined British, French, and Russian support for the Greeks. The protocol of 1830, which anticipated the war's final agreement in 1832, declared the formation of an independent state in Greece and offered poignant illustration of the decisive nature of European intervention.

The European powers often approached the western Ottoman provinces of Algiers, Tunis, and Tripoli as a block. This was true in the 1819 Franco-English fleet that forced the three capitals to accord them with commercially advantageous terms. Yet this brief flexing of military muscle did not produce the expected results, as the clauses of the treaty were only haphazardly enforced. The French colonial occupation of Algiers in June of 1830 had immediate ramifications for the bey, who had been warned since April of that year that he should maintain strict neutrality during the impending expedition, insisting that any assistance to the Algerians would be viewed as an act of war. In August, French ships docked in the harbor and carried a treaty explicating the consequences of their occupation on relations with the bey. He was instructed that if he "did not adhere to the treaty the King proposed within eight days, His Majesty would be obliged to use force." This accord granted exclusive rights to coral fishing, established trade privileges for French subjects, and extended the sultan's Capitulations agreements to Tunis.[4] Again, these provisions were not uniformly implemented. As the French commitment to colonizing Algeria deepened over the ensuing decades, so did the scrutiny of French colonial officials. Wary of maintaining their influence over the bey to protect the borders of their colonial possession and secure their rule, French diplomatic personnel were reliant on the governor's goodwill and suspicious of any potential competition from the province's growing Italian community, British support of the sultan, and Istanbul's hold over its autonomous vassal.

The concomitant recourse to gunboat diplomacy to persuade the governor of Tripoli, Yusuf Pasha Qaramanli, to award the French greater privileges in 1830 foreshadowed increasing interference in that province as well. The Qaramanli family had held a hereditary monopoly on the governorship since 1711 that was quite similar to the monopoly on the governorship of their counterparts in Tunis. Yet in the early nineteenth century, problems over succession were exacerbated by a series of local revolts favoring different members of the family, with the French and the British intervening on opposing sides. Both the pasha of Tripoli and its population solicited the support of Husayn Bey, who served as an intermediary with the sultan in the fall of 1834. As the conflict escalated, the

Ottoman envoy to Tripoli requested military assistance from Tunis, and the bey obliged with twelve warships, a frigate, and two smaller ships with 300 horses, under the command of two of his most trusted ministers, Shakir Sahib al-Taba'a and Mustafa Agha (both of whom were his in-laws).

As the Porte attempted to negotiate an agreement, British obstinacy led the sultan to depose the entire Qaramanli family in 1835. Replacing them with a bureaucrat sent from Istanbul, the sultan hoped to contain the conflict and circumvent further European meddling in provincial matters.[5] Since he was closely involved in the political affairs of the neighboring provinces, these two lessons made the stakes of international politics crystal clear for the bey, compounded by rumors that his own removal at the hands of the *qubtan pasha* was imminent.[6]

The vast changes to the international and regional balance of power, namely, the resurgence of European colonial empires, posed a potential threat to the continuity of hereditary government in Tunis, as did imperial actions to prevent the fragmentation of Ottoman territory. Subsequent sovereigns alternately took advantage of the rivalries between Istanbul and the Great Powers, or maintained a course of neutrality, intended to preserve their own government from European conquests and the centralizing forces of the Ottoman state. One result was that provincial resources were redirected towards the expansion and modernization of the military. This led to administrative and legal reforms, similar to government restructuring and industrialization projects underway across the empire. The governors and ministers in Tunis surpassed their reform-minded counterparts by their experiment with constitutional government from 1861 to 1864. These efforts at centralization and bureaucratic rationalization weakened the influence of the palace families and diminished the political relevance of the household model of government.

While the bey initially focused on building the military, ministers in Tunis explored alternative means to strengthen the state, considering the benefits of European Enlightenment thought and drawing inspiration from the Muslim past. Two of the most notable and well-published voices from Tunis were ibn Dhiaf and Khayr al-Din. While ibn Dhiaf's family was from the western part of the province, and Khayr al-Din was a mamluk, both were writers who had long careers in government service, represented the bey on diplomatic missions abroad, were major proponents of reform, and had ties to the ruling family. In their writings, they actively engaged with and challenged Orientalist notions of European superiority evoked to justify foreign domination. They identified security in financial stability, a balanced budget, and the rule of law. In this respect they echoed the flourishing intellectual debates across the Ottoman Empire (in Arabic known as the *nahda* or literary renaissance) and in the neighboring Qajar and Mughal Empires.[7] While the myriad reformulations of modernization projects contributed to conceptualizing Europeans through an "Occidentalist" lens and inspired internal civilizing missions, in the case of Tunis, it contributed to the push for a more equitable government.[8]

The shifting balance of power around the Mediterranean contributed to a range of diplomatic, cultural, intellectual, and social changes. By the early nineteenth century, Tunis was home to an expanding diplomatic community with about a dozen foreign consulates in the capital and a few smaller offices in cities of the interior, thanks to its *eyalat-i mumtaze* status. On the one hand, by fulfilling its obligation of military contribution to imperial campaigns, the province often sparred with European powers. Yet on the other, the province had long-standing ties to Europe that were continuously manifest in the ability of the beys to converse in Italian and the presence of European professionals at court, augmented by the temporary sojourn of instructors, skilled artisans, and engineers. Even in the eighteenth century, Bardo differed from more homogenous courts, particularly on the European side of the Mediterranean, in its diverse composition, later allowing for Europeans such as the Tunis-born Sardinian Raffo to function from 1820 to 1860 as a veritable liaison between the bey and European powers.[9]

This chapter contextualizes the place of Tunisia in the historiography of the Ottoman Tanzimat and examines how the modernization process, including the meaning of wealth, affected the ruling family. Financial problems challenged the redistributive model of government and made conspicuous consumption less sustainable as a political model. Building on the discussion of state finances, I consider how reforming the financial administration influenced the family's access to resources and how new formulations of legitimacy relied on law more than the family as the source of political power. Women's political roles were complicated by their lack of official sinecure, limited access to resources, and an intellectual trend towards viewing spending as a problem instead of an asset, just as the number of households doubled, consuming greater portions of the palace budget.[10] While modernization meant a trend away from conceptualizing the state as family, the palace and its household networks remained entangled with political life, however marginalized.

Ottoman military reforms date to the reign of Sultan Selim III (1789–1807) with the first unit of his restructured military corps, the *nizami jedid*, or the new order, established by 1794. Over the ensuing decades, subsequent sultans embarked upon a broad spectrum of administrative, judicial, and bureaucratic reforms while expanding state-funded education, creating an industrial base, and funding public works. Judicial reforms were symbolized in the two decrees promulgated by Sultan Abd al-Majid (1839–1861), the *Hatt-i Sherif* of Gulhane (1839) and the *Islahat Fermani* (1856), transforming the confessional structure of the Ottoman system by proclaiming equal civil status for all subjects regardless of their faith. Administrative councils composed of officials and prominent members of the Muslim and non-Muslim religious communities were established in 1840 to facilitate the participation of local representatives in the government.

Nizami troops became a significant force within the Ottoman military, serving as a model for provincial armies in their organization, uniforms, and even the name. Throughout this period, imperial edicts were delivered to provincial capitals that announced the reforms and demanded local compliance, as the redefinition of administrative hierarchies altered provincial borders and the responsibilities of governors. In education and administrative restructuring, imperial precedents reverberated across the provinces, and ministers began to centralize fiscal powers, reduce corruption, and improve the efficiency of tax collection to help pay for reforms. The governor of Egypt, Muhammad 'Ali Pasha, offered a successful example of provincial centralization. He modernized agriculture and restructured the economy, which provided revenues for building small factories, strengthened the military, and implemented ambitious industrial projects such as digging a canal linking Alexandria to the Nile. He invested in education by supporting the translations of hundreds of European texts into Arabic, and, by the end of his four decades of rule, he could boast of having sent over three hundred students to study in Europe.[11] He skillfully transformed his appointment into a hereditary position that survived British colonial rule, ending only in 1952, with his family occupying a role in government similar to the palace families in Tunis.

Both the imperial precedent and the impressive panoply of reforms in Cairo inspired administrators to the western border of the Muslim world. In Algeria, 'Abd al-Qadir implemented one version of centralization under the rubric of renewal (*tajdid*) in the disciplining and training of his resistance army, and even the 'Alawi Sultan of Morocco utilized Egyptian military manuals and the language of *nizam* in his own reform projects.[12] A number of observers in Tunis noticed the impact of Egyptian reforms. Calligaris, an instructor at the polytechnic school, thought that they constituted a precedent, since the powerful Sahib al-Taba'a was a "great admirer of Mehemed-Ali and tries to imitate him in the reforms that he sponsors."[13] The British vice-consul in Tunis drew similar conclusions about Ahmad Bey's source of inspiration.[14] Even if such assessments were merely impressionistic, there remained a number of similarities between Tunisian reforms and the Egyptian and imperial models.

Reforms in Tunis were inaugurated with the arrival of an imperial *firman* in 1831, when the bey was given a *nizam al-jedid* sash symbolizing the sartorial transformation of the court. As Husayn Bey reorganized the military and formed *nizami* units, their uniforms were redesigned along imperial models.[15] The attire reflected the streamlined image of the sultan's troops that dated to the 1829 decree (mandating the fez as official headgear). While clothing retained its social significance, instead of designating rank, corporal, or communal identity in fabric, colors, or turban style, it now suggested imperial unity and the state as sole arbiter of identity.[16] According to one description of the troops in Tunis:

> On their heads they wore the red Fez, distinguished from that of the other inhabitants not only by a long blue tassel, but by having the whole crown covered by a fringe of the same colour. The uniform was a blue kulka, or jacket, with a blue cloth waistcoat, cut in our [European] manner. Round the body they wore a red and white striped sash; and underneath, blue cloth pantaloons.[17]

European tourists were often disappointed with the sobriety of the uniforms that Temple associated with those worn in Istanbul, pointing out that the "Bey, his family, officers, household, and all the Moorish nobles who come on business to the Bardo, are all dressed in the lately-introduced and highly-unbecoming dress adopted from the Turks" (see Figure 5.1).[18] Husayn Bey carried the clothing reform to the grave, modeling the turban above the headstone into a fez (see Figure 5.2).[19]

Wide-ranging military reforms were concentrated during the government of Ahmad Bey, such as the formation of infantry regiments in 1842 and 1846 and the building of barracks to house them in the capital, its suburbs, and major towns across the province. He established support industries such as a textile factory, a bakery, a tannery, an iron foundry,

FIGURE 5.1. *Muhammad Bey in new uniform,* Illustrated London News, *June 1855.*

FIGURE 5.2. *Grave of Husayn Bey with headstone modeled as a fez, Turbet al-Bey, photo by the author.*

a gunpowder mill, and a small arms factory, funded from public revenues based on taxation. In 1840, the bey established a polytechnic school at Bardo, and a military school in 1855, offering a curriculum in Arabic and theology, math, military history, topography, French, and Italian. European instructors were invited to contribute to the curricula of both institutions, including one instructor who had previously spent two years training Ottoman troops in Istanbul.[20]

Ahmad Bey was as proud of these projects as of his modernizing reputation, inviting foreigners to watch the troops practice or taking them to visit the military hospital. Kennedy, a captain in the Irish military, viewed one such exercise in 1845, remarking that the troops were "armed and equipped like European light cavalry." He was then taken to the barracks where he recording being

> much surprised to find the barracks scrupulously clean, the bedsteads, of iron, with the bedding neatly arranged, as were their arms, kits, and saddlery, all of a fair quality and in very good order. We visited the different regimental workshops, where the soldiers are employed in making their own clothing, appointments, &c. In the armourer's shop were several carbines, of equal finish to the French models, and an ophicleide for the band was receiving the finishing touches.[21]

As Pückler-Muskau "praised the deportment of the troops organized after the European model," the bey responded with polite modesty: he "offered to let them manouvre before me, and added, without being blinded by any prejudice, that I should certainly find them far behind their model."[22] As Kennedy reported, they deliberated "the affairs of Europe and the present condition of Africa, upon which topics he spoke with such just, clear-sighted views, as convinced me the report I had before heard of his being a man of talent was correct. But what surprised me most was his knowledge of geography. . . . It was evident from his incidental remarks that he was well versed in the subject."[23] The bey's reference to European standards among European guests was intended to demonstrate the enlightened nature of the government and the strength of its military, and it contributed to their positive assessment of the bey's character.

Modernization went beyond defensive concerns to transform traditional practices such as the patronage of education and the charitable obligations of the elite by broadening them into state services. For instance, in 1840, Ahmad Bey bought a number of costly works from his bibliophile minister Husayn Khoja, and drew from the personal library of his family, to create a library in the Zaytuna mosque. This was sustained by an endowment that provided salaries for administrators who recorded which volumes were lent to students.[24] A second public library was established during the government of Muhammad al-Sadoq Bey (1859–1882), and the government revised the curriculum at the Zaytuna, bringing it under state control. He sponsored the eponymous Sadiki School to offer instruction in natural science and math, and the government funded programs to send students to study in Paris and Istanbul.[25] The bey financed a new hospital with the capacity to treat one hundred patients, providing services at no charge for those who could not afford to pay, which opened its doors in 1879.[26]

The concern for public health and the ramifications of epidemics led Mustafa Bey to create a board of health, based largely on the voluntary services of resident European doctors. They served primarily in an advisory capacity, regarding matters such as quarantine and urban hygiene, though sanitary control in the capital was delegated to the municipal council after its founding in 1858.[27] Headed by the mamluk-minister General Husayn, it set goals to clean the streets, improve the sewers, facilitate circulation, repair roads, and reduce crime. In the process, the council undertook a census of the buildings in the capital. To cover the costs of maintaining the streets, its members planned to license carriages as a form of taxation, but unfortunately, the British and French consuls blocked such measures, limiting the municipality's ability to implement their projects.[28] With agents appointed in ten different ports along the coasts, these preliminary measures demonstrated the government's concern for health matters.

While centralizing reforms increased the power of the government, judicial reorganization began to circumscribe the personal authority of the bey. The Bardo tribunal had been the highest court in the province, though the bey often consulted with ministers and *'ulama'* and Ahmad Bey reinstated weekly meetings of the shari'a council in 1838. The 1857 proclamation of the *'Ahd al-aman* (the Fundamental Pact) significantly transformed the legal system.[29] This move was almost identical to the sultan's *Hatt-i Sherif* of the previous year, which had established a separate branch of the judiciary for Europeans, awarding them a legal immunity that they hoped to extend to Tunis by invoking imperial pressure.[30] The *'Ahd al-aman* proposed a restructuring of judicial and legislative affairs and gave foreigners the right to own property, guaranteeing security and equal citizenship for all. It also established commercial and criminal courts and a mixed tribunal, though it maintained the bey's tribunal as a higher court where non-Muslims and foreigners could be tried.[31] Following their inauguration in 1848 at the imperial level, and dealing primarily with commercial matters, these mixed courts expanded the range of consular authority, releasing foreign nationals from the bey's jurisdiction so that they became virtually exempt from local legislation.[32]

The major accomplishment of the reform movement, and the one with the greatest repercussions for the household nature of politics, was the constitution promulgated in 1861. The product of at least three years of ministerial deliberations that began under Muhammad Bey (1855–1859), the final document contained thirteen sections and over one hundred articles. It dealt with the responsibilities of the bey, the authority of ministers and governmental employees, the organization of the budget, and legal guarantees to subjects and foreign residents (along the lines of the *'Ahd al-aman*). Significantly, its third article limited the authority of the bey by establishing a ministerial council (or grand assembly) that would combine administrative and judicial functions. Advisors in the ministries were organized with a clearer division of tasks and greater accountability. This structure eliminated the possibility of the bey reigning as an absolute monarch and was intended to prevent any one minister from consolidating a number of functions and acquiring supreme authority (over the bey), as in the case of Mustafa Khaznadar. Finally, it further amended the legal system, attempting to make Europeans liable under local legislation.[33] While the first Ottoman constitution was not completed until 1876, the Tunisian document reflected the comparable restructuring undertaken by Sultan Mahmud II, who divided the administration into three branches: the military, the bureaucracy, and religious and juridical affairs. Each was headed respectively by the *qadi al-'asker*, the Grand Vizir, and the shaykh al-Islam, in the attempt to limit the accumulation of power under any individual (in this case, the Grand Vizir).

Most sources on the reform era are silent on the contributions of palace women to such projects. Ibn Dhiaf, however, was clear about the close relationship between Ahmad Bey and his mother, a *jaria* brought to the palace as a child.[34] She served as the patron of Mustafa Khaznadar, whose powerful position among the bey's inner circle began when he was only twenty years old and may have encouraged his marriage to Ahmad's sister Kalthum around 1841.[35] The fact that her son sought her approval before undertaking important actions (most notably his voyage to France in 1846) hints at her involvement in political affairs.[36] Kalthum may have also been an active partisan of her husband's career. As noted above, she contributed her jewelry to financing military reform, and their children were interested in administrative careers.

Centralization projects were not easily carried out, as the subject population resented what was viewed as increasing government interference in their lives. For instance, when Mustafa Bey sought to swell the ranks of his troops through a military draft, he requested that the *'ulama'* in the capital compile a register of all men between the ages of ten and twenty-five.[37] Since these men had minimal interest in serving in the military, they requested that the shaykhs intervene on their behalf, and the initiative was abandoned.[38] Another popular protest occurred in September of 1861 when some 200–300 men marched to the palace complaining about the increasing cost of living and the problems of the new judicial organization, preferring the return to the former system of beylical justice.[39] Such sentiments were echoed in a protracted uprising that spread across much of the countryside in the spring and summer of 1864; it primarily was protesting unfair taxation but also demanding the suppression of the tribunals and a return to justice at the hands of the bey. Muhammad al-Sadoq used this as a pretext to cancel the constitution, presenting it as a conciliatory gesture to the rebels (though it is not at all certain that this was one of their demands).[40] These laws were similarly unpopular with the European diplomatic and merchant communities, since despite their encouragement of judicial reforms, European consuls refused to relinquish the privileges of consular jurisdiction.

Whether directly or indirectly, the financial, legislative, and judicial structures outlined in the fundamental laws of 1861 altered the authority of the bey and the position of the ruling family. This was true for sections devoted to state revenues and their distribution among members of the ruling family, the salaries of its personnel, the military, and other state needs (Chapter 4) as well as the proposed restructuring of higher courts (Chapter 3).[41] The constitution included procedures for filing complaints against ministers and government employees (Chapter 8), described the rights and responsibilities of civil servants and members of the military (Chapter 11), and standardized a retirement pension (Article 80). As it detailed the responsibilities of each branch of government and the benefits owed to officials, it made clear that they were not immune from criticism but accountable before the law.

While only briefly implemented, the constitution outlined a role for the palace families that was different from what they had exercised under less formal political structures. The first article of the constitution confirmed that "the eldest member of the Husaynite family is the governor" (*wali al-mamlaka*), but it specified that a change in the order of succession was possible "in case of infirmity." He was assigned 1,200,000 Tunisian piasters annually to cover all necessities and personal items, including his personnel, horses, carriages, and provisions for his family (Chapter 4). The remainder of the document restricted his role in government. For instance, the bey was accountable before the law, as he was required to swear by oath to uphold the *'Ahd al-aman* and all the laws that ensued from it before receiving the investiture (Chapter 1, Article 9). He was further obliged to act in conjunction with the relevant ministries (Chapter 5) and the Council of Ministers (Chapters 6 and 7), who had been delegated administrative, judicial, and legislative functions. This created an official procedure to depose the bey, and the new government resembled a constitutional monarchy.

These measures offered an introductory system of checks and balances in government while still preserving patriarchal structures within the governing family. The first chapter established the bey's control over his relatives in personal and financial matters, and its third article elaborated that "the head of state is also head of the ruling family." None of his family members were permitted to dispose of their money or marry, without his permission, regardless of age. The bey was granted "authority over them like that of a father over his young children," and in turn they "owe him the obedience of children." The reassertion of the bey's authority within the family was an attempt to curb spending and prevent debt, by providing the bey legal backing to control or sanction his adult male relations. It attributed the principle of guardianship over all children in the family to the bey as his permission was required for marriage, perceived as a family matter and not an individual prerogative.

Subsequent articles placed clear limitations on the bey's authority; the bey was not the ultimate arbiter of family affairs. The entire beylical family was accountable before the law, according to the final three articles of Chapter 1, which outlined provisions for addressing problems between members of the family, penalties for minor crimes committed by members of the family, and the prosecution of serious infractions. While the bey was given leeway in determining culpability, and the family was exempted from appearing in tribunals, they were to be sentenced according to the penal code.

The Reformed Budget

The bey maintained authority in matters of personal status, but he was left with little control over its financial or judicial affairs as pertaining to the family. Much of the fourth chapter regulated the distribution of stipends within the remainder of the family. Roughly based on previous hierarchies, entitlement increased substantially at marriage, and the establishment of the household showed deference to seniority. It formally divided members of the bey's family into distinct financial categories, based on sex and marital status. For instance, married men were given annual stipends of 66,000 piasters (or 5,500 per month), of which 8,000 (approximately 666 per month) was considered the spending money of their wives. Unmarried men living in their father's households could claim only 500 piasters per month (6,000 annually), unless their fathers were deceased, in which case this doubled. The daughters of the beys were given 20,000 annually once they were married, and only 3,000 if they were not, though similar to boys, this increased significantly (to 8,000 piasters) if their father was deceased. The widows of former ruling beys were allocated 12,000 piasters per year (other wives, as mentioned in the second article, were given 8,000, which was included in the allocation to their husbands).[42] Children of both sexes were given money for their weddings, boys 15,000 and girls 50,000, to prepare the trousseau, though neither young boys nor girls in the family were allowed to contract a marriage without the permission of the bey (Chapter 1, Article 5).

The commission preparing the constitution also deliberated specific legal provisions delineating compensation for mamluks, promulgated as a separate code in 1860. The first part detailed the common practice of preceding generations: all mamluks were to be given food and clothing (one set of winter clothing and one for the summer), gifts on the two 'id, soap, bedding, and fodder for their animals. Yet it added what appears to expand the definition of mamluks to include all their children after the age of fifteen. By 1860, piecemeal restrictions on the slave trade within the Ottoman Empire, and Ahmad's Bey's 1846 decrees against the slave trade, had begun to take their toll. While not intended to abolish slavery or to include the white slaves from the Caucasus, abolitionist pressures and prohibitive costs meant a scarcity of new recruits to the mamluk corps.[43] (The ownership of slaves continued into the French protectorate, with only lukewarm efforts to persecute human trafficking, in part, because the Resident General Massicault was a slave owner.[44]) Initiated by mamluks to secure employment for their sons, similar to other corporations, this measure provided alternative means to incorporate additional recruits into state service. This transformed mamluks from members of the ruling households into salaried employees, and they gained a fixed income and legal rights from the process.[45]

Despite targeting the bey's ability to redistribute state wealth by fixing stipends within the family, it is not clear if, or when, these became the source of unconstrained spending. From the first record of such stipends in 1782 until at least 1835, most men in the family consistently received 300 piasters per month (or 3,600 annually). Similarly, between 1758 and 1835, the monthly amounts designated to their households were fifteen, thirty, or fifty piasters, based on seniority. Facing inflation, currency devaluation, and the growing size of the extended palace family living at Bardo, Ahmad Bey had attempted to drastically reduce the number of recipients on the salary lists in March 1842.[46] Even before the formal promulgation of the constitution, the family appeared to follow its salary limitations, as Muhammad al-Sadoq Bey's monthly salary was 100,000 piasters and those of the various palace households were 500 or 5,000 piasters.[47] These contours were still adhered to over a decade later when, for instance, the children of Hafsia and her deceased husband 'Allala were given 200 a month and the widow of Muhammad al-Taher Bey was given 666½ piasters.[48] In addition, in 1863, Muhammad al-Sadoq attempted to control palace spending by paying some of his brother's creditors and issuing a circular to all the foreign consuls absolving him of further responsibility for debts that went beyond the necessities of clothing and food.

The legal provisions outlined in the constitution divided members of the family and adjusted their salaries depending on sex, marital status, and the presence of a male guardian, in the case of minors. By writing regular stipends according to family hierarchies into the constitution, the state took a certain degree of jurisdiction over family affairs. The 1861 document limited the bey's patriarchal role by preventing him from distributing money at whim, so that the *nafaqa*, which constituted the husband's duty towards his spouse and children and a mark of paternal benevolence, became a state responsibility. The reformed government redefined the family by removing mamluks from the household context, designating them as state personnel. In beginning to define and regulate familial matters, these measures show the continued relevance of family to the state, though instead of a symbol of authority, it was an object to be governed.[49]

STATE BUDGETS AND THE CRITIQUE OF CONSUMPTION

Across the empire, attempts at financial management strove to keep pace with the expansion of global trade, costly modernization plans, and unproductive debts.[50] While court spending and lack of accountability were part of the problem, economic difficulties were complicated by the advantageous practices of European merchants and their recourse to consular support. In Tunis, enterprising but dishonest officials such as Farhat al-Jalluli, Mahmud ibn Ayad, and Nassim Shemama pilfered state coffers, decreasing government revenues, and utilized their European citizenship to abscond with the money.[51] Despite periodic financial instability throughout the nineteenth century, recent research succinctly locates the point of crisis with the first foreign loan in 1863. Contracted by Muhammad al-Sadoq Bey under the influence of the French consul, this loan was destined for the restoration of the Roman aqueduct in Zaghwan and for remodeling the French embassy.[52] Similar to earlier industrial projects that were either unnecessary or primarily to the benefit of Europeans, the aqueduct offered little to the government and population at great expense. The telegraph installed in 1861, for example, was built and staffed by European laborers and technicians, and its services were mainly utilized by the foreign community. Further debts were incurred after a second loan (partially disbursed in kind with used munitions but repayable in cash), under steep interest rates. These led to the 1869 establishment of an international financial commission, with English, French, and Italian representation to service these debts.[53]

Foreign control of provincial finances coincided with the increasingly vociferous denigration of courtly customs. French Enlightenment critiques of the aristocracy were scornful of luxury, wealth, and extravagance as politically superficial and indicative of poor statecraft, stigmatizing consumption as a passive and feminine activity.[54] Roughly comparable presumptions were transposed onto Ottoman practices, in which the chaotic financial situation was considered a hallmark of Oriental despotism. The shift in French rhetoric surrounding gift giving illustrates how, with the rise of imperial expansion, early modern norms and transregional court practices became stigmatized as a sign of irrationality or inferiority. As soon as they established representation in the province, European consuls contributed to the circulation of luxury goods because foreign governments were obliged to present gifts for the inauguration of a new bey, a change in consul, and the signing or renewal of treaties. The United States paid $93,000 dollars to found a consulate and secure amicable commercial relations in 1799. Representatives from Denmark, England, Holland, Portugal, Naples, Sardinia and the two Sicilies, Spain, Sweden, Tuscany, and Venice brought jewels, gold, and munitions.[55] At times, the bey requested that consuls offer him rare imports. Considering how these treaties generally conferred favorable tariffs, fiscal exemptions, or access to natural resources such as coral, their purchase via cash and gifts filled an economic role and served as a source of income for the bey.

As a diplomatic practice, gifting fostered an atmosphere of competition between foreign powers, whereby any breach in etiquette threatened a consul's ability to wield influence at court. Earlier generations viewed this practice favorably, especially when it could secure advantageous alliances. In 1786, the consul Jean Baptiste du Rocher (1779-1787) was accorded 9,000 French livres to purchase gifts for the bey and the minister Mustafa Khoja, "whose good disposition towards us it is essential to preserve."[56] Mathieu de Lesseps (consul general 1827-1832) fretted about the negative political ramifications his modest gifts would create, as they represented "a breach in manners," whereas respect for such customs could "crown the success of certain Consuls in the Orient."[57] When Paris voiced its disapproval, it was not on moral or ideological grounds but, as the minister of foreign affairs remonstrated, because the consul's "service expenses regularly attain heights that are much too considerable."[58]

By the 1850s, bountiful gifts connoted the excess and irrationality that was emblematic of financial disorder, and the threat of force could achieve diplomatic goals. This contributed to the development of a French consensus that government ineptitude and corrupt ministers brought chaos to the fiscal situation in the province.[59] By the time financial reforms were envisaged, Alphonse Rousseau (French consul in Tunis, 1855) strongly advocated taking a "severe" approach to the ruling family by "reducing all of the superfluous and abusive expenses of the bey [Husayn] and his wives." He blamed the luxury of palace clothing and celebrated "the disappearance of turbans and cashemires and all of the gold embroidery" from their closets.[60] Léon Roches (consul 1855–1863) pitied the bey's "horrible financial situation," asking his government to help "deliver" them from their suffering.[61] Yet he responded to the bey's circular on family spending by declaring an "obvious insufficiency of the annual pension accorded to them," proposing that the definition of necessities should include "carriages and horses."[62] While blurring the distinction between luxury goods and staples, Roches clearly had in mind the financial interests of the French merchant community. Either way, the bey's efforts had limited impact, because according to François Botmiliau (consul general in Tunis, 1867–1873), greedy ministers were "prolonging the chaos that reigns in the financial affairs of the country."[63] Jules Barthélémy de Saint-Hilaire (minister of foreign affairs, 1880–1881) concurred that the realm of financial affairs was "the one in which the most absurd abuses" occurred.[64]

The stereotypes of irresponsibility within the palace and unbridled spending were reproduced in public discourse via papers such as *La republique française*, a prominent spokespiece of the republican faction and proponent of colonial expansion.[65] It published a series of articles in 1874 and 1875 that attacked Khayr al-Din by denouncing his taste for luxury goods and displays of wealth. One article accused him of clandestinely preparing two thousand robes, garnished with silver and gold, intended as gifts for Prussian diplomats (reminiscent of the gold embroidery criticized by Rousseau). Another mocked his efforts at parsimony and transparency by claiming that his personal retinue consisted of nineteen domestics and that he bought off members of the foreign press with gifts of jewels.[66] While articulating French fears of being supplanted by another European power, this author found that everything was in excess: the number of cloaks, their elaborate decorations, and the secrecy of the act. Rather than an economic practice, or a component of court culture, gifting could be reduced to an Oriental particularity, associated with unbridled spending, irresponsibility, and the general disorder of the Ottoman government, useful stereotypes for justifying colonial pretentions. Rhetoric aside, even French consuls recognized that the bey was attempting to head off financial problems, which resulted from the "onerous loans made to the princes by certain money lenders always in a hurry to benefit from the position of their debtor."[67]

Ibn Dhiaf and Khayr al-Din

Regardless of the accuracy, Orientalist criticisms of Ottoman governmental disorder did not fall on deaf ears. As bureaucrats and intellectuals debated the way to strengthen the state, they were cognizant of the necessity of financial stability to preserve imperial sovereignty. Though Cairo was the intellectual center of the *nahda*, the trajectory of Tunisian scholars of every generation transcended provincial borders, as many sojourned in Cairo, Istanbul, and the Hijaz.[68] Advocates of pan-Islamic solidarity, such as Jamal al-Din al-Afghani, had a clear following in Tunis, as did Muhammad 'Abduh, who visited Tunis in 1884 and in 1903.[69] Ibn Dhiaf's work was influenced by Rifa 'a al-Tahtawi's writings, which he cited as an authority on European law.[70] He kept current on Arabic publications, whether reprints of classics in Paris or translations of European texts out of Cairo, which he praised for having "produced excellent fruits and radiated its lights in this age."[71]

Ibn Dhiaf was one of the central partisans of modernization who advocated for government based in the rule of law. He spent close to ten years theorizing, contemplating, and writing his multivolume history of Tunis that was first revealed after his death in 1874. Though he structured it as an event-based narrative or chronicle, in many ways his political experience and turbulent current events influenced the content, resulting in a criticism of the government, with the mismanagement of finances a recurring theme especially for the history of the nineteenth century. To begin with, while he recognized how the limited harvest of 1825 meant a drop in government revenues, he claimed that the treasury also suffered "because of increased spending on luxuriously decorated clothes, ornamental saddles, gold-plated armor, [and] purchasing well-bred horses." When the government responded by modifying the balance between silver and copper in coins, he blamed devaluation as "the primary reason for the decline and weakness of the country."[72] He drew the same conclusion here as in his other discussions of taxes and tax collectors, arguing that when they became too onerous for the population, the population would revolt.

Much of ibn Dhiaf's synopsis of Ahmad Bey's government was structured to illustrate the negative repercussions of military expansion on the livelihood of the population. First, he warned that the unprecedented

number of soldiers "harmed the Tunisian dominions," since the taxes created to fund the troops burdened the people and stretched their limited
resources. This was especially true as there was no defensive need for
mounted troops.[73] Subsequent passages detailed the charges on soap and
olive oil and the bey's decision to farm out the rights to a tobacco concession to generate further revenues for the armed forces. As the bey relied
on taxation to increase the number of soldiers, he "caused the weaken-
ing and diminishing of the kingdom's livelihood."[74] The rapaciousness of
individual tax collectors further complicated the situation. Muhammad
ibn Ayad, for example, was zealous in his task to collect the *ashr* tax on
wheat and barley, "which burdened the people more than ever and their
harvests were smaller to the point where farmers almost abandoned planting. [The bey] feigned inattention because of his need to nourish the military and feed the horses, and it resulted that wheat and barley were imported to the kingdom from abroad." Finally, when protests began in the
Aradh region later in 1840, ibn Dhiaf stated, "Its cause was that the bey
was concerned with the expansion of the army with no attention to the
[financial] capacity of the state."[75]

The introduction to the *Ithaf* discussed ideal government by comparing absolutism, republicanism, and constitutionalism. Though an obvious
jab at Muhammad al-Sadoq Bey, ibn Dhiaf firmly grounded the critique
of absolutism in the shari'a. Elaborating on the "religious sanction to for-
bid evil," his examples of wrongdoing include "excessive taxes" and "the
debasement of coins" because of the detrimental impact on the population. Beginning with the seventh-century Ummayad governor 'Ubayd
Allah ibn Ziyad as the first person in the history of the Muslim community to mint a spurious coin, ibn Dhiaf incorrectly claims that ibn Ziyad
was "the killer of Husayn ibn 'Ali [ibn Abi Talib]."[76] The association between the assassin of the prophet's grandson with fiscal dishonesty underscored the gravity of the latter and foreshadowed the later critique of beylical policy. Treating coins as a commodity was thus a central attribute
of despotism, a sign of greed and excess, intended for personal profit, or
excessive displays of luxury. In contrast, he used the Qur'an, *hadith* (say-
ings and anecdotes relating to the Prophet Muhammad), and references
to early Islamic history to explain his support for constitutionalism, defined as rule based in law.

Wealth itself was value neutral for ibn Dhiaf. He cites a *hadith* to maintain that "the fruit of justice is prosperity" and to show that when used
productively, riches were a sign of strength, especially when directed
towards collective, as opposed to individual, gains. This was juxtaposed

with personal enrichment. Al-Mazari, the eleventh-century jurist, de-
cried arbitrary acts such as "taking revenue from the subjects and spending it for their proper interests." Furthermore, rulers should not build objects such as "castles, for which there is no need except personal pleasure
stemming from love of haughtiness, majesty, and excess."[77] This was an
explicit attack on Ahmad Bey, who transferred the court to the Muhama-
diyya, and possibly on Muhammad al-Sadoq Bey for comparable expenses
when establishing Qsar al-Said as an official residence.

Though ibn Dhiaf approved of the ruler earning a stipend from public
revenues (as outlined in the 1861 constitution) and justified such a practice as being one that existed under the first four caliphs, his general atti-
tude towards the bey was one of bitterness. Spurned by sympathies for the
1864 uprising as a popular critique of taxation and the abuse of privilege,
ibn Dhiaf considered the protest an appropriate response to burdensome
taxation.[78] His vision of revenues did not equate personal wealth with
political power but instead encouraged public resources to be invested for
the benefit of the entire community.

Khayr al-Din Pasha was an early figure of the *nahda* movement, along
with Rifaʿa al-Tahtawi in Egypt and Butrus al-Bustani in Lebanon, who
attempted to balance reform with the material realities of financial dif-
ficulty and the meddling influences of Europeans.[79] His path from slave
recruitment to a palace upbringing and a marital alliance with the ruling
family made his biography similar to that of prominent mamluks of the
preceding generations. As an adult, his ties to Tunis and Istanbul were
both physical and ideological. First a minor figure in the palace military,
he entered the ministry in the early 1850s, holding a series of prominent
positions in Tunis and abroad, for instance, representing the bey in Istanbul, Austria, Belgium, Denmark, England, France, Italy, Holland, and
Sweden. In 1862 he married Jannat, the daughter of Kalthum bint Mustafa Bey and Mustafa Khaznadar.[80] A published advocate of reforms, he
penned an 1867 treatise on government that made him a public figure,
a vocal proponent of strengthening the province who advocated solidi-
fying relations with Istanbul. The French consulate kept a close eye on
his activities, with regular updates exchanged between offices in Tunis,
Paris, and Istanbul regarding his travels, conversations with ministers at
the Ottoman capital, and rapprochement with the sultan.[81] His career and
writings suggest how the peregrinations of scholars, intellectuals, and bureaucrats fostered the exchange of ideas that contributed to educational,
administrative, legislative, and financial reforms throughout the empire.

Khayr al-Din's writing was informed by the local political context, though he demonstrated an awareness of broader trends within the empire and actively engaged with European scholars. For instance, his essay on reforms, *Aqwam al-masalik fi maʿrifat ahwal al-mamalik* [The Surest Path to Knowledge concerning the Condition of Countries], detailed the history, political structure, and military organization of European states, with recommendations for reform. He personally supervised the French translation as *Réformes necessaries aux états musulmans*, which appeared the year after the Arabic version was first printed.[82] His active participation in the production of the French edition included altering the text, turning it into a defensive essay on the qualities of Muslim civilization, its contributions to Europe, and its modernity. He carefully included references to the ideas of Voltaire, Montesquieu, Jean-Jacques Rousseau, and John Stuart Mill, as well as minor political figures such as Victor Duruy, Napoleon's minister of education, to demonstrate familiarity with Enlightenment rationalism and liberal economics.[83] Though he saved his longer elaboration on European political thought for an Arabic audience presumably unfamiliar with these texts, he presented his own views as consistent with Arab, Muslim, and European thought.

Much of his reform program was directly aimed at addressing the political and economic problems of the Ottoman Empire, defined by the apathy of its rulers and the decadence of contemporary society. Even if Khayr al-Din obliquely referred to the situation of Tunis, he addressed his proposals to the entire Muslim community, grounding them in the shariʿa and citing a range of Muslim theologians and intellectuals typical of a classical education. He criticized the Capitulations, encouraged administrators to work with the *ʿulama*, and propounded a system based on accountability to the public.[84] Of particular interest was an explicit and pointed criticism of consumerism that is worth quoting at length:

> However, if we examine the habits of those Muslims scornful [of innovation], we find that, just as they refuse to imitate foreigners in their useful institutions, they do not hesitate themselves to consume their products on a scale that is harmful to the interest of the country, without any concern for national production. This can be proven by their clothing, furniture, arms, war equipment, and a thousand other necessities that come only from abroad. It is easy to understand how such a system of consumerism is humiliating, anti-economic and anti-political.[85]

Revealing on a number of counts, this critique presumed that consumption was economically beneficial. He did not rally against luxury items per se but against foreign imports because they were harmful to local manufacture. The references to furniture and clothing targeted the habits of Tunisia's upper classes, while the inclusion of war equipment points towards the wasteful military expenses of Ahmad Bey as seen in ibn Dhiaf. Finally, the distinction between superficial westernization and modernization as the beneficial adoption of European institutions echoed a recurrent theme of reformist writings.

Taking a strong stance against the arbitrary nature of rule by reference to Ibn Khaldun and the lack of justice, Khayr al-Din supported the legalistic basis of government, encouraging "state reform based on justice and equity" as essential conditions to foster prosperity. Corruption contributed to only the climate of "disorder, injustice, and abuses [that] delivered the country to the French."[86] By the time he penned his memoirs from exile in Istanbul sometime around 1888, he was candid about the source of problems in Tunisia. In a virulent attack on ministerial irresponsibility, he targeted the powerful and wealthy mamluk Mustafa Khaznadar and Mustafa ibn Ismail, the favorite of Muhammad al-Sadoq Bey, a local orphan whose vertiginous ascent depended upon ruining the careers of top mamluks. Mismanagement, Khayr al-Din argued, was not an inherent characteristic of the government but the result of the dishonest habits of Mustafa Khaznadar and to a lesser extent ibn Ismail, who was "as useless and ignorant as he was ambitious and corrupt."[87] Khaznadar was "immoral," his administration was "disastrous," his taxation schemes were "abusive," and he "exhausted and destroyed" the revenues of the province. He not only treated the province as his "personal jurisdiction" but would "stop at nothing in order to satisfy his insatiable thirst for wealth."[88] Mustafa Khaznadar and his lackeys had been "exploiting at their whim the poor Regency for twenty years."[89]

The immorality of these men stood as a foil to Khayr al-Din's political career, his astute management of revenues, and commitment to public welfare. By fixing the blame on two individuals, whose characters he thoroughly denigrated, Khayr al-Din disassociated financial problems from governmental structures. Neither were abusive practices inherent to government nor had they left an irremediable situation: Tunisia was full of resources, and he marshaled his own experiences in the government and on the financial commission to substantiate this. He was a strong proponent of state-sponsored education and involved in the reorganization of primary schooling, revising the curriculum at the Zaytuna mosque (which he brought under state control). He created student scholarships and coordinated the founding of the Sadiki School.[90] While he wrote little about the benefits of charity, he personally donated over a thousand manuscripts to the public library founded by Muhammad al-Sadoq Bey.

Adding up tallies for his years as prime minister (1873–1877), he boasted, "Upon leaving power, I left Tunisia in a state more orderly, peaceful, and prosperous than what had been known for ages."[91] During this time, he recalculated taxation rates, offered fiscal exemptions to encourage the planting of new crops, reorganized customs, and fought against corruption and abuse, measures that he credited with facilitating the return to productivity and prosperity.[92] Under his guidance, the Financial Commission balanced the budget, allowing the government "to simultaneously pay the interest on the debt, family stipends, the pensions of princes and the salaries of employees, and in a word to ensure the routine functioning of all the branches of administration."[93] In these assessments, wealth was positively associated with security. Financial resources were for collecting, counting, and calculating into the budget to preserve the solvency and independence of the government when properly managed and invested in public services such as education.

Many of the beys and top advisors whom ibn Dhiaf and Khayr al-Din criticized had been entirely cognizant of the province's limited resources. This was evident when an imperial envoy requested monetary contributions to the imperial coffers from Ahmad Bey in 1838. The bey first responded that much of their revenues went towards paying the soldiers, and he invoked the imperial duty of protecting the borders of the province from the neighboring French. He then convoked a meeting of ʿulamaʾ and ministers to deliberate the matter, drafting letters to the sultan and the shaykh al-Islam and presenting a rational explanation for protecting provincial resources. The letters convincingly conveyed their allegiance to the sultan and respect for the unity of the Muslim community, while explaining the limits of provincial resources, including the problem of stretching the budget beyond its capacity, and politely declining the imperial request. The sultan did not insist.[94] On another occasion, a French diplomat reported Muhammad Bey's pragmatic assessment of agricultural resources and the considerable expenses of maintaining an army (as preface to and justification for honorably withdrawing the Tunisian contingent from the Crimean War).[95]

Even if the framing of their proposals in terms of absolutism versus the rule of law was a product of the *nahda*, ibn Dhiaf and Khayr al-Din's critique of wasteful spending was not a reform-era innovation. Ibn Yusuf's frequent references to the unnecessary extravagance of ʿAli Pasha's taste (his gold-bound books and gold-embellished porcelain glassware) were central to his eighteenth-century argument that conceit was one of the pasha's primary character traits.[96] Both ibn Dhiaf and Khayr al-Din contrasted the selfish acts of a few influential individuals who ruined the state financially with an ideal government in which justice and the rule of law were accompanied by investing resources into the country. For ibn Dhiaf, excessive spending was related to personal enrichment and corruption, which he derided as placing individual desires above communal welfare. Khayr al-Din's ideas about reform insisted on accountability for public revenues and support for local industry. His memoir also targeted individualism, and he accused a series of greedy and selfish ministers of destroying the government and lacking concern for the needs of the community.

While prosperity was a sign of a healthy government, both ibn Dhiaf and Khayr al-Din cautioned against the ruinous consequences of personal enrichment. Far from a derivate discourse, these concerns were distinct from the profoundly gendered terms of the debate in Europe that viewed consumption as a passive and feminine practice. For reformers in Tunis, spending alone was not a problem; they both distinguished between productive expenses destined to benefit the general public and useless ones devoted to personal welfare, as they urged for the rationalization of government in recognition of its responsibilities towards the subject population.

In the second half of the nineteenth century, Tunisia was increasingly the site of imperial interests, both Ottoman and European. Similarly to ministers in Istanbul and governors in Cairo, provincial bureaucrats undertook concentrated efforts to modernize government institutions and strengthen Tunisia's military capabilities, fixing boundaries on consular intervention to assert provincial sovereignty. Costly modernization programs, foreign loans, and corruption seemed to validate the consular depiction of a chaotic and irrational Orient.[97] Yet as late as the 1870s Khayr al-Din claimed that revenues were sufficient to cover all government expenses, including servicing the debt, and the balance in trade with Europe was relatively equal.[98] Khayr al-Din and ibn Dhiaf problematized spending when it benefited the individual to the detriment of the community, urging financial organization and ministerial responsibility instead of the selfish wasting of government resources. Expecting the government to provide for its subjects evoked a hierarchical relationship of obligation, similar to patriarchal models of the state, where the father's financial responsibility to support his family was projected onto the government and state servants.

Debates over the role of the state proposed new rationales for government and sought to recreate family roles to fit with changing conceptions of the social order. Ibn Dhiaf routinely provided biographical details about the beys' mothers and referenced their influence within the family and thus over matters of state. Yet while Khayr al-Din was part of a generation of "family mamluks" and considered the ability of the state to support the governing families a positive attribute, he wrote little about his own family, patronage networks, or household politics.[99] This silence reflects his fraught relationship with his father-in-law and a will to separate family life from his political career. Instead, he emphasized the importance of reason and justice in government, in contrast to the irrationality of personal politics such as nepotism and corruption that he associated with family networks. This implied a concentrated effort to impose a distinction between the state as a public domain and family as part of a private one, a process initiated in the middle decade of the nineteenth century and perpetuated by colonial powers.

While members of the governing family secured a stable income with the 1861 legislation, they did so in exchange for explicit subordination to the bey. Men retained access to titles and official sinecure, whereas women's avenues of power were becoming reduced. Though mamluks had benefited disproportionately from the informal nature of the patriarchal state, they were able to preserve their status despite reduced numbers through participation in reforms.[100] Such bureaucratic opportunities were not available to the palace women, who instead began to be transformed into a symbol of modernization. As the beys became aware of the stigma associated with polygamy, they framed their own marital decisions as monogamous by delegating one woman as the senior wife and downplaying concubinage.[101] In 1880 both Lubomirski and Hesse-Wartegg noted that the beys of Tunis orchestrated marital politics to give "the appearance of European civilization," since "in Tunis as well as in Constantinople and Cairo the fashion to have only one wife gains more and more followers."[102] An American reporter later commented that the government was Muslim "yet liberal," a qualification seemingly based on the impression that the "bey and all his chief officers have but one wife each, and divorces are discouraged and discountenanced."[103] Referring to Muhammad al-Sadoq Bey, who according to other sources married at least four times and may have practiced serial concubinage, this presentation of marital practices underscores how the beys of Tunis were aware of the ways in which family life represented modernity. Their private lives and domestic behaviors were the subject of political scrutiny, since equating the limited morality of the elite with their weak political capabilities could justify the civilizing mission.[104]

Chapter 6

INVENTING DYNASTIC TRADITIONS: FAMILY POLITICS OF FRENCH COLONIALISM

The 1861 constitution formalized the structural dependence of the family on the paternal authority of the bey, structures that were extended by the subjugation of the entire family under French colonialism. In May of 1881, a minor incident along the border with Algeria provided an opportunity for French warships to dock outside the capital, from where they delivered a treaty to the bey demanding continued trade privileges and the recognition of French suzerainty. This document inaugurated colonial rule by creating an official protectorate over the province, severing the bey's ties to the Ottoman center. Wary of the sultan's response, the French policed all correspondence between Tunis and Istanbul, removed Tunisian diplomatic personnel from their posts throughout the empire, and closely monitored Ottoman activities in neighboring Tripoli. The Porte sent a formal protest against this act of aggression to the integrity of its territory and dispatched two warships with sixteen hundred troops. The convoy was intercepted in Tripoli, and despite French intelligence reports that the sultan planned to grant the investiture to one of the younger men in the family to circumvent the treaty, the threat of French retaliation prevented any further military action from Istanbul.[1]

The colonial authorities justified their intervention on numerous counts, from the initial premise of the bey's inability to maintain security to the later moral imperative of educating, industrializing, and modernizing the country. Of interest here is the role accorded the bey and his family. In claiming to respect local sovereignty, protectorate authorities incorporated portions of the defunct constitution into the protectorate's legal edifice. These statutes confirmed the hereditary rights of the male line of descent and the bey's control over the extended family in an abridged version of the laws. As they omitted entire chapters and individual articles, primarily those relating to ministerial organization and the council of ministers, they also significantly modified the authority of the bey.[2] The bey became an agent of colonial domination, as matters of foreign relations were delegated to the highest French colonial official, the Resident General (by an accord dated 8 June 1881), as was the exercise of all judicial, administrative, and financial functions (the Convention of June 1883).[3] Though his executive prerogative was reduced to confirming French decisions, the bey's ceremonial role was expanded and developed in ways unique to the modern state.

While the French had dabbled in overseas expansion under the Bourbons, engaging with the slave trade, establishing sugar colonies in the Caribbean, and setting up trading outposts in the Atlantic and Indian Oceans, the resurgence in colonial activities over the course of the nineteenth century made empire a decisive component in the formulation of a modern national identity. The colonial project touched diverse sectors of metropolitan society, particularly after the founding of France's Third Republic in 1870. This era witnessed the flourishing of artistic and literary representations of empire, and geographical, anthropological, and scientific societies to classify the colonial world, and it was also one in which colonialism reached the masses. As the proliferation of exotic colonial products made them common consumer goods, information about the colonies was widely circulated in inexpensive and illustrated newspapers that targeted a broad readership.[4]

In fact, scholarly interests in colonial territories and their ability to provide popular entertainment often overlapped in international and universal expositions. These fairs were a quintessentially modern phenomenon, thanks to the emphasis on industrialization and a cataloguing of colonial exoticism in which the Middle East became an object on display. Instead of domination by force, colonial rule was envisioned as a form of guardianship in which civilizational terms overlapped with the familial. This relationship was depicted in images such as Pierre-Narcisse Guérin's *Bonaparte Pardoning the Rebels in Cairo* (1810). Despite the failure of the expedition, Guérin portrayed Egyptian insurgents as ashamed and beseeching, some on their knees, Napoleon stands over them in a position of moral and racial superiority, looking calm and paternal.[5] If liberalism could make the modernization of the backwards peoples of the world a national duty, it could also make paternal responsibility part of a subtle hierarchical discourse.[6]

Since the conquest of Algiers in 1830, France had taken a utilitarian approach to the governors of Tunis, whom they viewed as easier to manipulate than the Ottoman sultan, a policy that circumvented imperial authority. It served a cost-conscientious approach to colonial rule to leave parts of this system intact, subordinating the bey and local authorities in an associationist model of governance that sought to preserve colonial difference as opposed to one of assimilation with the metropole. At times, the French relied on the bey as an ally to pacify the local population and, at least initially, as a façade of local sovereignty. Their projects not only were threatened by rebellions within Tunisia (before and after May 1881), they were also frowned upon within European diplomatic circles and briefly challenged by the sultan. Thus began a struggle with both Italian and English diplomats to delicately play their card as a *fait accompli*, though they remained suspicious of both powers and their considerable resident communities for decades.[7]

Focusing on the position of Tunisia as the first major colonial acquisition of the Third Republic, this chapter considers how the deliberations over succession, the role of the bey in the state, and the marginalization of the ruling family reveal the interplay between French and Tunisian family politics.[8] It begins with a discussion of the tensions surrounding the public role of the royal family in France's turbulent nineteenth century, as bourgeois norms relegated family affairs to a separate, private sphere. Returning the focus to Tunisia, it then examines how patriarchal frameworks informed the relationship between the province and France and their later incorporation into the administration of the protectorate, pointing towards the continuity of Franco-Tunisian diplomatic interactions. The second half of the chapter explores the bey's ceremonial role and its significance to the legitimation of colonial rule to suggest what was modern about colonial structures and the performance of power. Finally, returning to the question of finances, I consider the contradiction between the state's responsibility towards, and monetary support of, the bey and the desire to divest much of the ruling family from official positions.

FAMILY POLITICS IN THE METROPOLE

French relations with the bey were informed by the political upheavals of the nineteenth century, their implications on the nature of the French state, and the understanding of power. The deposing, sentencing, and decapitating of Louis XVI and Marie-Antoinette offered a tragic end to the revolution's family romance, with filial remorse and tensions over gender roles crystalizing in the figure of the queen.[9] As the revolution was overturned by a succession of empire and monarchies, with only brief attempts at republicanism, the struggle between royal and representational government continued to find expression in accusations against royal women. The backlash against women's visibility during the French Revolution had first coalesced on the personage of Marie-Antoinette, by virtue of how her public and private functions came to represent the problem of women in the public sphere and threatened the masculinization of the public.[10] The ideal of a polity based on fraternity was more than a revolutionary slogan or a powerful metaphor; it contributed to the transformation of family law and the reform of inheritance laws to encourage egalitarian relations between brothers.[11]

Thanks to the ascendance of bourgeois values and the gendered conception of the public sphere, during the Napoleonic empires, Restoration, and July monarchies, royal women occupied a difficult position. They were not accepted as public figures, yet their lives were not immune from public scrutiny. While the necessity of producing royal heirs was women's responsibility (as attested by Napoleon Bonaparte's divorcing his first wife Josephine for her presumed failure to conceive) and constituted a political contribution, it was not recognized as a public role. This paradox was revealed when the Duchesse de Barry (the daughter-in-law of Charles X, 1824–1830) invited official figures to witness the birth of her son, creating a scandal. Though not even the royal family took her seriously as a political actor, this emphasis on the public and political nature of her reproductive role was a failed attempt to improve her image.[12] As bourgeois norms supplanted aristocratic codes of conduct at Versailles, palace women were expected to remain invisible.

The paradoxical position of the ruling family was particularly evident under the quasi-Bourbon King Louis-Philippe (1830–1848), whose self-presentation as an enlightened monarch or citizen king was full of contradictions. If he claimed to rule by virtue of not being in the direct royal line, he owed his throne to his lineage and relied on the symbols of kingship to bolster his legitimacy. In a modernist vein, he wanted the royal family to embody the nation, as he adhered to the bourgeois conceptualization of the family within the private sphere. One target of public criticism was the inclusion of his children on a civil list (an annual stipend for his household and the maintenance of their palaces, distinguishing the property of the sovereign from that of the state). Popular cartoons questioned why his family benefited from salaries paid by the state treasury as a form of personal enrichment at the expense of the nation.[13]

The idea of a fraternity of men and the ensuing masculinization of politics eliminated the possibility of the queen contributing to the public presence of the royal family. As Queen Marie-Amélie endeavored to navigate a public role that respected gender norms, she found that public displays of motherhood were unwelcome, and she retreated from even ceremonial appearances with the royal family. Political satires mocking royal domesticity brought to the fore the awkward position of familial metaphors of state because the king as father transgressed the separation between public and private spheres.[14]

If the position of the French ruling family within the state was resolved, it was only due to the removal of the monarchy and the founding of the Third Republic in 1870. Yet family continued to be a relevant model for social organization and a subject of state concern, as marriage served as a parable for the social contract. Debates over women's rights, gender roles, and their relation to national identity were informed by the colonial context and infused with civilizational language. Court life and the monarchy had been feminized by eighteenth-century Enlightenment figures such as Rousseau, with the harem as metaphor for such closed and feminine worlds and allusions to despotism implicitly referring to the Oriental.[15] Just as the heroic images of Napoleonic paintings reflected the cultural rationalization and celebration of French colonialism in the Orient into the nineteenth century, references to the Orient (as a symbol of what France was not) appeared in debates before the 1879 parliamentary decision to regulate divorce. In this way, the Orient consistently provided a reference point against which French national identity was defined. Whereas defenders of divorce argued that it constituted a patriotic act that would strengthen the family and nation, opponents viewed it as uncivilized and comparable to polygamy.[16] Rather awkwardly, women figured prominently in representations of the nation (the icon of Marianne, images of motherhood in literature and art), but "under cover of elevation to allegory or metaphor," women themselves were "refused political citizenship."[17] Even if family practices evoked normative social ideals and encouraged national unity, family hierarchies served as a prominent metaphor for the ordering of colonial races, where the French held a paternal responsibility to improve humankind.

THE ALTERED ADMINISTRATION
AND COLONIAL PATERNALISM

The language of paternal benevolence allowed charitable activities and redistributive structures of beylical government to legitimize the hierarchical nature of provincial society for much of the eighteenth and nineteenth centuries, a broad political resonance that continued into the modern era. Similar concepts appeared in diplomatic correspondence and informed French relations to the beys for much of the nineteenth century, so that the civilizing mission of colonialism did not mark a drastic break but merely the transposition of hierarchical ideologies onto administrative structures. While the Orient was often considered a civilization in decline, though not relegated to the level of primitive savages, the perception of the Orient as traditional or backwards was expressed by infantilizing descriptions of Orientals; as Consul General De Lesseps bluntly summarized, "These princes are big and ignorant children."[18] This perspective informed consular reports and ministerial deliberations about the beys of Tunis. Depicting the bey as an ineffective ruler implicitly suggested the need for supervision and guidance.

Though often depicted as "Arabophile" for his lengthy experience across the region (in Algeria, Morocco, and Tripoli) and his fluency in Arabic, Roches' brand of developmental utopianism was patronizing and condescending.[19] Shortly after beginning his tenure as consul (1855–1863), Roches described Muhammad Bey as a "poor little prince," urging the minister of foreign affairs that if the French were to help the bey "find a solution to his horrible financial situation," the bey would happily follow their advice.[20] He considered Muhammad al-Sadoq Bey no more capable of managing his government since "even the best of Muslims is nothing more than a pouting and overgrown child, who is easily discouraged, and whose education requires steadfastness and perseverance."[21] Yet Roches recognized that such character flaws were conducive to the perpetuation of French privilege, as his influence relied upon the bey's weakness and was threatened by the liberal approach of the 1861 constitution:

> It would not be in our greatest interests for the bey to relinquish too much of his authority in favor of an assembly. Foremost, because any French agent, who may be able to influence the whims of a Prince would have only a weak leverage upon the decisions of an assembly to which he would not be appointed.[22]

Those sharing these political calculations applauded Muhammad al-Sadoq's suspension of constitutional rule. Leverage over the government and preserving commercial and diplomatic interests were critical to what French administrators defined as the status quo since the occupation of Algiers. As Foreign Minister Drouyn de Lhuys said in 1864, French special interests in Tunis resulting from the colonization of Algeria relied upon "the continued rule of the family that is currently governing in Tunis."[23]

The structural subordination of the bey, and official deference to European superiority, was first concretized with the implementation of the 1869 Financial Commission, placing the bey under the joint tutelage of France, England, and Italy. The commission administered the tax collections, serving as guardians of their respective merchant and banking communities to "supervis[e] how [revenues] were used." The bey was deprived of the ability to dispose of government resources, and instead all financial powers were delegated to an executive committee (Article 9) that he was required to consult, and he could not act "without the approval of the mentioned committee."[24] As Marquis de la Valette, the minister of foreign affairs, concluded, the logical solution to the economic difficulties that plagued the regency was for the bey to "call upon the enlightenment of experienced men," such as the French.[25]

That this language of benevolence was only a thin cover for French interest in establishing suzerainty was apparent to the Tunisian court. The minister General Husayn complained to Khayr al-Din that "the French have one policy and one goal regardless of who the consul is. This is that they want the bey and his minister to ask for French protection on his own, and they want him to tell the Sublime Porte that this is his own doing." Or simply put, that "France's goal is to take our country with its consent."[26] He summarized the situation in June 1879 as follows:

> The French consul uses all his cunning means whether great or trivial to get what he wants; he thinks no one will understand what he is trying to achieve. He threatens the minister and the bey on the one hand, so he can get everything that he asks of them. On the other hand, he invites all of the important men from across the country and is kind to them and speaks to them in pleasant tones. He says: Anyone who has a problem, I will fix it, so that he is acting as if he is the bey, and the minister and the representative of the French.

Hardly naïve, the bey was cognizant of these ulterior motives but was left few options.[27]

The treaty of Bardo (the document signed at the adjacent Qsar al-Said palace in May 1881) concretized French suzerainty by superposing colonial administration on the beylical government. It relied on the cooperation or tacit acceptance of the bey in exchange for preserving his position among the elite and protection "against any danger threatening him as an individual, or his dynasty, or that might compromise the peace within his state."[28] Yet the bey's acquiescence was initially doubtful. The first Resident General, Theodore Roustan, worried that "the bey is our ally only in name," suspecting that he would "deal with the treaty in the same way that he dealt with our concessions, that is to say, to reduce it to insignificance by opposing each of its clauses one after the other," rendering it useless.[29] Therefore, officials in Tunis undertook considerable efforts to convince the bey that French sovereignty was for his own good, insisting that his position and the legitimacy of his entire family were threatened by the sultan, who planned to replace him, and only French intervention could save him from this "abyss."[30] In Paris, Prime Minister Jules Ferry optimistically proclaimed in the national assembly that the bey "has no other hope than French protection, and he is deeply attached to the French protectorate."[31]

With clear interests in controlling Tunisia to secure the fragile and volatile hold on Algeria, the French had surprisingly few concrete plans for colonial administration, which was instead constructed on an ad hoc basis by colonial officials, often informed by their failures in Algeria. The initial decision to build a government around the bey provided a covert form of colonial occupation so as not to offend Italy or Britain. Questions about the nature of protectorate rule arose when Muhammad al-Sadoq's health took a turn for the worse in the fall of 1882 as he approached his seventieth birthday. Paul-Henri-Benjamin d'Estournelles (the interim Resident General in 1882) nervously contacted his superiors in the metropole about the exact official position to adopt. He wondered if the French government intended to maintain the "altered administration" that they had put in place under the bey or whether this situation offered an opportunity to depose the family altogether.[32]

The French were suspicious of the two eldest men in the family, 'Ali and Taieb. Immediately following the signing of the 1881 treaty, 'Ali was forced to provide written proof of his submission, while Taieb was detained within the palace for his role in a plot that appealed to the sultan's authority.[33] Before the bey's imminent death, the Resident General capitalized on 'Ali's jealousy and apprehension of his younger brother, committing him to a secret agreement in which he swore to "never act other than in agreement" with the French government.[34] The promise of French backing for his candidacy as heir apparent confirmed the tactical reliance on the former ruling family in the protectorate government. This engagement in family politics became the cornerstone of an associationist approach to colonial governance.

The colonial apparatus was not integrated into the French metropolitan government, nor was it brought under the Ministry of Colonies; instead, French authorities doubled its offices as they built a parallel administration, leaving parts of the Tunisian government intact. As the colonial official Maurice Bompard later elaborated, dismantling the previous bureaucracy "would create futile difficulties," as it was inappropriate to replace them with "institutions and an administration born of another civilization and destined to meet different needs." Informed by a hierarchical order of civilizations, Bompard opined, "The existing government—despite its faults—was better than improvising another government, no matter how perfect."[35] This assessment presupposed an evolutionary understanding of human progress from primitive to modern, in which "French legislation, appropriate for a country with an ancient civilization, could not be easily adapted to the rudimentary administration and primitive customs in the regency [of Tunisia]."[36]

The judicial organization of the colony was based on the dual legal system already established in Algeria, where French citizens were governed by French laws, and a version of Islamic law that was compiled and codified under French supervision regulated colonial subjects.[37] Under the guise of respecting religion, this organization eliminated the previous flexibility of Islamic law allowed by interpretation, replacing it with a fixed body of texts that posed as tradition. Whether referred to as indirect rule or association, the dual structure of institutional segregation was anchored in the belief that the colonized were essentially different from their colonial benefactors. This dual system characterized French rule in Algeria and Tunisia and British rule in Egypt, and it was common across the African continent.[38]

French diplomats characterized the bey as a naïve and uneducated child, an image of colonial peoples prevalent in popular media such as advertisements and colonial expositions that depicted all of France's colonies as children under the paternal guidance of the metropole.[39] Imperial references to family were based on hierarchical presumptions of its organization, stemming from the authority of the father and the obedience and respect of his children. This image reasserted the civilizing premises of the colonial project that relied on liberalism's exclusion of children from exercising their rights.[40] Though purporting emotional solace, paternal and familial metaphors justified subordination and silenced dissent.

PRESERVING DIFFERENCE AND PERFORMING POWER

Through clothing, ceremonies, and galas, colonial authorities transformed the bey from a minor provincial governor into the prince of a hereditary dynasty with all the accoutrements due to such a rank. Regalia and festivities were central to the formation of modern identities in European cities such as Paris, London, Berlin, Vienna, or St. Petersburg. They became a popular way to demonstrate national or imperial unity, involve the masses in government (with or without permitting them a voice in politics), and create traditions, exalt royal authority, or signify national strength, making the late nineteenth century the "heyday of invented tradition."[41] The British in particular extended an appreciation for royal spectacle to the colonization of India, according titles and medallions to their local subordinates to transform and perpetuate a selection of Mughal traditions.[42]

Distinctions between French, or European, settlers and Tunisian subjects that were created by the legal system were imposed on other domains as well. Alongside the republican emphasis on rational government and the rule of law, the symbolic realm remained politically imperative. Whether preserving or modifying current practices, the protectorate administration created and bolstered traditions as stagnant and visible objects of a dynastic state. For instance, the first coins minted after 1881 preserved the style and design of the preceding years, though where one side had once been inscribed with the name of the Ottoman sultan, it merely read "minted in Tunis."[43]

The attention of colonial authorities to symbolic representations of continuity and difference was attested by efforts to enshrine these in legislation. By a decree of September 1883, the uniforms for the Tunisian military were fixed for infantry, cavalry, and artillery with specifics regarding tunics, jackets, pants, coats, shoes, equipment, and arms. All colonial troops wore a red fez with a blue silk tassel and a copper plaque on the front in the shape of the recently designed coat of arms of the beys, and they carried a sword.[44] The same uniform was proscribed for ministers and the bey's aides, with later protocol specifying, "Officers and soldiers in the Beylical Guard are no longer required to salute the princes in the Husaynite family when they are in Arab clothing," so that the act of wearing these clothes conferred official status.[45] The protectorate ensemble was partially based on the military uniform designed under Husayn Bey, reflecting the *nizami* units of the imperial troops, but the guard's beylical plaque and the addition of a sword were innovations (see Figure 6.1). The composite nature of Tunisia's colonial troops was reflected by the amalgam of local, Ottoman, and French elements. While felt hats signaled the specificity of Tunisia as an Oriental and Muslim country, the regiments were labeled according to their Ottoman names (with grades of *amir alai*, *kaimakam*, and *yuzbashi*), and all commands were given in French.[46]

Conversely, representations of Tunisian specificity were constructed to fit a particular late nineteenth-century understanding of French national identity and colonial tutelage. Though French republicans during both the Second Empire (1852–1870) and the Third Republic (1870–

S. A. Sidi Mohamed el Hadi, Bey de Tunis

Photo Garrigues Tunis - 288

FIGURE 6.1. *Muhammad al-Hedi Bey (1902–1906) wearing the full uniform as detailed under the French protectorate, undated postcard, author's collection.*

1940) derided pomp as a sign of royal absolutism and viewed popular festivals as peasant traditions, festive displays of empire served the political exigencies of garnering widespread popular support, associating national identity with colonial power, and boosting its international reputation.[47] Republicans sought to bridge class and political divides through national celebrations, declaring July 14 a national holiday (Bastille Day) and hoping new symbols of allegiance would discourage political factionalism and erase memories of territorial loss.[48] The most successful public events were the expositions, especially as the pedagogical content and scientific pretensions gave way to entertainment and the imperative of profit. Often supported by the colonial administration, colonial propaganda was a prevalent feature of the fairs.[49] While the 1878 Exposition in Paris celebrated national pride in science and technology, the Universal Exposition of 1889 glorified European colonial tutelage over Africa and Asia as part of this progress. In its spatial organization and ethnographic displays, the French portions of the exhibit portrayed the French as the peak of national and racial hierarchies, acting as a fatherly figure toward the less advanced peoples of the world.[50] Though the theatrical display of wealth in palaces, jewelry, and luxury goods was an early modern expression of power, the collection of colonial territories became its modern corollary for conspicuous consumption.

Tunisia was one of the few countries outside Europe and its colonies to participate in world fairs, beginning with the London Exhibition of 1851 (where there were also exhibits by the Ottoman sultan and Egypt). Over 190 items were included in the 1851 catalogue, ranging from raw materials such as wool, linen, tobacco, lead, iron, and 253 baskets of dates to finished products such as textiles, saddles, and 90 bottles of scented waters.[51] The exhibit was organized as a market, with stalls containing groups of items, the most popular of which seems to have been the display of local costumes.[52] Though the content of the 1867 fair was similar, including elaborate collections of clothing, furniture, musical instruments, and artisanal products, it was the structure itself that tantalized the crowds.[53] A replication of the Bardo palace designed by French architect Alfred Chapon, it contained a throne room, decorative items such as tiles and embroidery brought from Tunisia, the iconic lion statues that ornamented the staircase at its entrance, and an adjacent café and barbershop (see Fig. 6.2). Constructing an exclusive building to imply the nation's independence offered a physical embodiment of provincial autonomy that neatly corresponded to French imperial interests. This palace began a process of French investment in the creation of Tunisian royal traditions and a reinterpretation of Tunisian history that would continue under protectorate rule.

Whereas Tunisians participated in the organizing committee for the 1889 exposition, the decision-making process reflected the hierarchical construction of protectorate rule: Tunisians had little influence, and the bey was saddled with the bill.[54] Of the nine subcommittees that covered arts, education, furniture and accessories, textiles and clothing, industry, mechanics, foodstuffs, agriculture and viticulture, and horticulture, a Tunisian subject presided over only that on textiles. The organizing committee determined that the pavilion need not replicate a specific Tunisian monument but should serve as "a specimen of Tunisian style," so that the final product combined elements from mosques, shrines, and residential homes, with an extensive craft section designed as an Arab market, or *suq*, displaying dozens of artisanal trades (see Fig. 6.3).[55] If the exhibitions celebrated colonial achievement and the colonial future, the Tunisian one

PALACE OF THE BEY OF TUNIS.—SEE PAGE 2.
Palais du Bey Ahmed Le Bey de Tunis.

FIGURE 6.2.   *Pavilion of the bey of Tunis, Paris International Exposition 1867*,
Illustrated London News, *author's personal collection.*

was a success. As President Carnot remarked, the display demonstrated
"the progress achieved on a number of different arenas since the organization of the French protectorate in Tunisia."[56]

Henri Saladin was behind the design of the Tunisian section at both
the 1889 and the 1900 expositions, composed to produce "a gay and faith-
ful image of local art." His artistic acumen was upstaged by the hundred
or so Tunisians staffing the exhibit in a continuous ethnographic performance that formed the pavilion's central attraction.[57] It contained an expansive collection of antiquities and mosaics, and while the structure emphasized a tradition of royal extravagance, its interior evoked colonial
nostalgia and hinted at profits. Yet even though the beys had frequently
opted for a heterogeneous approach to interior décor, heavily influenced
by baroque style, these elements were eliminated since Saladin was explicit about his disapproval of Italian fads.[58] In eliminating the ways in

which the beys modernized their palaces to concentrate on Andalusian or Maghribi themes, the fairs of the early-protectorate era served as an additional site for the rearticulation of a particularly Tunisian tradition, as understood by French administrators and befitting colonial rule.[59]

In Tunisia, the emphasis on ceremonial protocol under the protectorate meant a new calendar of celebrations. No longer was the arrival of an imperial messenger an occasion for gathering notables, military, and religious officials at Bardo, with military music and the sounding of cannons. Circumcisions and weddings were no longer the elaborate festivities with days of feasting. Instead, the relatively sober commemoration of religious holidays became occasions for the celebration of French protection. Previous protocol for Muslim holidays, such as the two 'id, involved the gathering of members of the *diwan* and the *'ulama'* to listen to Qur'anic recitation and hadiths.[60] For Mawlid (commemorating the birth of the prophet Muhammad) as well, students from the Qur'anic schools gathered in the capital to read prayers as cannons sounded and the minarets of mosques were lit. On one occasion, Ahmad Bey traveled from the palace to the capital in a procession that included "two battalions from the heads of the army in their ceremonial clothes, [and . . .] two other battalions standing on either side." He joined the *'ulama'* and dignitaries for

Le Palais de la Tunisie.

FIGURE 6.3.   *The Tunisia Pavilion, Paris Universal Exposition 1889, from E. Monod's L'Exposition Universelle de 1889. Paris: E. Dentue, 1890.*

prayer in the Zaytuna mosque, after which they were served sweet drinks such as rosewater. Finally, the bey spent the evening mingling with the crowds in the market.[61]

In the context of imperial competition, French colonial officials sought to orchestrate holiday receptions to demonstrate their suzerainty as a lighter version of colonialism. The first opportunity arose when the holy month of Ramadan ended in July 1881. It was customary for the bey to receive visitors for two days: first, family, ministers, and local notables and then a broader public, including consular representatives, on the second day. Foreign representatives and other guests were admitted to the bey in the order that they arrived. Colonial officials found that this apparent lack of protocol took "no consideration for influence or seniority" and immediately demanded inclusion on the first day to distinguish French supremacy from the unofficial influence of other European powers. English and Italian representatives in particular had been "entirely hostile" towards French rule.[62]

The symbolic weight of holiday protocol did not go unnoticed by other European powers. When the Italian consul was obliged to wait before being admitted to visit the bey in 1890 and 1891, he complained about the "poor organization" and turned the incident into a diplomatic fiasco. Reports in the Italian press enflamed the matter, presenting it as a deliberate French affront to the nation, and an official complaint was subsequently sent to the French foreign minister.[63] While it was an imposition on previous beylical traditions, the colonial adjustment was intended for foreign audiences who carefully scrutinized ceremonial procedures.

By the end of France's first decade in Tunisia, the Resident General's office was issuing formal invitations to diplomatic personnel to attend holiday receptions hosted by the bey. Guests included the commander of the occupation forces and all the personnel of the Resident General's office, who arrived in a military cortege. The French minister of state was responsible for coordinating the bey's escort and planning the parade route from Bardo to Tunis.[64] On Mawlid in 1885, the bey's journey to the capital was not the former military procession but a train ride. He was met with fanfare and "saluted with beylical music," but instead of proceeding to prayers with the religious authorities and local notables, he "was received by Tunisian officers and administrators," after which the Resident General, Paul Cambon (1882–1886), took him to visit a local school. Later activities included a tour of the official printing press, speeches by various Tunisians in the colonial administration, and a brief concert by European schoolchildren. A synopsis of the events printed the next day reported how the bey was "following the traditions of his sovereign predecessors," that he "recognized all the progress accomplished under the protection of the French government," and thanked the administration for their "dedication to their mission."[65]

Attending the Mawlid celebration in February 1882, the colonial authorities boasted that by "associating ourselves with their official religious celebrations, they no longer doubt our intention to respect religion and national customs."[66] The Resident General similarly proclaimed in an address to the bey on *'id* that this was a time to

> renew our vow [to support] the prosperity of Tunisia, for the benefit of Your Highness and his family. In our dedication to sustaining the reign of justice and proper order, increasing production and its riches [. . .], we are acting in accord with the instructions and the goodwill of the government of the French republic.[67]

In exchange, the bey was invited to participate in the official celebration of Bastille Day, where as a French civil servant, he accompanied the Resident General in celebration of the revolution.[68] Though premised upon religious sanctity and French respect for Islam, the holiday agendas were oriented towards acting out French generosity and patronage.

French colonial administrators developed new ceremonials as well. Whereas Cambon utilized the coronation of 'Ali Bey in 1882 as an opportunity to give a public speech, his successors delivered the ceremonial schedule to later beys, escorting them to the Bardo for an official pronouncement and the presentation of the Legion of Honor medal to clarify its purpose as the French recognition of the new bey.[69] As of 'Ali Bey's death in 1902, the investiture was carried out under the authority of the Resident General, who invested the bey "in the name of France."[70] Other innovations included an investiture ceremony for the heir apparent, who continued to be referred to as the bey of the *mahalla*, though he had ceased to supervise tax collection since the beginning of protectorate rule, whose heir was given the title *bey of the table*, as his ceremonial role was limited to hosting dinners for Mawlid and the holiday of Laylat al-qadr.[71] After 1939, the anniversary of the bey's accession to the throne was also commemorated.

For all his devotion, the bey was not French, and to underscore this distinction, he was officially referred to by his Ottoman rank as "Pasha Bey of Tunis" (though the title *mushir* first awarded to Ahmad Bey was dropped).[72] With certain elements of procedural and symbolic continuity intending to convey the modicum of Tunisian sovereignty, the amalgam of Ottoman titles and French medallions created symbolic dissonance. If colonial administrators wanted to illustrate the inferiority of local particularities, they were unable to control how these events were received. One youthful spectator provoked the consternation of a dutiful police agent during the celebration of ʿid al-Fitr in 1894, when he remarked to a friend in the crowd, "The French are shit."[73] Local sarcasm similarly belittled the French gesture toward symbolic autonomy in their issuing of coins in the bey's name. A joke in circulation claimed that the Arabic script on the coin was incorrect, and that instead of saying "minted in Tunis," the coins were stamped: "Patiently we endure [French rule] in Tunis," transforming lip service to local sovereignty into a critique of French oppression.[74]

LEGISLATING FAMILY AFFAIRS

Protectorate rule furthered the process inaugurated by the constitution of separating the bey's family from the state administration. Bardo had been both the center of government and the primary residence of the governing families for almost two centuries, even when the beys frequently used the seaside palaces in the spring and summer and that at Hammam-Lif in the winter. Muhammad al-Sadoq Bey resided mainly at Qsar al-Said, opposite the Bardo gardens, enough distance for the protectorate administration to justify the piecemeal destruction of Bardo. First opting not to maintain the "secondary structures" such as the apartments of younger men in the family and ministers, they later demolished a number of annexed buildings.[75] The tribunal was closed and all administrative functions were relocated to the Dar al-Bey in the capital. ʿAli Bey apparently preferred the home in the coastal village of Marsa, and so Bardo no longer served as a symbol of family authority and instead was open to tourists, as it was transformed into a museum of antiquities in 1888.

Even without executive or judicial powers, the bey was a government employee entitled to a salary, and the protectorate agreement pledged to ensure that his standard of living "was not inferior to those of his predecessors."[76] The bey was allocated the annual sum of 2 million piasters for his family, which the French called his civil list. This total was divided into 1½ million for the bey's personal expenses; 200,000 for palace maintenance and its personnel; and 315,000 for his direct descendants (bringing the total to 2,015,000 piasters).[77] The stipend was initiated as a temporary solution to reduce the bey's control over the budget, since "it is only with time, and with a regime change, that we may seriously be able to modify these aspects of the budget if we wish to avoid hurting the feelings of the sovereign."[78] Hoping that the colony would eventually become financially self-sustainable, the minister of foreign affairs surmised, "It will probably suffice to revoke [from] the bey and his counselors [the] privilege of administering these revenues, instead guaranteeing His Highness with a regularly paid civil list."[79]

According to calculations made in 1881, the most significant drain on the colony's revenues was debt repayment at the rate of 4 million piasters per year, with palace expenses, including all costs related to the bey's household, consuming about 27 percent. The rest of the approximately 12 million piasters was divided among the army and the navy, religious personnel, the police, and an umbrella category of "diverse services." Three years into protectorate government, the colonial officials reviewing provincial accounting concluded that the lifestyle of the bey was far from extravagant and that "one should not believe that with the sum of 3,318,857 piasters the bey and his family find themselves in exceptionally good conditions."[80]

The parameters of the civil lists were restrictive enough so that in June 1883, 'Ali Bey sent his representative, Muhammad al-'Aziz bu 'Attur, to the ministerial council to request a raise.[81] He invoked Articles 29 and 30 of the 1861 constitution, which the French claimed to respect, according to which the bey and each member of the family received a fixed individual stipend instead of the lump sum divided between them. The minister of finances refused to apply the earlier legislation in its entirety, citing the additional expenses it would entail.[82] During the deliberations of the fiscal budget the following year, Bu 'Attur again raised the question of family stipends. The colonial assembly reiterated that revenues "must be allocated to administrative expenses and the repayment of protectorate costs," and considering that "court expenses cannot be included among either of these two categories," augmenting the stipend to 2 million was not justified. However, Cambon did agree to the modest increase to 1,500,000 so that "the beylical crown maintains all of the luster that it held under the regime of his predecessors."[83] Though protectorate legislation incorporated the constitution, money for the male and female members of the family and the maintenance of the bey's home were not included in the colonial budget, and the sum remained fixed, despite an 1888 plea towards the same end.[84] Instead, the colonial government assigned stipends only to members of his family who could be accommodated under the official limit.[85]

After a few decades of protectorate rule, French authorities became more explicit about the relevance of defining who belonged to the bey's family in order to reduce expenses. Around 1906, a project was under consideration that would limit the right to govern to the direct descendants of the bey, Muhammad al-Nasser (1906–1922), for financial and political reasons. First, excluding his agnatic relatives from the "community of heirs" would cut budgets and reduce state responsibilities toward the growing family that the French complained was composed of "countless princes added lazily to the list of stipends."[86] Instead, if they were dispersed outside the capital to manage rural estates or reoriented toward military careers, their ability to form a united block against the colonial state would be limited. It was hoped that Nasser's docile sons could be educated in a manner conducive to cooperation with the French. Though the plans never materialized, the administration later considered a possibility of divesting the majority of the ruling family and limiting succession to a direct line of descent in 1934. Fearful of popular outcry, the Resident General issued a statement declaring that "the protectorate government denounces all of these fanatic rumors, and confirms that there has never been a question of changing the regime in any manner."[87]

Despite this avowed commitment to noninterference, colonial authorities again examined the practice of succession during the Second World War, contemplating whether to nullify the claims of the man they had named heir apparent. They determined that while the order of succession to the eldest male in the family was included in the 1861 constitution, this legislation had been suspended by a decree in 1884. It concluded that "this rule is not written in any text of public legislation currently applicable," and it could therefore be altered as it suited the needs of the French government.[88]

The size of the bey's extended family continued to increase over the course of protectorate rule. Though an 1896 tally of men in the family included 21 names, in 1936 there were 77.[89] Even limiting recognition to the male line of descent, excluding the children of the beys' daughters from the benefits accorded to "blood princes and princesses," there remained over 200 beylical descendants on the salary roll in 1953.[90] Some of the decisions about who could be considered as part of the family had an adverse effect on women, as the French prioritized a male line of descent. Combined with the dwindling numbers of mamluks, the social group most likely to marry the beys' daughters, their potential disinheritance had the ironic effect of encouraging marriages between various degrees of cousins. By 1953, there were 124 princesses, of whom only 31 did not marry princes.[91]

The bey's retreat from urban spaces signaled his disassociation from public life, and it also distanced the palace family and women in particular from the administration. While Bardo still served ceremonial functions, the family lived in Marsa, and the colonial administration was located in the capital. Many of these summer homes were adjacent to the residences of European diplomats, who continued to socialize with the bey and his family. Here as well, informal relations between palace women and European diplomatic wives supplemented the official relations between their respective governments.[92] ʿAli Bey insisted that the colonial state fulfill its promise of protection and support, articulating a vision of the family as an integral part of the state and not as a domestic or private affair to depend on his own pocket money. Yet colonial authorities dedicated the budget to administrative needs and public expenses, and regardless of the official line promising support for the bey's family, they attempted to relegate the domestic to a private sphere beyond the concerns of the state. By placing a ceiling on the civil list, the colonial government circumscribed what could be done in the domestic sphere, while maintaining a façade of noninterference in family affairs.

The protectorate relied on the bey's symbolic acquiescence to colonial benevolence, but they were unable to control the multiple meanings of his symbolic role, particularly as they pertained to nationalist organizations. The mere fact that protectorate authorities contemplated altering succession practices or divesting branches of the beylical family indicates an awareness of the paradoxical repercussions created by maintaining the bey's position in government. For some strands of the nascent nationalist movement, the bey became an attractive sign of authority that predated French colonial rule. For instance, the Khaldunia scholarly circle, an elite group of men meeting for educational purposes, organized a conference in 1914 on Hammuda Pasha and Ahmad Bey, whom they characterized as the African "Sun King."[93] The iconic weight of the bey was similarly articulated by ʿAbd al-ʿAziz Thaalbi in his famous *La Tunisie martyre*, as a series of nationalist demands formulated around a program of constitutional monarchy. Lamenting that the bey was limited to stamping his approval on French decisions and was not responsible to the people, he nostalgically pointed to the reform projects of Ahmad Bey, Muhammad Bey, Muhammad al-Sadoq Bey, and the 1861 constitution.[94]

On the occasion of a visit to Tunis by the French president Alexandre Millerand in the spring of 1921, nationalists encouraged the bey to inquire about the validity of the 1861 constitution. When he failed to do so, the bey was accused of betrayal and denouncing the constitution, charges that Nasser Bey vehemently denied. The French refused to lend official support to his statement, and the distraught bey submitted his abdication that April. This news led to a popular strike and a large gathering in front of the bey's palace, and so the Resident General convinced him to stay in power to appease the situation.[95] The 1920s were a flourishing period of nationalist activity through political parties, labor unions, and women's groups, where the bey maintained relevance as one component of the nascent national imaginary.[96]

The familial metaphor of parental responsibility that upheld the scaffolding of the French colonial order could be deployed to question it. Munsef Bey (1942–1943), a known supporter of the nationalist cause, challenged colonial authority by requesting that the French properly fulfill their paternal duties. Shortly after his accession in 1942, he presented the French with a reform program, including administrative reorganization, increased Tunisian representation, equal salaries, and improvements in education, and that December he attempted to set up his own cabinet.[97] As he elaborated in a public speech given to the Resident General Jean-Pierre Esteva, the French representative "must consider himself, the same as I do, as the father of all Tunisians, and he has to work towards improving their conditions and their futures."[98] Neither his suggestions for reform nor his patriarchal proposition proved successful, and the French responded with an assertion of authority; falsely accused of collaborating with the Axis powers when the country was reoccupied by the Allies in 1943, the bey was invited to abdicate, and then the French forcefully deposed him. References to the bey as a symbol of sovereignty, or an agent of modernization in early phases of the nationalist movement, demonstrate the inability of French authorities to control the meanings of beylical rule.

For all its contradictions with the commitment to democratic and representative rule, colonial expansion was sanctioned throughout France's Third Republic to stave off international competition and bolster national pride.[99] Prominent republican figures such as Léon Gambetta and Jules Ferry (who was prime minister from 1880 to 1881) were staunchly in favor of the French occupation of Tunisia.[100] The presentation of the colonial project in Tunisia through paternal metaphors that emphasized protecting the bey from internal revolts, and preserving his dynasty, not only preserved the façade of a civilizing mission but eventually bolstered the decadence and elitism that the French associated with monarchical rule.

Tunis served as a template for the colonization of Morocco in 1912, initially construed to protect the sultan of Morocco from tribal uprisings that challenged his authority. Here, too, the semblance of local control was geared to legitimize the occupation. As Marshal Hubert Lyautey (Resident General in Morocco, 1912–1925) phrased it: "Administration must always appear to be supported by the native authorities under the supreme authority of the sultan, under our simple control."[101] The familial colonial discourse was deployed in French mandate rule over Syria and Lebanon (1919–1946), where references to colonial subjects as adopted children, with France as a sentimental mother and administrators as stern fathers, served again to make the hierarchical order more palatable under the guise of benevolent education.[102]

Portraying colonialism as the responsibility of a wise father over his young children was just one way that familial metaphors continued to be politically relevant despite the modern impetus to contain the family (and women) within the private sphere. Women in the palace were excluded from spectacles of local sovereignty in these re-created political traditions whereby hereditary rule passed between men. If their social lives continued to have diplomatic ramifications, they were circumscribed and subtle.[103] The gendered hierarchies of colonial rule often feminized the indigenous male elite, excluding them from the public sphere, and this was doubly true for colonized women. As colonial administrators elaborated the protectorate system, bolstering the trappings of authority compensated for any real judicial, legislative, or executive power, and the bey could at best claim a compromised patriarchy. Tensions surrounding the bey's elaborate ceremonial presence versus his practical insignificance stemmed from the decision to rely on the compliance of the bey, the hereditary rights of his descendants, and the support of his family financially, while limiting their ability to govern and reducing their access to state revenues. In Tunisia, the reliance on beylical rule helped create continuity between the patriarchal structures of Ottoman governance and the protectorate regime.

CONCLUSION

In January 2011 the international public discovered the corruption of Tunisia's President Zine al-Abidin Ben Ali (1987–2011); his wife, Leila Trabelsi; and their respective families, who had monopolized the nation's political and economic life for a substantial portion of his 23-year rule. In a number of respects, they perpetuated the worst attributes of a royal family: they built sumptuous palaces, flaunted their wealth, were immune to legal sanction, and used family connections for economic privileges.[1] In fact, before his deposition, many believed that Ben Ali was preparing to create a hereditary dynasty by passing on his position to his son-in-law Sakher al-Materi.

Yet while the influence of the Ben Ali–Trabelsi clan suggests the importance of family to political life, similar to what I have described under the beys in the eighteenth and nineteenth centuries, this minimalizes the profound differences between the two. Ben Ali's power stemmed largely from the dominant role of the ruling Constitutional Democratic Rally party (known by its French acronym, the RCD) and the traditions of the single-party state developed under the first president Habib Bourguiba (1956–1987). His authority was maintained through very modern technologies of surveillance and control from the bloated police force used to harass dissidents, infiltrate civil society organizations, and intimidate the population to a vast infrastructure of internet censorship, which severely curtailed online critiques of his regime and limited freedom of expression, as well as the acquiescence of vast sectors of the population.[2] Ben Ali was at least superficially accepted as a democratic sovereign in international diplomatic circles, praised by the International Monetary Fund for Tunisia's financial accomplishments, considered a reliable partner by the European Union, and viewed as a strategic ally in the War on Terror. While none of this protected his regime from the challenges posed by increasing socioeconomic and regional disparities, public resentment, and the estrangement of the military, they indicate that any connections with the familial nature of the state in the Ottoman period are either anecdotal or anachronistic.

This is not to contrast a corrupt or violent modern state with a harmonious and egalitarian Ottoman past, for such a nostalgic rendering of Tunisian society under the beys overlooks how state and society were clearly hierarchical and profoundly authoritarian. Though political power was accessible to the entire governing family, shared among the bey and his ministers, an inner circle made decisions with little accountability. Resources were confiscated for personal use at various points along the political spectrum and irregularly invested towards public good. If the practice of consultation was valued by some (Hammuda Pasha Bey, Ahmad Bey) more likely to consult with the ʿulamaʾ, or more accepting of a divergence of opinion, it was disparaged by others (Muhammad al-Sadoq Bey). Finally, while women were able to contribute to the economic and political strength of the ruling family, their actions did not shake its patriarchal foundations.

As indicated by generations of marriage alliances between the palace, the political elite, and the ʿulamaʾ, and the social networks linking Bardo to urban society, the palace families were keenly attuned to the importance of being accepted by provincial society. Women contributed to establishing and maintaining local ties, just as they factored into beylical relations with foreign powers. Over the course of the nineteenth century, women's status was increasingly a barometer by which foreigners judged Tunisian civilization. Since the foreign resident community had few contacts beyond governing circles, these assessments relied considerably upon impressions of the palace. Attentive to the political ramifications of social interactions, the beys presented themselves as monogamous, and provincial notables had their wives dine with foreign guests.

Family life informed how Ottomans, Muslims, and Orientals of all social backgrounds were written about in travelogues, academic studies, and the European press, some of which circulated in Tunis even before the colonial era. Not only was women's status a way to measure men's attributes and the advancement of civilizations, but such critiques often stigmatized Islamic law because of the husband's right to universal repudiation and the practice of polygamy. By the late nineteenth century, Arab and Ottoman intellectuals responded to these stereotypes in deliberating how state modernization projects applied to the family, household managements, gender roles, the marital couple, and child rearing. Such debates in newspapers, pamphlets, and published books incorporated local and regional conversations with Orientalist scholars in which family was shaped to represent social and cultural ideals whether nationalist, liberal, or conservative.[3]

One of the first Tunisians to enter this debate was the prominent *'alim* Muhammad al-Sanussi, who published a short study on women in 1897 that he subtitled "Women's Rights in Islamic Law."[4] Written in French, Sanussi's study sought to counter Orientalist critiques about women's inferior status in Islam through a series of explanations and justifications. Covering major subjects of contention such as polygamy, veiling, and divorce, he insisted upon Muslim women's financial rights, including inheritance and alimony, while he encouraged their education, and the development of occupational skills.[5] His conclusion that Islam was far from oppressive and instead protected women underscored the central issue at hand: that ensuring women's well-being was part of the Arab and Muslim (male) character. Thus, Sanussi set the stakes for the debates over women's status by gesturing towards their relevance for defining masculinity and national culture.[6]

Sanussi's writing reflects the adaptability of family structures and the flexible conceptualization of the ideal family over the course of the two centuries covered in this book. The eventual preeminence of the ruling family in the eighteenth century owed much to the anchoring of household structures, and the reconfiguration of political power under Murad Bey and his descendants, and was neither infallible nor eternal. Their position benefited from the tacit approval and renewed symbols of support from the sultan, as well as an anchoring in local elite culture. If the family used its wealth to demonstrate political power and belonging to a class of early modern courts, it also invested resources in public foundations, urban improvements, and support of a wide array of dependents, from household staff and servants to minor officials, artisans, merchants, and the urban poor. Women participated in the redistributive process, the representation of family authority, and palace politics while adhering to the boundaries of the patriarchal familial order. This respect for contemporary understanding of proper gender roles was indicated by ibn Yusuf and ibn Dhiaf, who recognized the significant bonds of marital affection between the beys and their wives, and the importance of maternal concern for their sons. In the early modern configuration of court life, the activities of women at Bardo were facilitated by the geographies of gender segregation, yet they relied upon the personal nature of political power that was dismantled by the reform process.

As part of the Arab cultural renaissance and an advocate of modernization, Sanussi also presaged over a century of deliberations over the relation between women, modernity, and Islam. These debates became increasingly vociferous throughout the protectorate era and during the nationalist movement, though this sustained interest in women's lives has not always been matched by serious consideration of their varied experiences. Interesting work has been done on women's education under the protectorate and their participation in the anticolonial nationalist movement, and histories of Tunisia continue to discuss women's status and women's rights to demonstrate the modernity or westernness of the nation-state.[7] Family life and personal status laws remain a privileged domain for gauging women's rights, justifying foreign political intervention and stigmatizing Arab culture.[8]

Different scholars have tried to challenge the consensus that the oppression of Arab and Muslim women begins in the family. For instance, Duben and Behar used demographic analysis to show that there was no one singular "Middle Eastern" or "Turkish" family type. Blili Temime's ethnographic discussion of family is a defensive gesture to demonstrate that Tunisian practices do conform to Western liberal standards, with examples to show the diversity of domestic arrangements and the rarity of polygamy. Mounira Charrad, for her part, insists that the modern state has liberated women by combating "tribal" mentalities responsible for their subjugation.[9] Yet these scholars reassert the centrality of Western liberal ideals of a monogamous, nuclear family and specific understandings of women's rights rooted in individualism by which women must be free of the family before they can be completely free. As Saba Mahmood has said, the problem of women's rights is not necessarily located within the family or women's position within the household since this model assumes that freedom and rights are based on individualism and the severing of women from their families.

My own approach to these questions has been to historicize family relations among one specific segment of the population in which family offered opportunities for women, as opposed to merely limitations. Though patriarchal, the state was based in family structures that allowed women to exercise economic and political power. Family and households were central components to building social and political networks throughout the Ottoman period, making a claim to transregional courtly culture, creating ties to provincial notables, and articulating the continuities between the Muradite and Husaynite beys. The financial centrality of the family to palace hierarchies and its general organization indicates the material basis for arguing that the familial is political. These microhistories of women's lives within the palace demonstrate their managerial roles, the importance of kinship, and how cultural affinities supplemented official ties to Istanbul.

In the seventeenth and particularly eighteenth centuries, households dominated Ottoman politics in the capital and a number of its provinces, corresponding to a period of relative decentralization and increasing provincial autonomy, of which Tunisia is a case in point. The governors participated in an early modern elite in which family and state overlapped at the courts of Europe, India, and Asia, and for whom the conspicuous consumption of luxury goods exemplified political power. Women in Tunis as elsewhere contributed to legitimizing the state in sartorial displays, the construction and patronage of religious endowments that concretized family investment in urban centers, their support for scholarly study, and respect for local saints. In a system in which wealth was redistributed, the sovereign extended his patriarchal authority in the family in charitable and benevolent acts towards his subjects.

During the nineteenth century, prominent ministers engaged with Ottoman and European intellectuals and cultural models, as shifting political exigencies led to modernizing the state and the family. This engagement occurred in conjunction with the ambitious reform program and constitutional experiment undertaken by the governors in Tunis (and their counterparts in Istanbul and Cairo). They corresponded with an increasing emphasis on military power and a shift away from family as the basis of the state to an increasingly gendered expression of political power as a uniquely male domain. These alternate conceptualizations of government as one based less on patriarchal benevolence and more on a depersonalized set of responsibilities transformed the relation between family and state, creating new boundaries between the public and private. One consequence was that reform of the financial administration limited the family's access to resources and its ability to fulfill the needs of the redistributive patriarchal state.

What does this suggest about the genealogy of reform? Was the process of modernization forced upon the beys by European consuls? This view relies on a simplistic equation between rational government and Europeans. In practice, consular officials and their protégés benefited from the system of arbitrary rule to a greater degree than the vast majority of the subject population. As is clear in diplomatic correspondence, the French had as little interest in supporting a constitutional monarchy as they did in establishing the rule of law. They preferred the immunity of consular jurisdiction to the mixed tribunals, encouraged luxury spending, and considered the contracting of loans to be a lucrative business for the merchant community. In addition, much of the interest in European learning, technology, and material culture was initiated by the governing elite. The beys had invited many of the European instructors and professionals to court, and the taste for European imports can be traced much earlier than the period of European ascendancy. While the discussion of consumerism indicates that there was a growing fad for European furniture and interior decoration in the second half of the nineteenth century, this trend was homegrown. Such particularities of taste reflected the personal impact on governing adopted by each bey: one had a penchant for collecting manuscripts, while another was fascinated with the military, so that the style and organization of government underwent frequent changes between 1700 and 1900.

Even when colonial bureaucrats attempted to absolve the state from responsibility towards the palace families, their efforts to define whether the bey was a public servant, and whether his family life was a state affair or a private matter, paralleled similar debates within France and the complex process of attempting to disentangle family from political life. While relatively more successful at excluding women from politics and the public sphere in the colonies, colonial rule was often framed through familial metaphors. In depictions of racial hierarchies as a family of nations, or of the colonized as children in need of patriarchal guidance, family continued to be intertwined with the conceptualization of the modern state.

The following six genealogies represent the main components of the palace families in the period discussed in this book. Aside from the first, which centers on 'Ali al-Turki, each begins with one of the beys who reigned (see the chronology for exact dates): 'Ali Pasha, Muhammad al-Rashid, 'Ali ibn Husayn, Husayn ibn Mahmud, and Mustafa ibn Mahmud. Though incomplete, they are based on archival documents and primary sources.

<u>Key</u>

△ male
○ female
— — marriage
— parent to child
| siblings

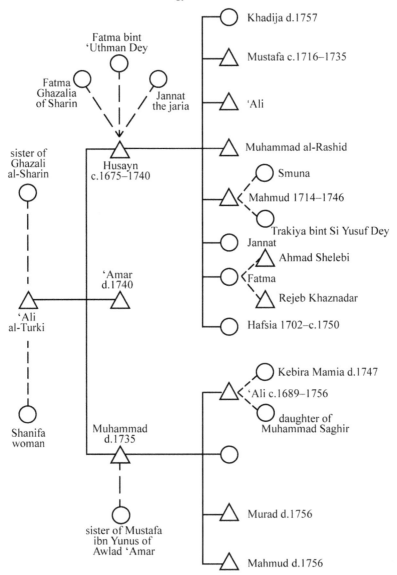

Genealogy 1. 'Ali al-Turki

Khadija d.1757

Fatma bint
'Uthman Dey

Fatma
Ghazalia
of Sharin

Jannat
the jaria

Mustafa c.1716–1735

'Ali

Muhammad al-Rashid

sister of
Ghazali
al-Sharin

Husayn
c.1675–1740

Smuna

Mahmud 1714–1746

Trakiya bint Si Yusuf Dey

Jannat

Ahmad Shelebi

Fatma

'Amar
d.1740

Rejeb Khaznadar

'Ali
al-Turki

Hafsia 1702–c.1750

Kebira Mamia d.1747

'Ali c.1689–1756

daughter of
Muhammad Saghir

Shanifa
woman

Muhammad
d.1735

Murad d.1756

sister of Mustafa
ibn Yunus of
Awlad 'Amar

Mahmud d.1756

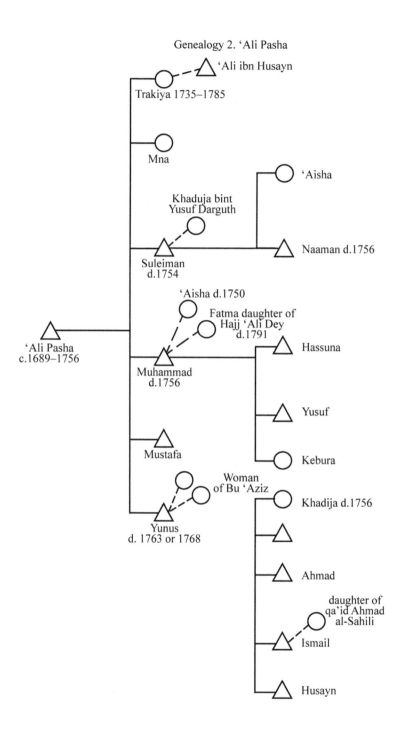

Genealogy 2. 'Ali Pasha

'Ali ibn Husayn

Trakiya 1735–1785

Mna

'Aisha

Khaduja bint
Yusuf Darguth

Naaman d.1756

Suleiman
d.1754

'Aisha d.1750

Fatma daughter of
Hajj 'Ali Dey
d.1791

Hassuna

'Ali Pasha
c.1689–1756

Muhammad
d.1756

Yusuf

Kebura

Mustafa

Woman
of Bu 'Aziz

Khadija d.1756

Yunus
d. 1763 or 1768

Ahmad

daughter of
qa'id Ahmad
al-Sahili

Ismail

Husayn

Genealogy 3. Muhammad al-Rashid Bey

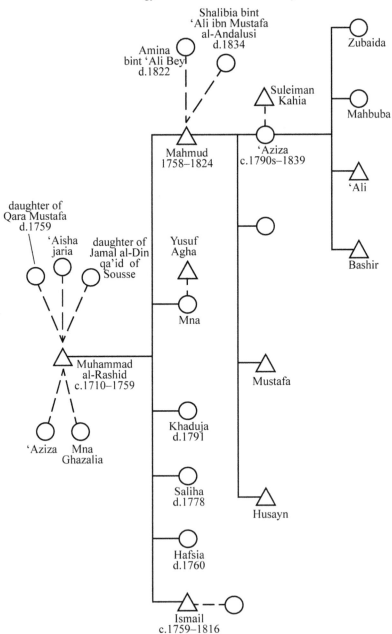

Genealogy 4. 'Ali Bey

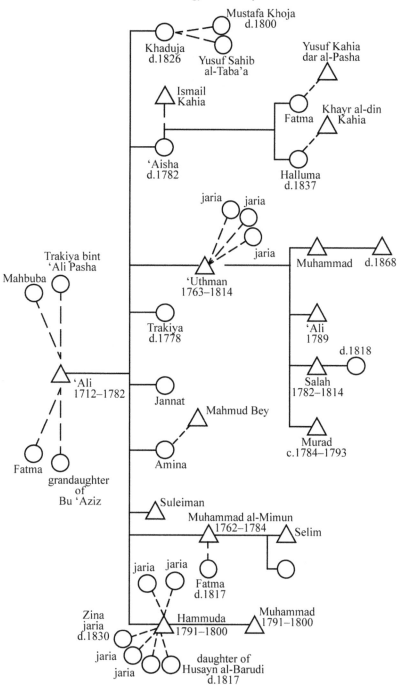

Genealogy 5. Husayn Bey

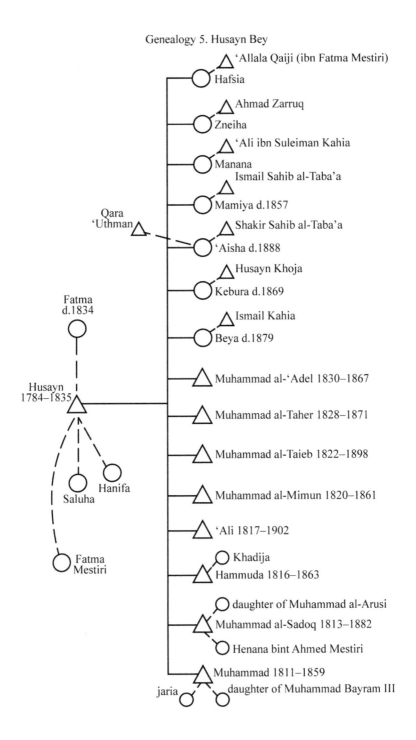

Genealogy 6. Mustafa Bey

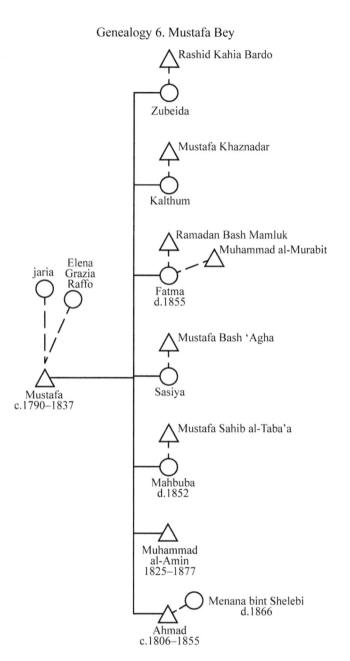

Rashid Kahia Bardo

Zubeida

Mustafa Khaznadar

Kalthum

Ramadan Bash Mamluk

Muhammad al-Murabit

Elena
Grazia
jaria   Raffo

Fatma
d.1855

Mustafa Bash 'Agha

Mustafa
c.1790–1837

Sasiya

Mustafa Sahib al-Taba'a

Mahbuba
d.1852

Muhammad
al-Amin
1825–1877

Menana bint Shelebi
d.1866

Ahmad
c.1806–1855

ANNUAL EXPENSE REGISTERS
OF THE PALACE TREASURY

Register Number	Date in Hijri Years	Approx. Christian Year	Register Number	Date in Hijri Years	Approx. Christian Year
83	1169	1755–1756	308	1214	1799–1800
99	1171	1757–1758	312	1215	1800–1801
175	1185	1771–1772	321	1217	1802–1803
180	1186	1772–1773	327	1218	1803–1804
184	1187	1773–1774	330	1219	1804–1805
187	1188	1774–1775	335	1220	1805–1806
192	1189	1775–1776	341	1221	1806–1807
201	1190	1776–1777	344	1222	1807–1808
209	1191	1777–1778	358	1224	1809–1810
214	1192	1778–1779	360	1225	1810–1811
216	1193	1779–1780	371	1227	1812–1813
220	1194	1780	376	1228	1813
224	1196	1781–1782	384	1229	1813–1814
229	1197	1782–1783	388	1230	1814–1815
233	1198	1783–1784	402	1231	1815–1816
239	1199	1784–1785	406	1232	1816–1817
243	1200	1785–1786	415	1234	1818–1819
246	1201	1786–1787	421/2	1236	1820–1821
247	1202	1787–1788	425	1237	1821–1822
251	1203	1788–1789	430/4	1240	1824–1825
260	1205	1790–1791	436/4	1242	1826–1827
266	1206	1791–1792	440/2	1245	1829–1830
270	1207	1792–1793	441/2	1246	1830–1831
273	1208	1793–1794	442/2	1247	1831–1832
279	1209	1794–1795	444/2	1249	1833–1834
289	1211	1796–1797	448/2	1250	1834–1835
295	1212	1797–1798	451/2	1251	1835–1836
300	1213	1798–1799	453/2	1252	1836–1837

Register Number	Date in Hijri Years	Approx. Christian Year	Register Number	Date in Hijri Years	Approx. Christian Year
385	1229–1230	1813–1815	468	1257–1258	1841–1843
395	1230–1231	1815–1816	472	1261–1265	1845–1852
403	1231–1232	1815–1817	479	1250–1265	1834–1847
411	1235–1236	1817–1821	483	1264	1848
427	1239–1240	1824–1825	491	1268	1851–1852
438	1245–1249	1829–1834	504	1271	1854
444	1248–1251	1833–1836	507	1273–1275	1856–1859
449	1251	1835	512	1276–1280	1860–1863
450	1251–1252	1835–1836	552	1276–1277	1860
456	1253	1837–1838	581	1297–1298	1881

NOTES

INTRODUCTION

1. See Appendix 1 for a complete genealogy of the family.

2. The basic unit of currency was the *nasr*, with fifty-two *nasri* to one *riyal*, or piaster, as it was called by Europeans. The approximate equivalents of weights and measures are listed in the glossary. Tunisian National Archives, Register 201 (hereafter listed as TNA).

3. Caroline Weber, *Queen of Fashion: What Marie Antoinette Wore to the Revolution* (New York: Henry Holt and Company, 2006), 11–47.

4. Anne Walthall, "Introducing Palace Women," in *Servants of the Dynasty: Palace Women in World History*, ed. Anne Walthall (Berkeley: University of California Press, 2008).

5. Julia Ann Clancy-Smith, *Mediterraneans: North Africa and Europe in an Age of Migration, c. 1800–1900* (Berkeley: University of California Press, 2010), 104.

6. This is the figure generally agreed upon by scholars, whereas estimates made by contemporary foreign sources often place the population between two and five million; Jamil M. Abun-Nasr, *A History of the Maghrib in the Islamic Period* (Cambridge: Cambridge University Press, 1987).

7. Julia A. Clancy-Smith, *Rebel and Saint: Muslim Notables, Populist Protest, Colonial Encounters (Algeria and Tunisia, 1800–1904)* (Berkeley: University of California Press, 1994).

8. Dalenda Bouzgarrou-Largueche, *Wtan al-Munastir: fiscalité et société (1671–1856)* (Tunis: Publications de la faculté des lettres de la Manouba, 1993); Lucette Valensi, *Fellah tunisiens: l'économie rurale et la vie des campagnes au 18ème et 19ème siècles* (Paris et La Haye: Mouton & Co., 1977).

9. Sadok Boubaker, *La régence de Tunis au XVII siècle: ses relations commerciales avec les ports de l'Europe méditerranéenne* (Toulouse: Université de Toulouse, 1978); Dalenda Larguèche, *Territoire sans frontiéres: la contrebande et ses réseaux dans la régence de Tunis au XIXe siècle* (Tunis: Centre de Publications Universitaire, 2002).

10. Lucette Valensi, "Islam et capitalisme: production et commerce des chéchias en Tunisie et en France aux XVIIIe et XIXe siècles," *Revue d'histoire moderne et contemporaine* 16, no. 3 (1969).

11. Ghislaine Lydon, "Writing Trans-Saharan History: Methods, Sources and

Interpretations across the African Divide," *Journal of North African Studies* 10, nos. 3–4 (2005); Lucette Valensi, "Esclaves chrétiens et esclaves noirs à Tunis au XVIIIᵉ siècle," *Annales, Economies, Sociétés, Civilisations* 22, no. 6 (1967).

12. There is a considerable body of literature on administrative decentralization and the prominence of local elites and families, notably Rifaʿat Abou-el-Haj, "The Ottoman Vezir and Pasa Households 1683–1703: A Preliminary Report," *Journal of the American Oriental Society* 94, no. 4 (1974); Albert Hourani, "Ottoman Reform and the Politics of Notables," in *The Modern Middle East: A Reader*, ed. Albert Hourani, Philip S. Khoury, and Mary C. Wilson (Berkeley and Los Angeles: University of California Press, 1993); Ehud R. Toledano, "The Emergence of Ottoman-Local Elites (1700–1900): A Framework for Research," in *Middle Eastern Politics and Ideas: A History From Within*, ed. Moshe Maʾoz and Ilan Pappé (London: Taurus Academic Studies, 1997).

13. Rifaʿat Abou-el-Haj, "An Agenda for Research in History: The History of Libya between the Sixteenth and Nineteenth Centuries," *International Journal of Middle East Studies* 15, no. 3 (1983): 305–319.

14. For Egyptian examples, see Ehud R. Toledano, *State and Society in Mid-nineteenth-century Egypt* (Cambridge: Cambridge University Press, 1990).

15. The expression is from Mohamed-Hédi Chérif, *Pouvoir et société dans la Tunisie de H'usayn Bin 'Ali (1705–1740)*, 2 vols. (Tunis: Publications de l'Université de Tunis, 1984).

16. Ernst von Hesse-Wartegg, *Tunis: The Land and the People* (New York: Dodd and Mead, 1882), 36.

17. The latter figure is taken from the papers of Pierre Grandchamp; see the Centre des Archives Diplomatiques de Nantes, France (hereafter CADN) Protectorats, Tunisie, 133.

18. Hermann Pückler-Muskau, *Semilasso in Afrika* (Stuttgart: Hallberger, 1836), vol. 2, 148–149.

19. On the use of rare and prestigious commodities, art, and architecture in the creation of the Empress Marie Theresa's monarchical identity, see the work of Michael Yonan such as Michael E. Yonan, "Veneers of Authority: Chinese Lacquers in Maria Theresa's Vienna," *Eighteenth-Century Studies* 37, no. 4 (2004).

20. Hesse-Wartegg, *Tunis*, 36–38.

21. Grenville T. Temple, *Excursions in the Mediterranean: Algiers and Tunis* (London: Saunders and Otley, 1835), 185.

22. See his biography in Ahmad Ibn Abi Diyaf, *Ithaf ahl al-zaman bi akhbar muluk Tunis wa 'ahd al-aman*, Ahmed Abdesselem ed. (Tunis: Publications de l'Université de Tunis, 1971), vol. 8, 94–95, as well as the biographical notes in André Raymond, ed., *Ahmad Ibn Abi l-Diaf Ithaf ahl al-zaman bi-ahbar muluk Tunis wa 'Ahd al-aman Chapitres IV et V: règnes de Husaine Bey et Mustafa Bey*, 2 vols. (Tunis: IRMC-ISHMN, 1994).

23. Indrani Chatterjee, *Gender, Slavery, and Law in Colonial India* (Oxford: Oxford University Press, 1999).

24. Leslie P. Peirce, *The Imperial Harem: Women and Sovereignty in the Ottoman Empire* (Oxford: Oxford University Press, 1993).

25. This was as true for the classic 1974 study of the nineteenth century as for recent scholarship, L. Carl Brown, *The Tunisia of Ahmad Bey, 1837–1855* (Princeton, NJ: Princeton University Press, 1974); M'hamed Oualdi, *Esclaves et maîtres: les mamelouks des beys de Tunis du XVIIe siècle aux années 1880* (Paris: Publications de la Sorbonne, 2011). See the critique in Julia A. Clancy-Smith and Cynthia Gray-Ware Metcalf, "A Visit to a Tunisian Harem," *Journal of Maghrebi Studies* 1–2 (1993).

26. Evelyn Sakakida Rawski, *The Last Emperors: A Social History of Qing Imperial Institutions* (Berkeley: University of California Press, 1998); Hata Hisako, "Servants of the Inner Quarters: The Women of the Shogun's Great Interior," in *Servants of the Dynasty: Palace Women in World History*, ed. Anne Walthall (Berkeley: University of California Press, 2008).

27. Ruby Lal, *Domesticity and Power in the Early Mughal World* (Cambridge: Cambridge University Press, 2005), 22.

28. There are a number of thoughtful studies on the representation of Oriental women; see, for instance, Rana Kabbani, *Europe's Myths of Orient* (Bloomington: Indiana University Press, 1986); Reina Lewis, *Gendering Orientalism: Race, Femininity and Representation* (London: Routledge, 1996); Billie Melman, *Women's Orients, English Women and the Middle East, 1718–1918: Sexuality, Religion and Work* (Ann Arbor: University of Michigan Press, 1992).

29. Louis Frank and J. J. Marcel, *Histoire de Tunis précédée d'une description de cette régence par le Dr. Louis Frank* (Tunis: Editions Bouslama, [1816] 1979), 106.

30. Hesse-Wartegg, *Tunis*, 71.

31. On the particular contributions of women to imperial projects, see Julia A. Clancy-Smith and Frances Gouda, eds., *Domesticating the Empire: Race, Gender and Family Life in French and Dutch Colonialism* (Charlottesville: University Press of Virginia, 1998).

32. The notion that Muslim women are imprisoned continues to inform scholarly and biographical writings on the Middle East as demonstrated by Farzaneh Milani, "On Women's Captivity in the Islamic World," *Middle East Report* 246 (2008).

33. Similar points have been made by a number of feminist scholars: Lila Abu-Lughod, "Do Muslim Women Really Need Saving? Anthropological Reflections on Cultural Relativism and Its Other . . ." *American Anthropologist* 104, no. 3 (2002); Chandra Mohanty, "Under Western Eyes: Feminist Scholarship and Colonial Discourses," in *Dangerous Liaisons: Gender, National and Postcolonial Perspectives*, ed. Anne McClintock, Aamir Mufti, and Ella Shohat (Minneapolis: University of Minneapolis Press, 1997); Gayatri Chakravorty Spivak, "Can the Subaltern Speak?" in *Marxism and the Interpretation of Culture*, ed. Cary Nelson and Lawrence Grossberg (New York: Macmillan Education, 1988).

34. If later age at marriage and small family size characterized northwestern

Europe from approximately 1500, current studies of the family in the Middle East can conclude only that family size and composition showed great variety. This does not seem sufficient to justify European exceptionalism; Mary S. Hartman, *The Household and the Making of History: A Subversive View of the Western Past* (Cambridge: Cambridge University Press, 2004).

35. Nara Milanich, *Children of Fate: Childhood, Class, and the State in Chile, 1850–1930* (Durham, NC: Duke University Press, 2009), 4; Nara Milanich, "Review Essay: Whither Family History? A Road Map from Latin America," *American Historical Review* 112, no. 2 (2007).

36. Tamara K. Hareven, "The History of the Family and the Complexity of Social Change," *American Historical Review* 96, no. 1 (1991).

37. Beshara Doumani, "Introduction," in *Family History in the Middle East: Household, Property, and Gender*, ed. Beshara Doumani (Albany: State University of New York Press, 2003).

38. Alan Duben, "Turkish Families and Households in Historical Perspective," *Journal of Family History* 10, no. 1 (1985); Alan Duben and Cem Behar, *Istanbul Households: Marriage, Family and Fertility 1880–1940* (Cambridge: Cambridge University Press, 1991).

39. Leïla Blili Temime, *Histoire de familles: mariages, repudiations et vie quotidienne à Tunis, 1875–1930* (Tunis: Editions Script, 1999).

40. Leïla Blili Temime, "La pratique du habous: fait de structure ou effet de conjoncture? Étude de cas," in *Hasab wa nasab: parenté, alliance et patrimoine en Tunisie*, ed. Sophie Ferchiou (Paris: Editions du CNRS, 1992); Sophie Ferchiou, "Structures de parenté et d'alliance d'une société arabe: les 'aylat de Tunis," in *Hasab wa nasab: parenté, alliance et patrimoine en Tunisie*, ed. Sophie Ferchiou (Paris: Editions du CNRS, 1992); Lilia Ben Salem, "Introduction à l'analyse de la parenté et de l'alliance dans les sociétés arabo-musulmanes," in *Hasab wa nasab: parenté, alliance et patrimoine en Tunisie*, ed. Sophie Ferchiou (Paris: Editions du CNRS, 1992).

41. Leila Hudson, "Investing by Women or Investing in Women? Merchandise, Money, and Marriage and the Formation of a Prenational Bourgeoisie in Damascus," *Comparative Studies of South Asia, Africa and the Middle East* 26, no. 1 (2006); Leila Hudson, *Transforming Damascus: Space and Modernity in an Islamic City* (London: Tauris Academic Studies, 2008), 67–84; Akram Fouad Khater, *Inventing Home: Emigration, Gender and the Middle Class in Lebanon, 1870–1920* (Berkeley: University of California Press, 2001); Judith Tucker, *Women in Nineteenth-Century Egypt* (Cambridge: Cambridge University Press, 1985); Nelly Hanna, *Making Big Money in Cairo in 1600: The Life and Times of Isma'il Abu Taqiyya, Egyptian Merchant* (Syracuse, NY: Syracuse University Press, 1998).

42. Homa Hoodfar, *Between Marriage and the Market: Intimate Politics and Survival in Cairo* (Berkeley: University of California Press, 1997); Annelies Moors, *Women, Property and Islam: Palestinian Experiences 1920–1990* (Cambridge: Cambridge University Press, 1995).

43. Judith Tucker, *In the House of the Law: Gender and Islamic Law in Otto-*

man *Syria and Palestine* (Berkeley and Los Angeles: University of California Press, 1998).

44. Saba Mahmood, *Politics of Piety: The Islamic Revival and the Feminist Subject* (Princeton, NJ: Princeton University Press, 2005).

45. Blili Temime, "La pratique du habous"; Sophie Ferchiou, "Catégorie des sexes et circulation des biens habous," in *Hasab Wa Nasab: parenté, alliance et patrimoine en Tunisie*, ed. Sophie Ferchiou (Paris: Editions du CNRS, 1992); Abdelhamid Henia, "Circulation des biens et liens de parenté à Tunis (XVIIᵉ-début XXᵉ siècle)," in *Hasab wa nasab: parenté, alliance et patrimoine en Tunisie*, ed. Sophie Ferchiou (Paris: Editions du CNRS, 1992).

46. Hesse-Wartegg, *Tunis*, 89.

47. Anne Walthall, ed., *Servants of the Dynasty: Palace Women in World History*, Berkeley: University of California Press, 2008.

48. Lisa Pollard, *Nurturing the Nation: The Family Politics of Modernizing, Colonizing, and Liberating Egypt, 1805–1923* (Berkeley: University of California Press, 2005), 5; Ann Laura Stoler, *Race and the Education of Desire: Foucault's History of Sexuality and the Colonial Order of Things* (Durham, NC and London: Duke University Press, 1995); Anne McClintock, *Imperial Leather: Race, Gender and Sexuality in the Colonial Context* (New York: Routledge, 1995).

49. See, in particular, Afsaneh Najmabadi, "Crafting an Educated Housewife in Iran," in *Remaking Women: Feminism and Modernity in the Middle East*, ed. Lila Abu-Lughod (Princeton, NJ: Princteon University Press, 1998); Omnia Shakry, "Schooled Mothers and Structured Play: Child Rearing in Turn-of-the-Century Egypt," in *Remaking Women: Feminism and Modernity in the Middle East*, ed. Lila Abu-Lughod (Princeton, NJ: Princeton University Press, 1998); Beth Baron, *Egypt as a Woman: Nationalism, Gender, and Politics* (Berkeley: University of California Press, 2005).

50. Partha Chatterjee, *The Nation and Its Fragments: Colonial and Post-Colonial Histories* (Princeton, NJ: Princeton University Press, 1993); Mrinalini Sinha, *Specters of Mother India: The Global Restructuring of an Empire* (Durham, NC: Duke University Press, 2006).

51. See Sinha, *Specters of Mother India*.

52. Marilyn Booth, "*Woman in Islam*: Men and the 'Women's Press' in Turn-of-the-20th-Century Egypt," *International Journal of Middle East Studies* 33, no. 2 (2001). On the relation between masculinity and bourgeois conceptions of respectability as they relate to national identity in Europe, see George L. Mosse, *Nationalism and Sexuality: Respectability and Abnormal Sexuality in Modern Europe* (New York: Howard Fertig, 1985); George L. Mosse, *The Image of Man: the Creation of Modern Masculinity* (Oxford: Oxford University Press, 1996).

53. Ilham Khuri-Makdisi, *The Eastern Mediterranean and the Making of Global Radicalism, 1860–1914* (Berkeley: University of California Press, 2010); Mohamad Tavakoli-Targhi, *Refashioning Iran: Orientalism, Occidentalism and Historiography* (Hampshire: Palgrave, 2001).

54. A number of scholars have argued that modernity was a global (and not Western) process in which colonialism was central; of relevance here are Dipesh Chakrabarty, *Provincializing Europe: Postcolonial Thought and Historical Difference* (Princeton: Princeton University Press, 2000); Dipesh Chakrabarty, *Habitations of Modernity: Essays in the Wake of Subaltern Studies* (Chicago: University of Chicago Press, 2002); Frederick Cooper and Ann Laura Stoler, *Tensions of Empire: Colonial Culture in a Bourgeois World* (Berkeley: University of California Press, 1997); Timothy Mitchell, ed., *Questions of Modernity* (Minneapolis: University of Minnesota Press, 2000); Timothy Mitchell, *Rule of Experts: Egypt, Techno-Politics, Modernity* (Berkeley: University of California Press, 2002).

55. Mohammed-Hédi Chérif, "La "déturquisation" du pouvoir en Tunisie: classes dirigreantes et société tunisienne de la fin du XVIᵉ siècle à 1881," *Les Cahiers de Tunisie* 117–118, no. 3–4 (1981). He also refers to Ottoman suzerainty over Tunis as a mere "formality": Chérif, *Pouvoir et société*, vol. 2, p. 208.

56. A reedition of a 1940s text: Hasan Hussine ʿAbdelwahab, *Khalasa tarikh tunis*, ed. Hamadi al-Sahli (Tunis: Dar al-Jenoub lil-Nashar, 2001).

57. These perspectives are explicit in the framing of a number of otherwise important studies such as Boubaker, *La régence de Tunis au XVII siècle*; Bouzgarrou-Largueche, *Wtan al-Munastir*; Khelifa Chater, *Dépendance et mutations précoloniales: la Régence de Tunis de 1815 à 1857* (Tunis: Publications de l'Université de Tunis, 1984); Valensi, *Fellah tunisiens*; Mohammed el Aziz Ben Achour, "Al-moassisat al-siyasiya fi ahd al-dawla al-husseiniya (al-qarnin al-thamin ashr wa al-tasʿa ashr)," *al-Majalla al-tarikhiya al-arabiya lil-diraset al-ʿathmaniya* 5–6 (1992).

58. A number of scholars scrutinize the relation between academic disciplines, area studies, and governmental interests in the twentieth century and following World War II and as pertains to the Middle East in particular. See Philippe Lucas and Jean-Claude Vatin, *L'Algérie des anthropologues* (Paris: François Maspero, 1975); Edward W. Said, *Orientalism* (New York: Vintage Books, 1978); Bernard S. Cohn, *An Anthropologist among the Historians and Other Essays* (Oxford: Oxford University Press, 1987); Zachary Lockman, *Contending Visions of the Middle East: The History and Politics of Orientalism* (Cambridge: Cambridge University Press, 2004).

59. This was less the case among an older generation of scholars who continue to take a broader approach to defining the region, including Charles Issawi, *An Economic History of the Middle East and North Africa* (New York: Columbia University Press, 1982); Albert Hourani, *Arabic Thought in the Liberal Age, 1789–1939* (Cambridge: Cambridge University Press, 1983); Suraiya Faroqhi, *The Ottoman Empire and the World around It* (New York: I. B. Tauris, 2004); André Raymond, *Tunis sous les Mouradites: La ville et ses habitants au XVIIe siècle* (Tunis: Cérès Editions, 2006).

60. Jarrod Hayes, *Queer Nations: Marginal Sexualities in the Maghreb* (Chicago: University of Chicago Press, 2000); Reda Bensmaia, *Experimental Nations: Or, the Invention of the Maghreb* (Princeton, NJ: Princeton University Press, 2003).

61. When possible, quotes from this text are taken from Ahmad al-Twili's Arabic version based on Manuscript 18688 of the Tunisian National Library. This covers only about 130 pages of the text published in French by Lasram and Serres and referred to as *Chronique tunisienne*.

62. These correspond to Hijri Years 1169–1258, though not all have been preserved, and the documents are particularly sparse for the final twenty years of this period (see Appendix 2). I have utilized all the available volumes.

CHAPTER 1

1. For detailed discussions of the complex transformations at the imperial center, see Abou-el-Haj, "The Ottoman Vezir and Pasa Households," I. Metin Kunt, *The Sultan's Servants: The Transformation of Ottoman Provincial Government* (New York: Columbia University Press, 1983); Cornell H. Fleischer, *Bureaucrat and Intellectual in the Ottoman Empire: The Historian Mustafa Ali (1541–1600)* (Princeton: Princeton University Press, 1986); Cemal Kafadar, *Between Two Worlds: The Construction of the Ottoman State* (Berkeley: University of California Press, 1995).

2. See, for instance, Dina Rizk Khoury, *State and Provincial Society in the Ottoman Empire: Mosul 1540–1834* (Cambridge: Cambridge University Press, 1997); Sarah D. Shields, *Mosul before Iraq: Like Bees Making Five-Sided Cells* (Albany, NY: State University of New York Press, 2000); Beshara Doumani, *Rediscovering Palestine: Merchants and Peasants in Jabal Nablus, 1700–1900* (Berkeley: University of California Press, 1995); Ussama Makdisi, *The Culture of Sectarianism: Community, History and Violence in Nineteenth-Century Ottoman Lebanon* (Berkeley: University of California Press, 2000); Linda Schatkowski Schilcher, *Families in Politics: Damascene Factions and Estates of the 18th and 19th Centuries* (Wiesbaden: F. Steiner, 1985).

3. Nabil Matar, *Turks, Moors & Englishmen in the Age of Discovery* (New York: Columbia University Press, 1999); Nabil Matar, *Britain and Barbary, 1589–1689* (Gainesville: University Press of Florida, 2005). On the formative role of piracy in Ottoman-Venetian diplomacy and the development of Ottoman legal codes, see Joshua M. White, "Catch and Release: Piracy, Slavery, and Law in the Early Modern Mediterranean" (PhD dissertation, University of Michigan, 2012).

4. On the economic impact of corsairing in Tunis, see Taoufik Bachrouch, *Formation sociale barbaresque et pouvoir à Tunis au XVIIe siècle* (Tunis: Université de Tunis, 1977); Paul Sebag, *Tunis au XVIIe siècle: Une cité barbaresque au temps de la course* (Paris: L'Harmattan, 1989).

5. Andrew C. Hess, *The Forgotten Frontier: A History of the Sixteenth-Century Ibero-African Frontier* (Chicago: University of Chicago Press, 1978), 60.

6. Alphonse Rousseau, *Relation de la prise de Tunis et de la Goulette par les troupes Ottomanes en 981 de l'Hegire*, trans. Alphonse Rousseau (Alger: Imprimerie de Gouvernement, 1845).

7. Khelifa Chater, "Le fait Ottoman en Tunisie: mythe et réalité," *Revue d'Histoire Maghébine* 31–32 (1983); Bachrouch, *Formation sociale barbaresque*, 110.

8. Rhoads Murphey, *Ottoman Warfare, 1500–1700* (London: UCL Press, 1999).

9. Asma Moalla, *The Regency of Tunis and the Ottoman Porte, 1777–1814* (London: Routledge Curzon, 2004), 11–13.

10. Ibn abi-Dinar, 207 and 209, cited in Moalla, *The Regency of Tunis*, 17. The central state experienced difficulties when requesting respect for treaties signed with England, France, and Venice, eventually leading to the English and French desire to open consulates in the North African ports. See White, "Catch and Release."

11. Moalla, *The Regency of Tunis*, 89.

12. Tal Shuval, "The Ottoman Algerian Elite and Its Ideology," *International Journal of Middle East Studies* 32 (2000).

13. Bachrouch, *Formation sociale barbaresque*, 33 and 45–46.

14. Oualdi, *Esclaves et maîtres*, 65–66.

15. For more on these political shifts, see Jamil M. Abun-Nasr, "The Beylicate in Seventeenth-Century Tunisia," *International Journal of Middle East Studies* 6 (1975); Robert Mantran, "L'évolution des relations entre la Tunisie et l'Empire Ottoman du XVIᵉ au XIXᵉ siècle," *Les Cahiers de Tunisie* 26–27, nos. 2–3 (1959).

16. Moalla, *The Regency of Tunis*, 29.

17. See also Hichem Djait, "Influences Ottomanes sur les institutions, la civilisation et la culture tunisiennes du XVIᵉ au XIXᵉ siècles," *Revue d'Histoire Maghébine* 6 (1976).

18. Moalla, *The Regency of Tunis*, 21.

19. Sevket Pamuk, *A Monetary History of the Ottoman Empire* (Cambridge: Cambridge University Press, 2000), 178–182. These were minted continually until the 1880s, when the French removed them. More aesthetic descriptions especially for the nineteenth century can be found in J. Farrugia de Candia, "Monnaies husseinites," *Revue Tunisienne* 11–12, no. 3–4 (1932); H. Hugon, *Les emblèmes des beys de Tunis* (Chalon-sur-Seine: Imprimerie E. Bertrand, 1913).

20. Gifts to Ottoman officials are mentioned for instance in TNA Registers 99, 184, 192, and 247. See also Muhammad Saghir ibn Yusuf, *Al-mashrʿaʾ al-mulki fi sultanat awlad ʿAli Turki*, Ahmed al-Twili, ed. (Tunis: 1998), 119.

21. Isabelle Grangaud, *La ville imprenable: une histoire sociale de Constantine au 18e siècle* (Paris: Éditions de l'École des Hautes Études en Sciences Sociales, 2002).

22. There were two ceremonies once the *firman*s arrived; see TNA Register 209.

23. Though this was not uniformly adhered to, and does not appear to have been enforced, the obligation was understood. TNA History Series, Carton 220, Dossier 349, Document 62, probably by Ahmad ibn al-Dhiaf.

24. See TNA Register 442/2. References to the upkeep of officials arriving from Istanbul, the ceremonial reading of imperial *firman*s, and gifts for Istanbul

are mentioned in TNA Registers 180, 184, 223, 239, 247, 266, 270, 273, 289, 308, 312, 330, 344, 358, 371, 384, 388, 402, 406, 430/4, 440/2, 442/2, and 451/2. Additional records of gifts sent to Istanbul or presented to imperial officials passing through Tunis are recorded in TNA History Series 220/349, especially Documents 54–58, 141–165.

25. See the royal *firman*s to this effect in TNA History Series, 220/340, such as Documents 7, 17, 31, 46, and 53, and the summaries in Robert Mantran, *Inventaire des document d'archives turcs du Dar-al-Bey (Tunis)* (Tunis: Presse Universitaire, 1961). On provisions see TNA register 275 and registers 209, 247, 295, and 384.

26. In the twenty-nine account books available for the period of Algerian supremacy (1168–1220 a.h.), at least nineteen boats were sent from Tunis to Algiers, on average more than every two years.

27. See the references in Béranger, *La régence de Tunis*, 116 and 144.

28. Kafadar, *Between Two Worlds*.

29. Peirce, *The Imperial Harem*, 39–42.

30. Rawski, *The Last Emperors*.

31. Lal, *Domesticity and Power*.

32. Abun-Nasr, "The Beylicate," 78.

33. Moalla, *The Regency of Tunis*, 26.

34. Raymond, *Tunis sous les Mouradites*, 34.

35. Muhammad Saghir Ibn Yusuf, *Mechra el Melki, chronique tunisienne (1705–1771)*, trans. Mohammed Lasram and Victor Serres (Tunis: Editions Bouslama, 1978 [1900]), 221.

36. This is the way that ibn Dhiaf phrases al-Sharif's actions: Ibn Abi Diyaf, *Ithaf ahl al-zaman*, vol. 2, 94.

37. Imperial *firman*s were delivered in 1702, with large gifts to the *kabiji*, and again that winter, Béranger, *La régence de Tunis*, 116 and 132.

38. Béranger transcribes her name as "Limbarque": ibid., 126–127, 138.

39. Moalla, *The Regency of Tunis*, 39.

40. See Genealogy 1 in Appendix 1.

41. See the endowment records of her sister Mna Ghazalia: TNA History Series 1/5/37.

42. Béranger, *La Régence de Tunis*.

43. M'hamed Belkhuja, "Cobbat Mamia," *Revue tunisienne* 26, no. 131 (1919).

44. Following Fatma bint Mami's death, ibn 'Ali offered Burteghiz a slave concubine to help assuage his grief and maintain these familial ties; see Ibn Yusuf, *Chronique tunisienne*, 124, 129, 225, and 335.

45. Ibn Yusuf states that Ahmad ibn Metisha, a commander of the *zawawa* troops, had married one of the daughters of ibn 'Ali before joining with 'Ali Pasha in 1728, though it is not clear which daughter; *Al-mashr'a al-mulki*, 92.

46. See the biographical references in Ibn Abi Diyaf, *Ithaf ahl al-zaman*, vol. 7, 29; Ibn Yusuf, *Chronique tunisienne*, 147.

47. See the lists of Fatma's property and endowments that make explicit her re-

lation to Ahmad Shelebi and Rejeb Khaznadar, TNA History Series 1/6/35. Additional references to her relation to the Shelebi family are in TNA History Series 1/6/13 and 1/6/41–47; ibn Yusuf, *Al-mashr'a al-mulki*, 142: and Ibn Abi Diyaf, *Ithaf ahl al-zaman*, vol. 7, 164.

48. This is where Muhammad ibn Husayn is buried: Ibn Abi Diyaf, *Ithaf ahl al-zaman*, vol. 7, 29.

49. Ibn Yusuf, *Al-mashr'a al-mulki*, 43. A reference to Fatma bint Husayn's mother as "Jannat al al-'aljia" is in TNA History Series 1/6/43.

50. Ibn Yusuf, *Al-mashr'a al-mulki*, 51.

51. See TNA Register 2250, entitled "The possessions of Husayn Bey's daughters," and TNA History Series 1/6/41 and 42, which lists the possessions of Fatma bint Husayn (here called the aunt of Hammuda and Mahmud). It is possible that this referred to her sister, Jannat.

52. Ibn Yusuf, *Chronique tunisienne*, 128.

53. Ibn Yusuf, *Al-mashr'a al-mulki*, 97.

54. Jane Hathaway, *The Politics of Households in Ottoman Egypt: The Rise of the Qazdaglis* (Cambridge: Cambridge University Press, 1997), 109–124.

55. Ibid., 116–119.

56. Mary Ann Fay, "Women and Households: Gender, Power and Culture in Eighteenth-Century Egypt" (PhD dissertation, Georgetown University, 1993).

57. Margaret L. Meriwether, *The Kin Who Count: Family and Society in Ottoman Aleppo, 1770–1840* (Austin: University of Texas Press, 1999), 119–120.

58. He frequented religious notables, participated in scholarly circles, copied manuscripts, and may have desired a position within the scholarly bureaucracy: ibn Yusuf, *Al-mashr'a al-mulki*, 17. The manuscript was copied numerous times in the nineteenth century and later referenced by the historian ibn Dhiaf: Ibn Abi Diyaf, *Ithaf ahl al-zaman*. See also B. Roy, *Extrait du catalogue des manuscrits et des imprimés de la Bibliothèque de la Grande Mosquée de Tunis*, Histoire avec la collaboration de Mhammed bel Khodja et de Mohammed el Hachaichi, ed. (Tunis: Imprimerei Générale [J. Picard et Cie], 1900), 40.

59. Ibn Yusuf, *Al-mashr'a al-mulki*.

60. Ibid., 68.

61. Ibid., 107.

62. Ibid., 161–162.

63. Chérif, *Pouvoir et société*.

64. Ibn Yusuf, *Chronique tunisienne*, 60–62 and 150–151.

65. Though ibn Yusuf, who discusses the presence of the Ghazalis at Muhammad al-Rashid's deathbed and the chagrin of his wife, infers the in-law relationship, and she is mentioned in archival documents as Ghazalia or the daughter of Ghazali. See TNA History Series 1/5/31, TNA Registers 175–360; ibn Yusuf, *Chronique tunisienne*, 181, 142.

66. Ibn Yusuf refers to him as "Bu 'Aziz the traitor," *Chronique tunisienne*, 171; ibn Yusuf, *Al-mashr'a al-mulki*, 148, 171.

67. She is not mentioned in secondary sources, though she is frequently listed among family members, for example, in an inheritance list in TNA History Series 1/5/31; for her ownership of properties in TNA Register 2250; and for household expenses from 1771 to 1784 in TNA Registers 175–239.

68. Ibn Yusuf, *Chronique tunisienne*, 162.

69. Food and clothing stipends to the house of ʿAli Pasha, his wives, and his children are noted in each of the palace expense registers dating from 1772 (the first register that details such expenses) through 1829; see TNA Registers 180–440/2.

CHAPTER 2

1. Robert Brunschvig, Abd-al-Basit ibn Halil, and Anselme Adorne, *Deux récits de voyage inédits en Afrique du nord au XVe siècle* (Paris: Larose, 1936), 21, 75.

2. Manuela Marin, "Cuisine d'Orient, cuisine d'Occident," *Médiévales* 16, no. 33 (1997); Manuela Marin, "Beyond Taste: The Complements of Colour and Smell in the Medieval Arab Culinary Tradition," in *A Taste of Thyme: Culinary Cultures of the Middle East*, ed. Sami Zubaida and Richard Tapper (London: Tauris Parke Paperbacks, 2000); Lilia Zaouali, *Medieval Cuisine of the Islamic World: A Concise History with 174 Recipes* (Berkeley: University of California Press, 2007), 106–107.

3. See *Kitab al-wusla ila al-habib fi wasf al-tayyibat wa al-tib* [Book of the Bonds of Friendship or a Description of Good Dishes and Perfumes] and Baghdadi's *Kitab wasf al-atʿima al-muʿtada* [The description of familiar foods]; Arthur John Arberry, Charles Perry, and Maxime Rodinson, *Medieval Arab Cookery = al-Tabikh al-ʿarabi fi 'l-ʿusur al-wusta* (Devon, England: Prospect Books, 2006), 143, 53, 344–346, 406, and 409.

4. Temple, *Excursions*, vol. 1, 127.

5. Rudi Matthee, *The Pursuit of Pleasure: Drugs and Stimulants in Iranian History, 1500–1900* (Princeton, NJ: Princeton University Press, 2005), 161; Susan Babie, *Isfahan and Its Palaces*.

6. Tulay Artan, "Ahmed I's Hunting Parties: Feasting in Adversity, Enhancing the Ordinary," in *Starting with Food: Culinary Approaches to Ottoman History*, ed. Amy Singer (Princeton, NJ: Markus Weiner Publishers, 2011); Dariusz Kolodziejczyk, "Polish Embassies in Istanbul or how to sponge on your host without losing your self-esteem," in *The Illuminated Table, the Prosperous House: Food and Shelter in Ottoman Material Culture*, ed. Suraiya Faroqhi and Christoph K. Neumann (Würzburg: Ergon in Kommission, 2003).

7. Rawski, *Last Emperors*, 132, 160; Jeroen Frans Jozef Duindam, *Vienna and Versailles: The Courts of Europe's Dynastic Rivals, 1550–1780* (Cambridge: Cambridge University Press, 2003); Mohammed Ennaji, *Soldats, domestiques et concubines: l'esclavage au Maroc au XIXe siècle* (Tunis: Cérès Productions, 1994); Arjun Appadurai, "Introduction: Commodities and the Politics of Value," in *The So-*

cial Life of Things: Commodities in Cultural Perspective, ed. Arjun Appadurai (Cambridge: Cambridge University Press, 1986).

8. Sidney W. Mintz, *Sweetness and Power: The Place of Sugar in Modern History* (New York: Penguin Books, 1985).

9. Emily Allen, "Culinary Exhibition: Victorian Wedding Cakes and Royal Spectacle," *Victorian Studies* 45, no. 3 (2003).

10. Suraiya Faroqhi, "Research on the History of Ottoman Consumption: A Preliminary Exploration of Sources and Models," in *Consumption Studies and the History of the Ottoman Empire, 1550–1922: An Introduction*, ed. Donald Quataert (Albany: State University of New York Press, 2000).

11. Michael Kwass, "Ordering the World of Goods: Consumer Revolution and the Classification of Objects in Eighteenth-Century France," *Representations* 82, no. 1 (2003). Consumer practices and the politics of taste also contributed to nineteenth-century representations of political power; Leora Auslander, *Taste and Power: Furnishing Modern France* (Berkeley: University of California Press, 1996).

12. Ariel Salzmann, "The Age of Tulips: Confluence and Conflict in Early Modern Consumer Culture (1550-1730)," in *Consumption Studies and the History of the Ottoman Empire, 1550–1922: An Introduction*, ed. Donald Quataert (Albany: State University of New York Press, 2000), 84. On the cultural and economic importance of consumption more broadly, see Suraiya Faroqhi and Christoph K. Neumann, eds., *Ottoman Costumes: From Textile to Identity* (Istanbul: Eren, 2004); Donald Quataert, ed., *Consumption Studies and the History of the Ottoman Empire, 1550–1922: An Introduction* (Albany: State University of New York Press, 2000); Dana Sajdi, *Ottoman Tulips, Ottoman Coffee: Leisure and Lifestyle in the Eighteenth Century* (London: Tauris Academic Series, 2007).

13. Ahmed Saadaoui, *Tunis, ville ottomane: trois siècles d'urbanisme et d'architecture* (Tunis: Publications de l'Université de Tunis, 2001).

14. The value of the Tunisian piaster was consistent throughout this period. The periodization is partially determined by the parameters of the archive, as there are few extant registers prior to 1770, and the format was altered due to experimentation with new accounting practices from the mid-nineteenth century; see Munsif Fakhfakh, *Mujaz al-dafatir al-idariya wa al-jabaʿiya bi-al-arshif al-watani al-Tunisi (Sommaire des registres administratifs et fiscaux aux archives nationales tunisiennes).* (Tunis: Publications of the Tunisian National Archives, 1990).

15. Duindam, *Vienna and Versailles*, 48–60.

16. Mona L. Russell, *Creating the New Egyptian Woman: Consumerism, Education, and National Identity, 1863–1922* (New York: Palgrave Macmillan, 2004); Toledano, *State and Society*.

17. Ibn Yusuf, *Chronique tunisienne*, 400.

18. TNA Register 312. See also the genealogies of Muhammad al-Rashid and ʿAli Bey in Appendix 1.

19. These units were regularly listed in accounting registers; see TNA Reg-

ister 260, which lists a combined total of ten houses; Register 436/2 lists sixteen units of *hawanib* and four *subahiya*. Moalla, *The Regency of Tunis*, 82–84.

20. Multiple bath attendants are mentioned from TNA Register 83 with one *ra'is hammam* added to the payrolls following a marriage; for instance, there were twenty-two bath attendants in 1821 and twenty-five in 1833. See TNA Registers 425/2 and 444/2.

21. The reference to the slave market in the capital is from TNA Register 395. Other notes for slaves bought from Ibrahim al-Sudani or another slave bought from Mustafa al-Tlemsani indicate that this was part of slave networks spanning Northern Africa and the Sahara; see TNA Registers 355 and 111 respectively. These estimates are based on partial documentation covering the period from 1781 to 1835. On *khedam* purchased in Tunis, see, for instance, TNA Registers 221, 286, 331, 385, 395, 403, 411, 427, 436–438, 443, 444, 449, and 450.

22. See the descriptions in Abdelhamid Larguèche, *Les ombres de la ville: pauvres, marginaux, et minoritaires à Tunis (XVIIIe et XIXe siècles)* (Tunis: Centre de Publications Universitaire Facultés des Lettres de Manouba, 1999), 400–402; Elisabeth Cornelia van der Haven, "The Bey, the Mufti and the Scattered Pearls: Shari'a and Political Leadership in Tunisia's Age of Reform, 1800–1864" (PhD dissertation, Leiden University, 2006).

23. Pückler-Muskau, *Semilasso in Afrika*, vol. 2, 194 and 254.

24. In some cases, the term was used for workers and employees who received forms of monetary compensation, though in others, mention of *'ataq* (or manumission), often following the deaths of members of the ruling family, makes their slave status clear; see, for example, TNA Registers 427, 436, 444, and 450.

25. Though derogatorily referred to by Europeans as "renegades," they were referred to as mamluks within the palace. See, for instance, references to a French mamluk who converted in 1788, two Spanish mamluks in 1793, or Mustafa the Maltese mamluk in 1830 in TNA Registers 247, 270, and 440/2. See also Oualdi, *Esclaves et maîtres*, 26–30.

26. In 1841 there were 100 *mamluks al-sqifa* recorded in TNA Register 470/2, while earlier records such as TNA Registers 201, 216, 220, 224, and 239 mention respectively 37, 34, 31, 32, and 33 *mamluks al-bit*, whereas Registers 184 and 187 indicate 54 and 35 *mamluks al-saghir*. The most detailed and comprehensive effort to tally the total number of mamluks is in Oualdi, *Esclaves et maîtres*, 91–98.

27. These terms appear in a range of sources from the account registers, to chronicles, to the correspondence of European diplomats; see the discussions in Oualdi, *Esclaves et maîtres*, 126–161; Nadia Sebaï, *Mustapha Saheb Ettabaa: un haut dignitaire beylical dans la Tunisie du XIXe siècle* (Carthage, Tunisia: Carthaginoiseries, 2007), 52, 71.

28. They were prominent in provincial government under the Hafsids and similarly served the French colonial authorities. Their economic and political standing is discussed in Pierre Grandchamp, "Documents concernant la course

dans la régence de Tunis de 1764 à 1769 et 1783 à 1843," *Les cahiers de Tunisie* 19–20, nos. 3–4 (1957); Ibn Abi Diyaf, *Ithaf ahl al-zaman*, vol. 7, 160 and vol. 8, 84, 240, 342; Medhi Jerad, "La famille Djellouli de la deuxième moitié du XVIIIe siècle à 1830," *al-Majalla al-tarikiyya al-Maghribiyya (li-al-ʿahd al-hadith wa-al-muʿasir) Revue d'histoire maghrébine*, no. 117 (2005).

29. Jerad, "La famille Djellouli," 74.

30. Sebaï, *Mustapha Saheb Ettabaa*, 55, and Ibn Abi Diyaf, *Ithaf ahl al-zaman*, vol. 8, 121.

31. For instance, there were three wet nurses in 1784: TNA Register 239.

32. Estimates per household are based on clothing purchases; see, for example, TNA Register 273 or Register 312. On the older reference, see Matar, *Turks, Moors & Englishmen*, 59. By the early twentieth century, Mzali and Pignon claim that the title *ʿaljia* was given to white slaves who had been freed and married to their masters, though this definition does not seem universally applicable, Mohammed Salah Mzali and Jean Pignon, eds., *Khérédine homme d'état: memoires* (Tunis: Maison Tunisienne de l'Édition, 1971). Others have translated this rather vaguely as "odalisque."

33. On the purchase of white slaves from Istanbul, see TNA Register 286 and TNA History Series 1, Dossier 10, Documents 4 and 5 (from the 1830s).

34. Ibn Yusuf, *Chronique tunisienne*, 161.

35. Ibn Yusuf, *Al-mashr'a al-mulki*, 211–212.

36. Expenses for the trousseau of Muhammad al-Rashid's *jaria* are noted in TNA Register 2144 and reference to Khadija can be found in TNA Register 175.

37. Ibn Abi Diyaf, *Ithaf ahl al-zaman*, vol. 3, 202.

38. Jawhara al-Habashia and Fatma the *ʿaljia*: Blili Temime, *Histoire de familles*, 57.

39. For instance, the lists of clothing often mention the *qazqat* directly after the *mamluks al-saray*, suggesting that they formed a similar group, while these lists do not use the term *mamluks al-sqifa*; see, for example, TNA Register 425.

40. On Ramadan, see TNA Registers 184, 327, and 360. Extra foods for the *qazqat* for their holiday cover a period from 1778 to 1811; see, for example, TNA Registers 214, 224, 260, 266, 273, 289, 308, 327, 330, 335, 341, 358, and 360. There is also one reference to them as Christians (*nasara*) in Register 184.

41. Nicolo *bash qazaq* received a salary from at least 1813 (Register 376) to 1832 (Register 444/2), and his wife Maria was provided stipends (*nafaqa*), TNA Registers 436/2 and 448/2.

42. There are scattered references to their numbers, TNA Register 192 (49 *qazqat*), Register 220 (35 *qazqat*), Register 273 (50 *qazqat*), and Register 289 (55 *qazqat*). Though European governments and private organizations raised money to purchase the freedom of some captives, many were salaried manual laborers receiving payment for work at the new house, Marnaqiya, Hafsia, fortresses, and the gunpowder manufacture; see, for instance, TNA Register 247 and Register 344.

43. Their exact number varied; only four are mentioned in 1757 (Register 94), while there were ten Sicilians in TNA Register 247, and Frank mentions six young Italians who were pages or valets in the bey's apartments; Frank and Marcel, *Histoire de Tunis*, 68.

44. H. A. R. Gibb and Harold Bowen, *Islamic Society and the West: A Study of the Impact of Western Civilization on Moslem Culture in the Near East*, 2 vols. (London: Oxford University Press, 1950), vol. 1, 334 and 342. By the late nineteenth century, one such individual was referred to as the *maître de la garde robe*; see the memoirs of Aïché Osmanoglu, *Avec mon père le Sultan Abdulhamid de son palais à sa prison*, trans. Jacques Jeulin (Paris: L'Harmattan, 1991).

45. TNA Register 83 mentioned two Christian doctors, one of whom was listed until 1784 having served three successive beys; see TNA Registers 239 and 442/2. See also Lucien Moatti, *La mosaïque médicale de Tunisie: 1800–1950* (Paris: Editions Glyphe, 2008).

46. Christian instructors were mentioned in TNA Registers 388 and 425/2.

47. A salary for Gian Battista the *manqalji* was mentioned in 1776 in TNA Register 201 (the position was later held by a Francisco the *manqalji*; see Register 260), which confirms the account in Jean-Claude Winkler, *Le Comte Raffo* (Berlin: 1967). The term presumably derives from *mongela*, the Tunisian word for "watch" or "clock."

48. Clancy-Smith, *Mediterraneans*, 48–53.

49. Midwives are mentioned frequently in TNA Register 2144. Other women in the palace are noted sporadically; for example, see Register 111.

50. The humble origins of some men were indicated by the simplicity of their names, Mustafa the cook, or Muhammad al-Wafi the painter. Small-scale construction on various foundations built by the governors involved thirty to forty workers per day: Saadaoui, *Tunis, ville ottomane*. Even the religious profession constituted a relatively accessible form of social mobility, according to Leon Carl Brown, "The Religious Establishment in Husainid Tunisia," in *Scholars, Saints, and Sufis: Muslim Religious Institutions since 1500* (Berkeley: University of California Press, 1972).

51. A few of the references to these individuals are in TNA Registers 2144 (Barukh the coppersmith), the jewelers Shalum and Yaqub in Registers 28 and 436, and a merchant named Yusuf Mushki is frequently mentioned in Register 425/2, or 344. The *taba'ji* who worked at the mint is listed as *al-dhimmi* and was successively held by men named Huda, Mordechai, and Yusuf; see TNA Registers 180 to 470/2. Jewish workers at the treasury are included in TNA Register 444/2. There are a number of archival registers written in Hebrew characters, listed in Fakhfakh, *Mojz al-dfatr*. Ibn Yusuf mentions that 'Ali Pasha had nine Jewish men who worked in the treasury: Ibn Yusuf, *Chronique tunisienne*, 238.

52. Recent scholarship elaborates on the imperial engagement with sartorial legislation in relation to social status, communal identity, and economic protec-

tionism. See Donald Quataert, "Clothing Laws, State, and Society in the Ottoman Empire, 1720–1829," *International Journal of Middle East Studies* 29, no. 3 (1997); Faroqhi and Neumann, eds., *Ottoman Costumes*.

53. An example of the former in 1794 is a note for a uniform for a new mamluk for 19 piasters (TNA Register 279); in Moharrem 1230 (January 1815) is the entry for "uniforms for ten new mamluk for 323 piasters" (TNA Register 388). Such entries are frequent throughout the registers. References to headgear and shoes are scattered throughout the registers, such as the note in Shaban 1230 for *burnous*es for mamluks, totaling 494 piasters: TNA Register 388.

54. For example, a note records shoes for the *qazqat* for six months for 108 piasters: TNA Register 279.

55. TNA Register 201. On Istanbul, see the memoirs of Emine Foat Tugay, *Three Centuries: Family Chronicles of Turkey and Egypt* (London: Oxford University Press, 1963).

56. The totals for the entire palace per month were 76 *qafiz*s of wheat; 81½ *metar*s of olive oil; 83 *qila*s of clarified butter (*samn*); 950 *ratl*s of rice; 382 *ratl*s of sugar; and 232 *ratl*s each of olives, honey, and cheese. See TNA Register 111.

57. Tulay Artan, "Aspects of the Ottoman Elite's Food Consumption: Looking for 'Staples,' 'Luxuries,' and 'Delicacies,' in a Changing Century," in *Consumption Studies and the History of the Ottoman Empire, 1550–1992: An Introduction*, ed. Donald Quataert (Albany: State University of New York Press, 2000).

58. For example, TNA Register 260.

59. On holidays, they served one *ratl* of meat for every three people: Saadaoui, *Tunis, ville ottomane*, 210–212, 214.

60. Each household contained an average of 150 dependents in the eighteenth century, and there were approximately 15,000 people fed at the main palace kitchens by the late sixteenth century: Artan, "Aspects of the Ottoman Elite's Food Consumption," 135–139.

61. Calculating smaller rations of 200 grams per person would result in households of 25, 50, 75, and 250 persons: TNA Register 111.

62. Artan, "Aspects of the Ottoman Elite's Food Consumption," 135–139 and 141.

63. TNA Register 261 for 1790 lists one *haml* of vegetables for three and one half piasters; the estimates are for the *haml*s noted in Register 260.

64. TNA Register 2144. Mordecai M. Noah, *Travels in England, France, Spain, and the Barbary States, in the Years 1813–14 and 15* (New York: Kirk and Mercein, 1819), 290, and Thomas Shaw, *Observations Relating to Several Parts of Barbary and the Levant* (Frankfurt: Publications of the Institute for the History of Arabic-Islamic Sciences, [1738], 1995), 223. Filippi similarly praised the variety of fruits and vegetables and the high quality of grapes and olives: Charles Monchicourt, *Documents historiques sur la Tunisie, relations inédites de Nyssen, Filippi et Calligaris (1788, 1829, 1834)* (Paris: Société d'Éditions Géographiques, Maritimes et Coloniales, 1929), 110.

65. Noah, *Travels*, 290.

66. Shaw mentioned *tamatas* in 1738: *Observations*, 289. While they cropped up in a few private gardens in late eighteenth-century Istanbul, they did not appear in imperial registers until the 1830s. Similarly, potatoes were not widely consumed by the sultans; see Özge Samanci, "Culinary Consumption Patterns of the Ottoman Elite during the First Half of the Nineteenth Century," in *The Illuminated Table, the Prosperous House: Food and Shelter in Ottoman Material Culture*, ed. Suraiya Faroqhi and Christoph K. Neumann (Würzburg: Ergon in Kommission, 2003), 174–176.

67. As indicated by Zaouali, who proposes the arrival of tomatoes in the sixteenth century: Zaouali, *Medieval Cuisine of the Islamic World*, 43.

68. This was regularly present during Ramadan across the Muslim world and is mentioned in medieval recipe collections; see Zaouali, *Medieval Cuisine of the Islamic World*, 36; al-Muzaffar ibn Nasr Ibn Sayyar al-Warraq et al., *Annals of the Caliphs' Kitchens: Ibn Sayyar al-Warraq's Tenth-Century Baghdadi Cookbook* (Leiden: Brill, 2007), 413–417.

69. In earlier examples, the bey's mother received four and eight *ratl*s of each; see, for example, TNA Register 233. From 1778 to 1826, there was only a period of about ten years (all within the reign of Hammuda Pasha) when these lists are not mentioned; they then resumed before his death.

70. Zaouali, *Medieval Cuisine of the Islamic World*, 79.

71. See the note in Moharrem 1241, totaling 415 piasters: TNA Register 436/4.

72. Based on TNA Register 111.

73. See the lists for the winter of 1198 (December 1783 and January 1784) in TNA Register 111.

74. Muhammad Bey himself was fond of hunting deer, and he modified the route according to where game might be found; see N. Davis, *Evenings in My Tent; or, Wanderings in Balad Ejjareed. Illustrating the Moral, Religious, Social, and Political Conditions of Various Arab Tribes of the African Sahara*, 2 vols. (London: A. Hall, Virtue, & Co., 1854), vol. 1, 44, 88–89, 120–121.

75. See especially TNA Register 111.

76. TNA Register 111. Rose water, jasmine, and amber were often used to perfume sweets; Temple, *Excursions*, 200.

77. André Raymond, *Artisans et commerçants au Caire au XVIIIe siècle*, 2 vols. (Damas: Institut français de Damas, 1973), vol 2, 470–476.

78. Lucette Valensi, "Consommation et usages alimentaires en Tunisie aux XVIIIᵉ et XIXᵉ siècles," *Annales. Histoire, Sciences Sociales* 30, no. 2 (1975).

79. This marble nook was part of Husayn Bey's early nineteenth-century remodeling; Jacques Revault, *Palais et résidences d'été de la région de Tunis, XVIe–XIXe siècles* (Paris: Editions du Centre national de la recherche scientifique, 1974), 330.

80. Mocca from Yemen was brought via merchants in Alexandria and the caravan from Mecca; see Thomas MacGill, *An Account of Tunis, of Its Government, Manners, Customs, and Antiquities, Especially of Its Productions, Manufacturers and*

Commerce (Glasgow: J. Hedderwick & Co., 1811), 176; Raymond, *Artisans et commerçants au Caire au XVIIIe siècle*, vol. 2, 156; Andre Raymond, "Les problemes du café en Egypte au XVIIIᵉ siecle," in *Le café en Mediterranée: histoire, anthropologie, economie, XVIIIe–XXe siècle*, ed. J.-L. et al. Miège (Aix-en-Provence: Université de Provence, CNRS, 1981); Jean-André Peyssonel, *Voyage dans les régences de Tunis et d'Alger* (Paris: La Découverte, 1987), 78–79.

81. The *qahwaji* was included in a salary list as receiving monthly supplies of coffeepots. Other examples include a note in Moharrem 1205 (October 1790) for the purchase of teacups and saucers: TNA Register 60. Similar terms were used to refer to personnel responsible for coffee in Istanbul (the *kahveci başi*) and in Safavid Persia (*qahvahchi-bashi*): Gibb and Bowen, *Islamic Society and the West*, vol. 1, 344; Matthee, *Pursuit of Pleasure*, 144–174. On the social significance of coffee, see Ralph S. Hattox, *Coffee and Coffeehouses: The Origins of a Social Beverage in the Medieval Near East* (Seattle: University of Washington Press, 1985); Alan Mikhail, "The Heart's Desire: Gender, Urban Space and the Ottoman Coffee House," in *Ottoman Tulips, Ottoman Coffee: Leisure and Lifestyle in the Eighteenth Century*, ed. Dana Sajdi (New York: Tauris Academic Press, 2007).

82. Ibn Yusuf, *Chronique tunisienne*, 161; Pückler-Muskau, *Semilasso in Afrika*, vol. 2, 151 and 157; Temple, *Excursions*; Davis, *Evenings in My Tent*, vol. 1, 166.

83. TNA Register 111.

84. See TNA Registers 2249/2, 2306, and 2276.

85. These are too frequent to enumerate. Examples include TNA Registers 216, 260, and 308.

86. An account of Ismail Bey lists tomatoes and Turkish cheese; see TNA Register 2254.

87. TNA Registers 436/2 and 444/2.

88. Ibn Sayyar al-Warraq et al., *Annals of the caliphs' kitchens*, 30–33.

89. Hedda Reindl-Kiel, "The Chickens of Paradise: Official Meals in the Mid-seventeenth Century Ottoman Palace," in *The Illuminated Table, the Prosperous House: Food and Shelter in Ottoman Material Culture*, ed. Suraiya Faroqhi and Christoph K. Neumann (Würzburg: Ergon in Kommission, 2003), 63–64, 81. The Abbasids were certainly indebted to Persian culinary traditions: Arberry, Perry, and Rodinson, *Medieval Arab Cookery*, 97, 230; Zaouali, *Medieval Cuisine of the Islamic World*, xv, 37.

90. Zaouali, *Medieval Cuisine of the Islamic World*, xvi, xix.

91. Valensi, *Fellah tunisiens*, 245–246.

92. Honey and cheese were common enough to warrant separate accounting, though the two were routinely coupled together with the monthly totals inserted into the main expense registers; see, for example, TNA Register 300.

93. An entire *haml* of dates for the grade called *timr* cost six piasters in 1790; see TNA Register 261. For honey prices in Hijri year 1207 (1792–1793), see TNA Register 270. Similarly in 1202 (1787–1788), it was between forty and fifty-four piasters per *qintar*: Register 247.

94. *Samn* was measured in *qila* and oil per *metar*; for sample prices, see TNA Register 261.

95. Sami Zubaida, "National, Communal and Global Dimensions in Middle Eastern Food Cultures," in *A Taste of Thyme: Culinary Cultures of the Middle East*, ed. Sami Zubaida and Richard Tapper (London: Tauris Parke Paperbacks, 2000), 38, 41–43.

96. Valensi, *Fellah tunisiens*, 245–246.

97. John Clark Kennedy, *Algeria and Tunisia* (London: H. Colburn, 1846), vol. 2, 85 and 124.

98. Ibn Yusuf, *Al-meshra' al-mulki*, 64–65.

99. Twenty sheep for the kitchen were purchased for forty-five piasters in 1793; see TNA Register 273. Three cows and nineteen sheep were purchased for the burial of Salah ibn 'Uthman Bey in July 1829, at prices of about twenty-eight and fifteen piasters each: TNA Register 437.

100. Peyssonel, *Voyage*, 70.

101. Moalla, *The Regency of Tunis*, 99; Temple, *Excursions*, vol. 1, 239. There are only scattered references to tobacco purchased for the palace. For instance, one *qintar* and twenty-five *ratls* were bought for seventy-five piasters in 1815; see TNA Register 388.

102. They also had clarified butter, oil, honey, and almonds, and their daily total for meat was one *qintar* and seventy-two *ratls*; see TNA Register 111.

103. TNA Register 261.

104. In 1790, one *qintar* of rice, which contained about 100 pounds, cost eighteen piasters, whereas the *qintar* of wheat, which cost twenty-five piasters, held the equivalent of around 900 pounds: TNA Register 261. At least some of the rice was imported from Egypt: André Raymond, "Tunisiens et Maghrébins au Caire au dix-huitième siècle," *Cahiers de Tunisie* 7, nos. 26–27 (1959).

105. Pückler-Muskau, *Semilasso in Afrika*, vol. 2, 70; Frank and Marcel, *Histoire de Tunis*, 10. This was despite the apparently high price of coffee, which MacGill placed in 1811 at eighty-five to ninety piasters per *qintar*: MacGill, *An Account of Tunis*, 176.

106. Kennedy, *Algeria and Tunis in 1845*, vol. 2, 101.

107. Ibid., 111–112.

108. Ibid., 25.

109. Temple, *Excursions*, vol. 1, 127.

110. TNA Register 451/2, though prices varied as almonds were fifty-five piasters per *qintar* in TNA Register 266.

111. Even in the early twentieth century, *zlabia* was a rare treat "only made during the holy month of Ramadan and by a few specialists": J. Vehel, *La veritable cuisine tunisienne: Manuel pratique et complet*, presentation par Yassine Essid, ed. (Tunis: MediaCom, 2003), 117.

112. Ibn Yusuf, *Chronique tunisienne*, 161–162.

113. TNA Register 192.

114. Saloua Darghout, "Le dar es-Seqeli à Tunis," in *L'habitat traditionnel dans les pays musulmans autour de la Méditerranée*, ed. Groupe de recherches et d'études sur le Proche-Orient (Le Caire: Institut Francais d'archéologie orientale, 1988), 103; Jacques Revault, *Palais et demures de Tunis (XVIIIe et XIXe siècles)* (Paris: Editions du CNRS, 1971); Valensi, "Esclaves chrétiens et esclaves noirs à Tunis au XVIIIe siècle."

115. Mohammed el Aziz Ben Achour, *Catégories de la société Tunisoise dans la deuxième motié du XIXe siècle* (Tunis: Institut Nationale d'Archeologie et d'Art, 1989), 311; Revault, *Palais et résidences d'été*, 105.

116. Mohammed el Aziz Ben Achour, "Une famille et sa demeure dans la medina de Tunis: dar al-Jalluli (XVIIIe-XXe siècles)," in *L'habitat traditionnel dans les pays musulmans autour de la Méditerranée*, ed. Groupe de recherches et d'études sur le Proche-Orient (Le Caire: Institut Francais d'archéologie orientale, 1988), 575.

117. Ben Achour, *Catégories de la société tunisoise*, 141, 262–263.

118. Mohamed Beji Ben Mami, "Le dar Rassa'a à Tunis," in *L'habitat traditionnel dans les pays musulmans autour de la Méditerranée*, ed. Groupe de recherches et d'études sur le Proche-Orient (Le Caire: Institut Francais d'archéologie orientale, 1988), 101; Jacques Revault, "L'habitation traditionelle d'après le dar el-Hedri," in *L'habitat traditionnel dans les pays musulmans autour de la Méditerranée*, ed. Groupe de recherches et d'études sur le Proche-Orient (Le Caire: Institut Francais d'archéologie orientale, 1988), 124.

119. Blili Temime, *Histoire de familles*.

120. He mentions drinking coffee, eating sweets, and smoking pipes at other social visits with the Bu 'Ashurs and in Hammam-Lif: Temple, *Excursions*, vol. 1, 22, 77, 127.

121. Clancy-Smith, *Mediterraneans*, 117; Anne-Marie Planel, "De la nation à la colonie: la communauté française de Tunisie au XIXe siècle d'après les archives civiles et notariées du consulat général de France à Tunis" (PhD dissertation, École des hautes études en sciences sociales, 2000), 81.

122. Bartholomeo Ruffin, "Journal de l'ambassade de Suleiman Aga à la cour de France (janvier–mai 1777)," *La Revue Tunisienne* (1917); van der Haven, "The Bey, the Mufti and the Scattered Pearls."

123. Antoine de Latour, *Voyage de S. A. R. monseigneur le duc de Montpensier à Tunis, en Égypte, en Turquie et en Grèce: Lettres* (Paris: Arthus Bertrand, 1847), 230, 234, 238.

124. Ibn Abi Diyaf, *Ithaf ahl al-zaman*, vol. 4, 108–123.

125. Revault, *Palais et résidences d'été*, 419.

126. Pückler-Muskau, *Semilasso in Afrika*, vol. 2, 155–156.

127. Davis, *Evenings in My Tent*, vol. 1, 3.

128. These were not from his inheritance as his father was still living, André Demeerseman, "Inventaire des biens d'un Caïd en 1826: Bakkar Djellouli, traduction annotée," *IBLA* 45 (1982): 300–302.

129. Ben Achour, *Catégories de la société tunisoise*, 269–271.

130. Hesse-Wartegg, *Tunis*, 95.

131. Henri Saladin, *Tunis et Kairouan* (Paris: H. Laurens, 1908), 42.

132. Ibrahim Chabbouh, "La maison Buras à Kairouan," in *L'habitat traditionnel dans les pays musulmans autour de la Méditerranée*, ed. Groupe de recherches et d'études sur le Proche-Orient (Le Caire: Institut Francais d'archéologie orientale, 1988); Ali Zouari, "Le dar Jalluli et le dar Hintati à Sfax," in *L'habitat traditionnel dans les pays musulmans autour de la Méditerranée*, ed. Groupe de recherches et d'études sur le Proche-Orient (Le Caire: Institut Francais d'archéologie orientale, 1988).

133. Quoted in Clancy-Smith and Metcalf, "A Visit to a Tunisian Harem," 48.

134. Hesse-Wartegg, *Tunis*, 91–94.

135. Vicomte Begouen, "La Condamine: Tunis, Le Bardo, Carthage," *Revue Tunisienne* 5 (1898): 82.

136. Ruffin, "Journal de l'Ambassade de Suleiman Aga." Calligaris mentioned an entire room filled with clocks: Monchicourt, *Documents historiques*, 326.

137. Samanci, "Culinary Consumption Patterns," 161–162.

138. Fatma Müge Göçek, *Rise of the Bourgeoisie, Demise of Empire: Ottoman Westernization and Social Change* (New York: Oxford University Press, 1996), 98–106. By the end of the nineteenth century a wider variety of western objects were utilized as signs of status, education, culture, and class identity: see Nancy Micklewright, "Personal, Public, and Political (Re)Constructions: Photographs and Consumption," in *Consumption Studies and the History of the Ottoman Empire 1550–1922: An Introduction*, ed. Donald Quataert (Albany: State University of New York Press, 2000); Toufoul Abou-Hodeib, "Taste and Class in Late Ottoman Beirut," *International Journal of Middle East Studies* 43, no. 3 (2011).

139. Abou-Hodeib, "Taste and Class in Late Ottoman Beirut."

140. Latour, *Voyage de S. A. R. monseigneur le duc de Montpensier*, 5.

141. Haris Exertzoglou, "The Cultural Uses of Consumption: Negotiating Class, Gender, and Nation in the Ottoman Urban Centers during the 19th Century," *International Journal of Middle East Studies* 35, no. 1 (2003); Elizabeth B. Frierson, "Cheap and Easy: The Creation of Consumer Culture in Late Ottoman Society," in *Consumption Studies and the History of the Ottoman Empire, 1500–1922: An Introduction*, ed. Donald Quataert (Albany, NY: State University of New York Press, 2000).

142. Grehan estimates the total number of daily calories to be around two thousand, similar to the diet in France and Japan at that time: James Grehan, *Everyday Life & Consumer Culture in 18th-Century Damascus* (Seattle: University of Washington Press, 2007).

143. Suraiya Faroqhi, *Subjects of the Sultan: Culture and Daily Life in the Ottoman Empire* (London; New York: I. B. Tauris, 2000), 204–221.

144. Arjun Appadurai, "How to Make a National Cuisine: Cookbooks in Contemporary India," *Comparative Studies in Society and History* 30, no. 1 (1988).

1. The combination of an urban citadel and garden palace was typical of the early modern and modern era; see Gülru Necipoğlu, "An Outline of Shifting Paradigms in the Palatial Architecture of the Pre-Modern Islamic World," *Ars Orientalis* 23 (1993).

2. Ahmed Saadaoui, "Palais et résidences des Mouradites: apport des documents des archives locales (la Tunisie au XVIIᵉ s.)," *Comptes-rendus des séances de l'Académie des Inscriptions et Belles-Lettres* (2006).

3. ʿAli Pasha "loved reading and had read in one of his books marvelous descriptions of the Zohra in Cordoba, in Andalusia. He conceived of a plan to build constructions worthy of such admiration": Ibn Yusuf, *Chronique tunisienne*, 226–227.

4. This *wakil* was an important position, held for a long time by al-ʿArbi Zarruq, with access to significant sums of money, often thousands of piasters per month. See, for example, TNA Register 300, where 3,810 piasters were spent in two months, or notes in the month of Moharrem for 2,877 piasters, tiles from 2,697 piasters, and a subtotal of 11,291 piasters in TNA Register 436/3.

5. By the 1860s Muhammad al-Sadoq Bey found that the intramural space had been exhausted, and he moved to an annex about two hundred meters from its walls, known as Qsar al-Said, holding court there; Revault, *Palais et résidences d'été*, 337.

6. Marilyn Booth, *Harem Histories: Envisioning Places and Living Spaces* (Durham: Duke University Press, 2010).

7. Revault, *Palais et résidences d'été*, 329–331.

8. Ibn Yusuf, *Chronique tunisienne*, 161; Pückler-Muskau, *Semilasso in Afrika*, vol. 2, 193–196.

9. Pückler-Muskau, *Semilasso in Afrika*, vol. 2, 194. This was also mentioned in the secondhand information recounted a few decades later by Hesse-Wartegg, *Tunis*, 89–90.

10. For one of the lengthy lists of such items, see TNA History Series 1/8/3-10.

11. For instance, see the notes about bringing flowers to press: TNA Register 273.

12. Ernest-Gustave Gobert, *Usages et rites alimentaires des Tunisiens: leur aspect domestique, physiologique et social; [suivi de] les références historiques des nourritures tunisiennes* (Tunis: MediaCom, 2003); Valensi, "Consommation et usages alimentaires."

13. See the comments by Miss Smith, who passed through in 1840, in Clancy-Smith and Metcalf, "A Visit to a Tunisian Harem," 47.

14. Ibn Abi Diyaf, *Ithaf ahl al-zaman*, vol. 3, 202. Planel found that at least one of these doctors (Laurant Gay, a surgeon at court from around 1790 to 1823) was familiar with pediatrics, speculating that he may have provided obstetric and gynecological care for the palace women: Planel, "De la nation à la colonie," 53.

15. Yusuf's wet nurse received a few piasters in 1763 after his death, and Suleiman was buried in 1765; see TNA Register 2144. Register 214 is the only one mentioning Mahmud's daughter (around 1778).

16. There were funeral preparations for the daughter of the deceased bey, Muhammad al-Rashid, the daughter of Ghazalia, in Rejeb 1173 (February 1760); see TNA Register 2144 and Register 94 as well. Trakiya bint ʿAli Bey was buried in the family mausoleum at Turba al-Bey, and Hammuda Pasha's son Muhammad (1791–1800) and ʿUthman's son Murad (1784–1793) appear, for example, in Registers 266 and 270. On Hammuda Pasha's mourning, see Ibn Abi Diyaf, *Ithaf ahl al-zaman*, vol. 3, 48–49.

17. TNA History Series 1/4/27.

18. See the reference to clothes for a *jaria* of Muhammad al-Rashid in 1170 (1756) in TNA Register 2144, and the newborns mentioned in Registers 239 and 266.

19. For examples, see the preparation and celebration of births in 1816 and 1817 mentioned in TNA Registers 402 and 406.

20. The three *hawanib*, doctor, and two others were given 100 piasters for announcing the birth of Hammuda in November 1759, as was the *qaʾid* who announced Mahmud's birth in July 1757; see TNA Register 2144.

21. The mother of Muhammad al-Rashid Bey's daughters was listed consistently from 1758 until her death in 1803 (see TNA Registers 99–327); another wife was listed either as Mahmud's or Husayn's mother and received the same amounts and was mentioned until her death in 1810 (see TNA Register 360). Muhammad al-Rashid Bey was also outlived by Mna Ghazalia, who received the same amounts as the other women and died around 1812.

22. Each time ʿAli Bey's daughters completed a *sura* (or chapter of the Qurʾan), their teacher received a bonus; see, for instance, TNA Registers 214, 216, and 220.

23. A female instructor for the bey's daughters was mentioned in TNA Registers 2144 and 239, and Fatma the Genoese, in TNA Register 2144 (for 1761).

24. Pückler-Muskau, *Semilasso in Afrika*, vol. 2, 153 and 194; Temple, *Excursions*, 196.

25. Clancy-Smith, *Mediterraneans*, 261–262.

26. See TNA Register 187, TNA History Series 1/8/3, and the reference in Henry Dunant, *Notice sur la régence de Tunis* (Tunis: Société Tunisienne de Diffusion, 1975 [1858]), 72.

27. See, for example, TNA Register 360.

28. The first record of Fatma in the expense registers appears in TNA Register 99, dating to the reign of Muhammad al-Rashid Bey, in 1757–1758.

29. See, for example, TNA Register 436/2.

30. All three were ibn ʿAli's children with the female slave from Sardinia, Jannat. See the reference to properties that Fatma owned that originally belonged to her mother "Jannat, the *ʿaljia*": TNA History Series 1/6/43.

31. The house of Hammuda Shelebi was mentioned in TNA Registers 175–341; he was listed as *marhum*, or deceased, in her property records.

32. Bonuses were distributed to various households for the *milak* and *'ares bint okht al-m'atham Sidna* in identical amounts to those for the bey's marriage to *bint al-Ghazali* in Moharrem, Sfar, and Ramadan 1170 (October and November 1756, June 1757), and 800 piasters of diamonds the following year: see TNA Register 2144.

33. *Dar bint okht Sidna* was included in salary and clothing lists from 1757 to 1775, when a note that her salary was discontinued indicates she passed away around May 1775; see TNA Registers 99, 175, 180, 184, 187, and 192.

34. Her labor was in 1172, and the circumcision of the bey's sister's grandson was in 1180. See TNA Register 2144. It seems probable that this grandson died at a young age, as did Fatma's daughter, since Rejeb Khaznadar mentioned only Fatma and his daughter Hafsia (by another woman) in a *waqf* he made in 1780; Ben Achour, *Catégories de la société tunisoise*, 53.

35. Fatma died in Rejeb 1207 (February 1793), and partial expenses for her *farqa* and *ziara*, including cumin, caraway, and garlic for seventy-four piasters, were recorded in Dhou al-Qa'ada; see TNA Register 270.

36. 'Aziza's son 'Ali married his cousin Menana (the daughter of his maternal uncle Husayn). 'Aziza married the prominent mamluk Suleiman Kahia, and the children are often referred to as the Kahia's children—for example, in TNA Register 246.

37. Seniority often coincided with a postsexual phase. Leslie Peirce, "Seniority, Sexuality, and Social Order: The Vocabulary of Gender in Early Modern Ottoman Society," in *Women in the Ottoman Empire*, ed. Madeline C. Zilfi (Leiden: Brill, 1997).

38. Ben Achour, *Catégories de la société tunisoise*, 124.

39. This presented a significant divergence from Ottoman imperial practices, as the sultans preferred concubinage over royal marriages and rarely married slave concubines. In Tunis, there was a celebration when Muhammad al-Rashid married a *jaria* in 1757. For marriage contracts between Hammuda, 'Uthman, and Mustafa and freed slaves named "bint 'abdallah," see TNA History Series 1/6. On instances of marriages with slave women in the al-Asram, 'Agha, Bahri, Jalluli, Zarruq, Sharif, and 'Abd al-Wahab families, see Ben Achour, *Catégories de la société tunisoise*, 178–216.

40. Mustafa Bash Agha married Sasia bint Mustafa Bey in the 1830s, and her sister Kalthum married Mustafa Khaznadar shortly thereafter. The Aghas married a number of old notable families, while the Khaznadars conducted marriage alliances with the Bakkush and Sharif families, who were *'ulama'*; Ben Achour, *Catégories de la société tunisoise*, 177–178, 184, and 206.

41. Mohammed el Aziz Ben Achour, "Les 'aylat du corpus: notes historiques," in *Hasab wa Nasab: parenté, alliance et patrimoine en Tunisie*, ed. Sophie Ferchiou (Paris: Editions CNRS, 1992).

42. Such transformations are discussed by Abdelhamid Henia, "Origine et évolution d'un patrimoine familial tunisios (XVIIᵉ–XIXᵉ siècles)," *IBLA* 17, no. 154 (1984).

43. Revault, *Palais et demures de Tunis*; Ben Achour, *Catégories de la société tunisoise*, 55–66. See also Ben Mami, "Le dar Rassaʾa à Tunis"; Chabbouh, "La maison Buras à Kairouan"; Revault, "L'habitation traditionelle d'après le dar el-Hedri."

44. Ben Achour, *Catégories de la société tunisoise*, 75, 208.

45. See the biographies of these families in Ben Achour, *Catégories de la société tunisoise*, 176–206.

46. Blili Temime, *Histoire de familles*, 102.

47. The study is based on data related to 135 families: Blili Temime, *Histoire de familles*, 121 and 123. Blili's results resemble eighteenth- and nineteenth-century families in Aleppo and Nablus (averaging 3.3 children), where upper-class and polygamous families tended to be slightly larger (with 3.6 children); see Meriwether, *The Kin Who Count*, 79–80.

48. Valensi, *Fellah tunisiens*, 286–290. Emilie de Vialar was performing clandestine baptisms on deathly ill Muslim and Jewish children under her care. In the 1850s, she claimed that these numbered in the hundreds: Clancy-Smith, *Mediterraneans*, 274–275. Rouissi suggests that infant and child mortality may have been as much as 35 percent: Moncer Rouissi, *Population et société au Maghreb* (Tunis: Cérès Productions, 1977), 44.

49. Ben Achour, *Catégories de la société tunisoise*.

50. Blili Temime, *Histoire de familles*, 151–155.

51. See, for instance, Henia, "Origine et évolution d'un patrimoine familial tunisios." In Aleppo and Cairo, few families had the means and space to support multiple generations under one roof, and if they did, it was for a few years, with the average household splitting into smaller simple family arrangements following the death of the patriarch; Kenneth M. Cuno, "Joint Family Households and Rural Notables in 19th-Century Egypt," *International Journal of Middle East Studies* 27, no. 4 (1995); Meriwether, *The Kin Who Count*, 82–95.

52. Ferchiou, "Structures de parenté," 141 and 144.

53. Ben Achour's study includes eighteen of the same families and two different ones, and provides a detailed breakdown of the figures. Ben Achour, *Catégories de la société tunisoise*, 222–223.

54. This is according to a study of 125 men over multiple generations. See Arnold H. Green, *The Tunisian Ulama, 1873–1915: Social Structure and Response to Ideological Currents* (Leiden: E. J. Brill, 1978), 87–89.

55. See Appendix 1, Genealogies 1, 2, 4, and 5.

56. As mentioned in Chapter 1, there were three of these before 1750: Hafsia bint Husayn ibn ʿAli with ʿAli Pasha (in 1714) and those of Husayn ibn ʿAli and his son Muhammad al-Rashid with their maternal cousins from the Ghazali family.

57. Lilia Ben Salem, "Structures familiales et changement social en Tunisie," *Revue tunisienne de science sociales* 27, no. 100 (1990); Monia Hejaiej, *Behind Closed*

Doors: Women's Oral Narratives in Tunis (New Brunswick, NJ: Rutgers University Press, 1996), 19.

58. Charles Lallemand, *Tunis et ses environs: texte et dessins d'après nature* (Paris: Maison Quantin, 1890), 167; Samira Sethom, "Étude de quatre contrats de mariage Sfaxiens du XIXᵉ siècle," *Cahiers des arts et traditions populaires: revue du Centre des Arts et Traditions Populaires* 6 (1977).

59. Ben Achour, *Catégories de la société tunisoise*, 66.

60. Revault, *Palais et demures de Tunis*, 53; Lallemand, *Tunis et ses environs*, 186.

61. Alia Baïram, "Le Bit-el-Mùna ou chambre à provision dans l'habitation traditionnelle à Tunis," *Cahiers des arts et traditions populaires* 7 (1980).

62. Oualdi, *Esclaves et maîtres*, 137–139; Ben Achour, *Catégories de la société tunisoise*, 185, 190, 209; Green, *The Tunisian Ulama*, 54–56.

63. Ibn Abi Diyaf, *Ithaf ahl al-zaman*, vol. 7, 13–14 and 38–39. Du Roches says he paid Trakiya 100,000 piasters to return to favor; see Eugene Plantet, ed., *Correspondance des Beys de Tunis et des Consuls de France avec la cour, 1577–1830* (Paris: Félix Alcan, 1899), vol. 3, 114–115.

64. Her opinions held sway over her son, who was very respectful of her; see the repeated references to this in L. Carl Brown, *Tunisia of Ahmad Bey*, 43, 209, and 327.

65. The latter continued to live in the palace and received financial support; see the allocations for 'Uthman's two houses from 1815 through 1822, and for the wife of Salah ibn 'Uthman until her death in 1829, in TNA Registers 388–440/2. Ibn Dhiaf notes that he "adopted the sons of his assassinated cousin 'Uthman Bey, and installed them with him in his house, they were young boys": Ibn Abi Diyaf, *Ithaf ahl al-zaman*, vol. 2, 135.

66. The French consul—who personally approved of this regime change—claimed that "everyone, whether Turk, Arab, Moor, is happy" with this outcome: Plantet, ed., *Correspondance des beys*, vol. 3, 530.

67. The section on 'Uthman consists mainly of an explanation of the coup and its chronology; the only other anecdotes are that Imam Ahmad al-Barudi died and that 'Uthman ordered the burning of marijuana fields: Ibn Abi Diyaf, *Ithaf ahl al-zaman*, vol. 3, 119–131.

68. See the stipend lists in Dhou al-Qa'ada and then Moharrem in TNA Registers 384 and 388.

69. The religious scholar Mahmud al-Mahjub said that if Mahmud was angry or resented this, he would be the first to take his side: Ibn Abi Diyaf, *Ithaf ahl al-zaman*, vol. 3, 124.

70. Ibid., 135, 195, and 251–252.

71. See Appendix 1, Genealogy 4. Halima was mentioned by name as the wife of Khayr al-Din Kahia on her tombstone in the family *turba* (mausoleum) and TNA History Series 1/9/2; Fatma bint Ismail Kahia was also buried in the family *turba*.

72. 'Aisha's daughters were married in December 1815 or January 1816. See partial expenses included in TNA Registers 388 and 402 and History Series 1/8/15.

73. See his biography in Ibn Abi Diyaf, *Ithaf ahl al-zaman*, vol. 7, 124–125.

74. See Appendix 1, Genealogy 5. TNA History Series 1/8/14.

75. Ibn Abi Diyaf, *Ithaf ahl al-zaman*, vol. 3, 202–203.

76. Guy's letter dated 27 March 1827 is quoted in Raymond, ed., *Ahmad Ibn Abi l-Diaf*, vol. 2, 141.

77. Temple, *Excursions*, 194.

78. Calligaris was also director of Ahmad Bey's military school at Bardo. Calligaris purports that she was rewarded for her role in the 1814 violence by marriage with Husayn, though they were likely married a few years earlier, as both ibn Dhiaf and Raymond say that she was the mother of Muhammad and Muhammad al-Sadoq, born in 1811 and 1813, respectively, and the latter directly contests Calligaris' dating of the marriage: Raymond, ed., *Ahmad Ibn Abi l-Diaf*, vol. 2, 141. There are a number of other inaccuracies in his account; he dates Hammuda Pasha's death to 1808 and claims that Mahmud was one of his brothers, in Monchicourt, *Documents historiques*, 340–350.

79. Ibn Yusuf, *Chronique tunisienne*, 161–162.

80. Pierre Grandchamp, "A propos du sejour à Tunis de Caroline de Brunswick, princesse de Galles (4–12 avril, 1816)," *Revue tunisienne* (1934).

81. Filippi and other European dignitaries attended a reception in the winter of 1833–1834: Monchicourt, *Documents historiques*, 326.

82. Pückler-Muskau, *Semilasso in Afrika*, vol. 2, 192.

83. See Dunant, *Notice sur la régence de Tunis*, 72; Monchicourt, *Documents historiques*, 326.

84. Clancy-Smith, *Mediterraneans*, 302–303.

85. Temple, *Excursions*, 196–200, 127, 205, and 300; Monchicourt, *Documents historiques*, 236.

86. Pückler-Muskau refers to his source as "one of the consular ladies." Much of his account is identical to the quotes from Berner's report submitted to the British embassy and discussed in Clancy-Smith and Metcalf, "A Visit to a Tunisian Harem."

87. Pückler-Muskau, *Semilasso in Afrika*, vol. 2, 193–194.

88. It was not clear which of his wives this referred to, since she was not mentioned by name, and by this date both Fatma Mestiri and Shelbia were deceased: ibid., 195.

89. Temple, *Excursions*, 196, 200.

90. Pückler-Muskau, *Semilasso in Afrika*, vol. 2, 195.

91. Temple, *Excursions*, 200, 205.

92. Pückler-Muskau, *Semilasso in Afrika*, vol. 2, 194.

93. Ibid., 196.

94. Temple, *Excursions*, 196.

95. Ibid., 202–203.

96. Pückler-Muskau, *Semilasso in Afrika*, vol. 2, 196–197.

97. These were the prices in 1814 and 1828; see TNA Registers 384 and 436/2.

98. Temple, *Excursions*, 201.

99. Ibid., 197–199.

100. Ibid., 189.

101. Pückler-Muskau, *Semilasso in Afrika*, vol. 2, 198.

102. Temple, *Excursions*, 202–203.

103. Pückler-Muskau, *Chroniques*, vol. 3, 301–303; Mounir Fendri, "L'audience de 9 mai 1835, Le Prince de Pückler-Muskau chez Hussine Bey," *Les Cahiers de Tunisie* 30, nos. 121–122 (1982).

104. Quoted in Pückler-Muskau, *Semilasso in Afrika*, vol. 2, 196.

105. In Egypt, Muhammad 'Ali Pasha used these visits to demonstrate economic and political power: Khaled Fahmy, *All the Pasha's Men: Mehmed Ali, His Army and the Making of Modern Egypt* (Cairo: University of Cairo Press, 1997), 6–9.

106. Gülru Necipoğlu, "Framing the Gaze in Ottoman, Safavid, and Mughal Palaces," *Ars Orientalis* 23 (1993).

107. Lal, *Domesticity and Power*.

108. On female travelers in the Ottoman Empire, see also Lewis, *Gendering Orientalism*; Melman, *Women's Orients*.

109. Much as has been argued for the twentieth century; see Cynthia Enloe, *Bananas, Beaches and Bases: Making Feminist Sense of International Politics* (Berkeley: University of California Press, 2000), 93–123.

110. Clancy-Smith and Metcalf, "A Visit to a Tunisian Harem."

111. Peirce, *The Imperial Harem*, 30, 57–90.

112. Lynn Hunt, *The Family Romance of the French Revolution* (Berkeley: University of California Press, 1992); Weber, *Queen of Fashion*; Lynn Hunt, "The Many Bodies of Marie Antoinette: Political Pornography and the Problem of the Feminine in the French Revolution," in *Eroticism and the Body Politic*, ed. Lynn Hunt (Baltimore: Johns Hopkins University Press, 1991); Sarah Maza, "The Diamond Necklace Affair Revisited (1785–1786): The Case of the Missing Queen," in *Eroticism and the Body Politic*, ed. Lynn Hunt (Baltimore: Johns Hopkins University Press, 1991).

113. Rawski, *Last Emperors*, 127–128.

114. Abbas Amanat, *Pivot of the Universe: Nasir al-Din Shah Qajar and the Iranian Monarchy, 1831–1896* (Berkeley: University of California Press, 1997).

115. Andre Schmid, *Korea between Empires, 1895–1919* (New York: Columbia University Press, 2002), 27–28; Keith L. Pratt, Richard Rutt, and James Hoare, *Korea: A Historical and Cultural Dictionary* (Richmond, Surrey, England: Curzon Press, 1999), 288–289.

1. On the decentralized nature of the Tunisian interior, see Abdelhamid Henia, *Le grid et ses rapports avec le Beylik de Tunis (1676–1840)* (Tunis: Publications de l'Université de Tunis, 1980).

2. For examples of this, see Linda T. Darling, *Revenue-Raising and Legitimacy: Tax Collection and Finance Administration in the Ottoman Empire, 1560–1660* (Leiden: E. J. Brill, 1996); Rifa'at Ali Abou-el-Haj, "Aspects of the Legitimation of Ottoman Rule as Reflected in the Preambles to Two Early *Liva Kanunameler*," *Turcica, Revue d'études turques XXI–XXIII* (1991).

3. On the symbolism of the ceremony and the procession, see Babak Rahimi, "*Nahils*, Circumcision Rituals and the Theatre State," in *Ottoman Tulips, Ottoman Coffee: Leisure and Lifestyle in the Eighteenth Century*, ed. Dana Sajdi (New York: Tauris Academic Press, 2007).

4. Artan, "Aspects of the Ottoman Elite's Food Consumption," 143. Similarly, at the Daulatkhane royal precinct in Isfahan, the kitchen, bakery, and storehouses opened onto an alleyway where extra food was handed out so that the Safavid Shah symbolically fed his subjects; Sussan Babaie, *Isfahan and Its Palaces: Statecraft, Shi'ism and the Architecture of Conviviality in Early Modern Iran* (Edinburgh: Edinburgh University Press, 2008), 136.

5. Mine Ener, *Managing Egypt's Poor and the Politics of Benevolence, 1800–1952* (Princeton, NJ: Princeton University Press, 2003), xviii; Amy Singer, *Constructing Ottoman Beneficence: An Imperial Soup Kitchen in Jerusalem* (Albany: State University of New York Press, 2002); Amy Singer, "The 'Michelin Guide' to Public Kitchens in the Ottoman Empire," in *Starting with Food: Culinary Approaches to Ottoman History*, ed. Amy Singer (Princeton, NJ: Markus Weiner, 2011).

6. Davis, *Evenings in My Tent*, vol. 1, 5.

7. Ben Achour, *Catégories de la société tunisoise*, 269.

8. TNA Register 275.

9. See Amy Singer, "Charity's Legacies: A Reconsideration of Imperial Endowment Making," in *Poverty and Charity in Middle Eastern Contexts*, ed. Michael Bonner, Mine Ener, and Amy Singer (Albany: State University of New York Press, 2003).

10. See, for instance, Ulku U. Bates, "Women as Patrons of Architecture in Turkey," in *Women in the Muslim World*, ed. Lois Beck and Nikki R. Keddie (Cambridge: Cambridge University Press, 1978); Carl F. Petry, "Class Solidarity versus Gender Gain: Women as Custodians of Property in Later Medieval Egypt," in *Women in Middle Eastern History: Shifting Boundaries in Sex and Gender*, ed. Beth Baron and Nikki R. Keddie (New Haven, CT: Yale University Press, 1991); Fay, "Women and Households."

11. Peirce, *The Imperial Harem*, 198–210.

12. Singer, *Constructing Ottoman Beneficence*.

13. Peirce, *The Imperial Harem*, 198.

14. See Grangaud, *La ville imprenable*; Miriam Hoexter, *Endowments, Rulers and Community: Waqf al-Haramayn in Ottoman Algeria* (Leiden: Brill, 1998).

15. Meriwether, *The Kin Who Count*, 178–206.

16. Larguèche, *Les ombres de la ville*, 107; Saadaoui, *Tunis, ville ottomane*, 73–74.

17. Saadaoui, *Tunis, ville ottomane*, 107.

18. Ibid.

19. These were recorded in a register of his *ahbas*; see TNA Register 2306. On their relation to public health, see Nancy Elizabeth Gallagher, *Medicine and Power in Tunisia, 1780–1900* (Cambridge: Cambridge University Press, 1983), 15–16.

20. Béchir Sfar, *Assistance publique musulmane en Tunisie* (Tunis: Imprimerie Rapide, 1896), 13; Saadaoui, *Tunis, ville ottomane*, 210–212, 14.

21. Larguèche, *Les ombres de la ville*, 127–128.

22. Sfar, *Assistance publique musulmane en Tunisie*, 25–26; Jean Poncet, "Un problème d'histoire rurale: le habous d'Aziza Othmana au Sahel," *Les Cahiers de Tunisie* 31, no. 3 (1960); Sadok Zmerli, *Les précurseurs* (Tunis: Éditions Bouslama, 1979), 7–15; Gallagher, *Medicine and Power*, 22.

23. Ibn Yusuf, *Chronique tunisienne*, 247.

24. See Appendix 1, Genealogy 2.

25. Khadija's was recorded in TNA History Series 1/5/46 and ʿAisha's in 1/5/49.

26. This implies that the girls were already dead and that one died in 1760; TNA History Series 1/5/37.

27. Ministry of State Domains, *al-ihzab* Files 34 and 39. Archives stored in this ministry are only partially catalogued, and individual documents are not numbered.

28. See Ministry of State Domains, *al-ihzab* Files 30 and 40.

29. Ferchiou, "Catégorie des sexes," 257.

30. Henia, "Circulation des biens," 228, 234.

31. Green, *The Tunisian Ulama*, 112.

32. The records say these were given to *koloughli*, a term referring to the sons of former soldiers or their descendants. In later years they were listed as "Hanafi," after the legal school followed by the Ottoman ruling class (as opposed to that of the general population, which was Maliki); see, for example, TNA Register 251 or 260.

33. Saadaoui, *Tunis, ville ottomane*, 215, 232.

34. Larguèche, *Les ombres de la ville*, 61.

35. A note in 1764 says the burial of six poor people cost nine piasters, whereas in Moharrem 1190 and 1213 (February or March 1776 and June 1798) the cost was one piaster each; see TNA Registers 2144, 201, and 300 respectively.

36. These were first recorded in TNA Register 175; appear regularly after Register 229, with additions from Register 321 (for eight piasters each, and four to Sidi ʿAli ibn Ziyad); and are mentioned in every register through the next four decades.

37. Ibn Yusuf, *Chronique tunisienne*, 239.

38. TNA Registers 220 and 221.

39. TNA Registers 214 and 286.

40. Leon Carl Brown, "Religious Establishment in Husainid Tunisia"; Green, *The Tunisian Ulama*.

41. Abdelhamid et Dalenda Larguèche, *Marginales en terre d'Islam* (Tunis: Cérès Editions, 1992), 113–136. Her biography has also been utilized by feminists praising her as a "free spirit" and "human rights activist" whose strong character "alienated her from the traditional family life reserved for women of her era": Emna Ben Miled, "Aicha el Manoubiyya: une tunisienne libre," *Quaderns de la Mediterrània* 12 (2009).

42. The total *sadaqa* from the month of Jamada al-thani (February 1759), 1172, TNA Register 2144.

43. TNA Registers 229 and 239.

44. Larguèche, *Les ombres de la ville*, 109–112.

45. TNA Register 2143.

46. TNA Register 2144.

47. Ibn Abi Diyaf, *Ithaf ahl al-zaman*, vol. 4, 61, and TNA Register 216.

48. On the death of the bey's grandson, see TNA register 214. Frank and Marcel, *Histoire de Tunis*, 119. Pückler-Muskau guessed that there were 800 freed slaves at the funeral of Husayn Bey: Pückler-Muskau, *Chroniques*, vol. 2, 251.

49. These were noted in the month of Jamada al-ula (beginning in April 1817); TNA Register 403.

50. Ibn Yusuf, *Chronique tunisienne*, 412.

51. Ibn Abi Diyaf, *Ithaf ahl al-zaman*, vol. 3, 202; Clancy-Smith, *Mediterraneans*, 105.

52. The clothes and monetary gifts to all those circumcised as well as payments to the barbers are described in TNA Register 2144 for the year 1178. These totaled some 3,400 piasters; the shoes alone (priced at one-half piaster and three *nasris* each) equaled 276 piasters.

53. TNA Registers 286, 2144, and 2145.

54. TNA Register 2144.

55. TNA Register 436/4.

56. Ibn al-'Aziz's *Kitab al bashi* quoted in Larguèche, *Les ombres de la ville*, 117.

57. See TNA Register 2144, for the year 1180.

58. For the month of Rabia' al-thani (June 1775) 1189; TNA Register 2144.

59. Amos Perry, *Carthage and Tunis, Past and Present: In Two Parts* (Providence, RI: Providence Press Company Printers, 1869), 479.

60. When ibn 'Ali headed for Beja with the army, he also brought "his family, domestic servants, and elderly women": Ibn Yusuf, *Chronique tunisienne*, 148. See also TNA Register 2144.

61. Though later, Hammuda Pasha remained permanently in the capital, sending Suleiman Kahia as his deputy; see Ibn Abi Diyaf, *Ithaf ahl al-zaman*, vol. 3, 19.

62. See Silvia Marsans-Sakly, "Extracting Revenue and Legitimating Power: The Mahalla in the Regency of Tunis" (paper presented at the 17th Annual

MEHAT Conference, University of Chicago, 2002); Dalenda Larguèche, "The *Mahalla*: The Origins of Beylical Sovereignty in Ottoman Tunisia during the Early Modern Period," in *North Africa, Islam and the Mediterranean World: From the Almoravides to the Algerian War*, ed. Julia A. Clancy-Smith (London: Frank Cass, 2001).

63. These are all listed in TNA Register 2144, by region, dating from 1176 to 1186 (about 1762 to 1772). Similar notes can also be found in TNA Register 2143: for example, "money to the individual who brought two rabbits."

64. On the role of gift giving as demonstrations of elite loyalty in Morocco, see Rahma Bourqia, "Don et théâtralité: reflexion sur le rituel de don (hadiya) offert au sultan au XIXᵉ siècle," *Hespéris-Tamuda* 31 (1993). Indrani Chatterjee emphasized the honor associated with giving and the subsequent dishonor of receiving; see Chapter 4: I. Chatterjee, *Gender, Slavery, and Law*.

65. TNA Register 2145.

66. There were poor harvests from 1816 to 1820. For the increase in 1819, see TNA Register 415.

67. Ibn Abi Diyaf, *Ithaf ahl al-zaman*, vol. 3, 208.

68. Ahmad Ibn Abi Diyaf, *Min rasa'il ibn abi al-Diyaf*, Mohammed al-Salah al-Mzali ed. (Tunis: 1969), 17.

69. Larguèche, *Les ombres de la ville*.

70. See the note in 1179 (1765): TNA Register 2144.

71. Larguèche, *Les ombres de la ville*, 132.

72. In 1875 the functions of the hospice were taken over by the Sadiki hospital. Shifting bureaucratic practices and the insufficiency of its resources from the *awqaf* revenues meant that by the late nineteenth century, there was limited space, making it necessary to obtain a certificate of need from a judge to be admitted into the hospice. A similar situation prevailed in Egypt: Mine Ener, "Getting into the Shelter of Takiyat Tulun," in *Outside in: On the Margins of the Modern Middle East*, ed. Eugene L. Rogan (London: I. B. Tauris, 2002).

CHAPTER 5

1. Ibn Abi Diyaf, *Ithaf ahl al-zaman*, vol. 4, 173.

2. Devoize's letters regularly complain about the poor treatment of French subjects throughout this period and their veritable imprisonment in the *funduq*. He notes the regular arrival of imperial envoys: Plantet, ed., *Correspondance des beys*, vol. 3, 367–372, 377 and 382, 389, 398–399. He also mentions the influence the Algerian governors held over the bey, supporting Moalla's conclusion (*The Regency of Tunis*, 60) that they were behind a brief truce signed with France that the sultan forced them to annul.

3. Ibn Abi Diyaf, *Ithaf ahl al-zaman*, vol. 3, 201–202.

4. The threats were communicated by De Lesseps; see Plantet, ed., *Correspondance des beys*, vol. 3, 700–704. See Articles 5, 6, and 7 in the copy of the treaty

in Alphonse Rousseau, *Les annales tunisiennes* (Tunis: Editions Bouslama, 1983), 513–515. On the French occupation of Algiers and the effects on Tunis, see also Ibn Abi Diyaf, *Ithaf ahl al-zaman*, vol. 3, 215–218.

5. Lisa Anderson, "Nineteenth-Century Reform in Ottoman Libya," *International Journal of Middle East Studies* 16, no. 3 (1984); Abou-el-Haj, "An Agenda for Research in History."

6. There is a lengthy discussion of the affairs in Tripoli and its impact on the bey in Ibn Abi Diyaf: *Ithaf ahl al-zaman*, vol. 3, 243–246.

7. Tavakoli-Targhi, *Refashioning Iran.*

8. On the Ottoman civilizing mission and "Occidentalism," see Selim Deringil, "'They Live in a State of Nomadism and Savagery': The Late Ottoman Empire and the Post-Colonial Debate," *Comparative Studies in Society and History* 45, no. 2 (2003); Carter Vaughn Findley, "An Ottoman Occidentalist in Europe: Ahmed Midhat Meets Madame Gulnar, 1889," *American Historical Review* 103, no. 1 (1998); Ussama Makdisi, "Ottoman Orientalism," *American Historical Review* 107, no. 3 (2002); Eve M. Troutt Powell, *A Different Shade of Colonialism: Egypt, Great Britain, and the Mastery of the Sudan* (Berkeley: University of California Press, 2003).

9. Though according to Brown (*The Tunisia of Ahmad Bey*, 227), he "possessed influence but not power."

10. Between 1830 and 1860, the number of palace households listed as receiving food and stipends from the palace treasury, aside from the numerous *juar*, went from seventeen to about thirty.

11. Fahmy, *All the Pasha's Men.*

12. Amira K. Bennison, "The "New Order" and Islamic Order: the Introduction of the *Nizami* Army in the Western Maghrib and Its Legitimation, 1830–1873," *International Journal of Middle East Studies* 36, no. 4 (2004).

13. Monchicourt, *Documents historiques*, 314.

14. Brown quotes foreign office reports from 1837, but he regrets that the vice-consul did not detail these claims: Brown, *The Tunisia of Ahmad Bey*, 232.

15. See the records for the sewing and outfitting of uniforms for the *nizam jedid* troops: TNA Register 442/2. Brown says that this change was prompted by an imperial *firman*: *The Tunisia of Ahmad Bey*, 263–265.

16. Quataert, "Clothing Laws, State, and Society in the Ottoman Empire, 1720–1829."

17. Pückler-Muskau goes on to regret that these were "so paltry compared with the former splendid Mamluke costume, glittering with gold and jewels"; Pückler-Muskau, *Semilasso in Afrika*, vol. 2, 115–116.

18. Temple, *Excursions*, 188–189.

19. Turba al-Bey, Tunis. This is mentioned by Mohammed el Aziz Ben Achour, "'Tourbet el Bey' sépulture des Beys et de la famille husaynite à Tunis," *IBLA* 48, no. 155 (1985).

20. See the reference to three French instructors in a letter dated 16 December

1837, Number 52, ISHMN—Tunis, Archives of the Ministry of Foreign Affairs (Quai d'Orsay), Ministry of Foreign Relations, Political correspondance 1/3.

21. Kennedy, *Algeria and Tunis in 1845*, 159. An ophicleide is a bugle or a type of wind instrument that is similar to a bugle.

22. Pückler-Muskau, *Semilasso in Afrika*, vol. 2, 155.

23. Kennedy, *Algeria and Tunis in 1845*, 10–11.

24. It took a battalion of soldiers to carry them all, amd they filled twenty book cases; see Ibn Abi Diyaf, *Ithaf ahl al-zaman*, vol. 4, 56–57.

25. Noureddine Sraïeb, *Le Collège Sadiki de Tunis, 1875–1956: enseignement et nationalisme* (Paris: CNRS, 1995).

26. Larguèche, *Les Ombres de la ville*, 134–135.

27. Gallagher, *Medicine and Power*, 41–42; Joel Montague, "Notes on Medical Organization in Nineteenth-century Tunisia: A Preliminary Analysis of the Materials on Public Health and Medicine in the Dar el-Bey in Tunis," *Medical History* 17, no. 1 (1973).

28. This was because measures such as the taxation of carriages would have had an uneven impact on the foreign population, as most were owned by men with European protection. European residents contributed to a fair share of urban violence, further limiting the council's efforts to police the capital; see William L. Cleveland, "The Municipal Council of Tunis, 1858–1870," *International Journal of Middle East Studies* 9 (1978). As the poorest of European migrants, the Maltese community often took the blame for the general rowdiness and disorder: Clancy-Smith, *Mediterraneans*, 181–182.

29. Ibn Abi Diyaf, *Ithaf ahl al-zaman*, vol. 4, 30.

30. Van der Haven, "The Bey, the mufti and the scattered pearls," 102.

31. Mantran, "L'évolution des relations"; Chater, *Dépendance et mutations*, 596.

32. Egypt too founded mixed courts in 1876, and while associated with the Capitulations agreements and preferential treatment for Europeans, the Egyptian government hoped the courts would limit foreign interference and stall foreign domination; see Nathan J. Brown, "Law and Imperialism: Egypt in Comparative Perspective," *Law & Society Review* 29, no. 2 (1995); Nathan J. Brown, "The Precarious Life and Slow Death of the Mixed Courts of Egypt," *International Journal of Middle East Studies* 25, no. 1 (1993).

33. See the discussion and summaries in Nathan J. Brown, *Constitutions in a Nonconstitutional World: Arab Basic Laws and the Prospects for Accountable Government* (Albany: State University of New York Press, 2002); Theresa Liane Womble, "Early Constitutionalism in Tunisia, 1857–1864: Reform and Revolt" (PhD dissertation, Princeton University, 1997). Womble includes the complete text in Arabic and French (dating to 1931).

34. This was around 1798, following the raid of St. Pietro, a small island off the coast of Sardinia. She is not to be confused with Elena-Grazia Raffo, another wife of Mustafa Bey who was born in the palace and was from a Genoese family: Ibn Abi Diyaf, *Ithaf ahl al-zaman*, vol. 4, 11–12.

35. According to ibn Dhiaf, his mother viewed the young Mustafa as her grandson: *Ithaf ahl al-zaman*, vol. 8, 74. Kalthum was included for the first time as receiving a salary at the beginning of the Hijri Year 1258 (February 1842) but was not included in the previous year; see TNA Register 470/2.

36. *Ithaf ahl al-zaman*, vol. 4, 104–105.

37. Though as a rule the *'ulama'* preferred not to be involved in governing, the beys consistently sought their support for reform projects; see Green, *The Tunisian Ulama*, 103–128.

38. Ibn Abi Diyaf, *Ithaf ahl al-zaman*, vol. 3, 264–265. This is also mentioned by the French Consul Schwebel; see his letter dated 12 February 1837 in the ISHMN—Tunis, Archives of the Ministry of Foreign Affairs (Quai d'Orsay), Ministry of Foreign Relations, Political correspondance 1/3. Similar attempts in Egypt resulted in the flight of potential conscripts: Fahmy, *All the Pasha's Men*.

39. G. S. van Krieken, *Khayr al-Din et la Tunisie, 1850–1881* (Leiden: E. J. Brill, 1976), 64.

40. Their main point of contention, if any, would have been with the tribunals, and certainly not with the Council of Ministers, which was opposed by the bey and a number of European consuls. For further discussion, see Marsans-Sakly, "The Revolt of 1864," 47, 80–81, 204–205.

41. A number of these clauses were also detailed in the copy of the Constitution included in Dispatch 47, from Direction des Affaires Politiques et Commerciale, dated 17 October 1860, in CADN Protectorat-Tunisie, 1st Series, Carton 875.

42. This final point was specified in an earlier draft of the chapter; see TNA History Series 92/77/4.

43. Ehud R. Toledano, *Slavery and Abolition in the Ottoman Middle East* (Seattle: University of Washington Press, 1998), 113–119.

44. Mohsen Hamli, "The 1890 Legal Wrangles over Sudanese Slaves in Tunisia," *Journal of North African Studies* 16, no. 3 (2011): 424.

45. TNA History Series, 92/78/6. Most did not occupy important positions, and while grandsons of mamluks were added to the mamluk corps, so were native Tunisians; see Oualdi, *Esclaves et maîtres*, 311–315.

46. TNA Register 470/2.

47. TNA Register 552 for 1860.

48. Though only partial, these date to 1876 and 1879: TNA Registers 581 and 583.

49. On the relation between this cordoning of the religious within the public domain and how codification of the shari'a, particularly in the creation of family as an object of law, relates to modernization, see Talal Asad, *Formations of the Secular: Christianity, Islam, Modernity* (Stanford, CA: Stanford University Press, 2003), 227–231.

50. The first European loan was contracted by Sultan Abd al-Mejid in 1854: Issawi, *An Economic History*, 7–9, 62–68.

51. The details of these successive affairs and their financial machinations (particularly that of ibn Ayad) are discussed at length in a variety of secondary sources and will not be reiterated here. See, for instance, Jean Ganiage, *Les origines du Protectorat Français en Tunisie (1861–1881)* (Paris: Presses Universitaire de France, 1959).

52. The French embassy was housed in one of the beylical palaces in Marsa that 'Ali Bey had provided in 1774. The French were not required to pay rent and in exchange were expected to pay for maintenance, but the latter end of the bargain was not respected: Revault, *Palais et résidences d'été*, 81.

53. On the periodization of financial problems, see Silvia Marsans-Sakly, "The Revolt of 1864."

54. See the excellent discussions of this in Victoria de Grazia and Ellen Furlough, eds., *The Sex of Things: Gender and Consumption in Historical Perspective* (Berkeley: University of California Press, 1996); David Kuchta, *The Three-Piece Suit and Modern Masculinity: England, 1550–1850* (Berkeley: University of California Press, 2002); Auslander, *Taste and Power*.

55. See the lists of gifts in Plantet, ed., *Correspondance des beys*, vol. 3, lxvi–lxvii.

56. De Castries to Jean-Baptiste du Rocher, 15 January 1786, and du Rocher to de Castries, 13 January 1786: Plantet, ed., *Correspondance des beys*, vol. 3, 153.

57. Mathieu-Maximilien-Prosper, Conte de Lesseps (Consul General of Tunis) to Ayguste-Ferron, Conte de Laferronnays (Minister of Foreign Affairs), and de Lesseps to de Laferronnays, in Plantet, ed., *Correspondance des beys*, vol. 3, 670, and 678–679.

58. Paris, 14 December 1829, in CADN, Archives des Postes, 145. See also the letters from 1797; 11 January 1828; 1848; and September 1864.

59. See the file on Princely Debts, TNA History Series 1/11, covering the period of Muhammad al-Sadoq Bey's reign and focusing particularly on his brothers Muhammad al-Taher, Muhammad al-Amin and Muhammad al-Taieb.

60. Rousseau, *Annales*, 383–384.

61. CADN, Archives des Postes, 91, letter dated 18 December 1855.

62. See the letter from 20 June 1863, in CADN, Archives des Postes, Tunis, Consulat, 113.

63. BNF, Affaires d'Orient 1875–1877, Ministère des Affaires étrangères, France, Documents diplomatiques n. XII, Consul General Botmiliau to the Minister of Foreign Affairs, 6 July 1869.

64. CADN, Protectorats et Mandats, Protectorat Tunisie, 1st Series, 177, Letter 65 dated 19 May 1881. The consul of Sardinia similarly claimed that Husayn Bey "increasingly abandoned himself to uncontrolled luxuries," which could only be the ruin of the province, bringing "misery and disorder": Monchicourt, *Documents historiques*, 74.

65. William B. Cohen, "Gambettists and Colonial Expansion before 1881: The *République Française*," *French Colonial Studies* 1 (1977). Ganiage states that the French Consul Roustan intervened to put a stop to the articles because of nego-

tiations over a railway concession; see Ganiage, *Les origines du protectorat français*, 471–476.

66. *La republique française*, 18 December 1874 and 23 June 1875.

67. CADN, Archives des Postes, Tunis, Consulat, 113, letter dated 20 June 1863; he further details the debts of Taher, Taieb, and al-Amine in Letter 301.

68. Ahmed Abdesselem, *Les historiens tunisiens des XVIIe, XVIIIe et XIXe siècles: essai d'histoire culturelle* (Tunis: Publications de l'Université de Tunis, 1973).

69. Moncef Chenoufi, "Les deux séjours de Muhammad 'Abduh en Tunisie: et leurs incidences sur le réformisme musulman tunisien (6 décembre 1884–4 janvier 1885 et 9–24 septembre 1903)," *Les Cahiers de Tunisie* 12 (1968); Green, *The Tunisian Ulama*, 147–148.

70. On the influence of Tahtawi, see Ahmed Jdey, *Ahmed Ibn Abi Dhiaf son oeuvre et sa pensée: essai d'histoire culturelle* (Zaghouan: Publications de la Fondation Temimi, 1996); Béchir Tlili, *Etudes d'histoire sociale tunisienne du XIXe siecle* (Tunis: Publications de l'Université de Tunis, 1974). Ibn Abi Diyaf, *Min rasa'il ibn abi al-Diyaf*, 16; Ahmad Ibn Abi Diyaf, *Consult Them in the Matter: A Nineteenth-Century Islamic Agrument for Constitutional Goverment*, trans. L. Carl Brown (Fayetteville: University of Arkansas Press, 2005), 90.

71. Ibn Abi Diyaf, *Min rasa'il ibn abi al-Diyaf*, 16; Ibn Abi Diyaf, *Consult Them in the Matter*, 77.

72. Ibn Abi Diyaf, *Ithaf ahl al-zaman*, vol. 4, 44.

73. Ibid., 28–29.

74. Ibid., 33, 35.

75. Ibid., 42–44.

76. Ibn Abi Diyaf, *Consult Them in the Matter*, 57.

77. Ibid., 76, 99–100.

78. Marsans-Sakly, "The Revolt of 1864."

79. Hourani, *Arabic Thought in the Liberal Age, 1789–1939*, 87–95.

80. Much of his biographical information is taken from his memoir: Mzali and Pignon, eds., *Khérédine homme d'état*.

81. See, for instance, the notes regarding his intentions from 19 December 1864 and 6 January 1865, in BNF, Documents diplomatiques, Affaires étrangères, and again on 20 November 1871, in CADN, Archives des Postes, Tunis, Consulat, 113.

82. This was reprinted in Arabic in 1876 and in a Turkish translation in 1878.

83. Khayr ed-Din al-Tunisi and Magali Morsy, *Essai sur les réformes nécessaires aux états musulmans* (Aix-en-Provence: Edisud, 1987), 144, 87, 101, 112 respectively.

84. Ibid., 122, 128, 129, 133, 140.

85. Ibid., 90.

86. Ibid., 95; Mzali and Pignon, eds., *Khérédine homme d'état*, 31.

87. Mzali and Pignon, eds., *Khérédine homme d'état*, 40.

88. Ibid., 26–27.

89. Ibid., 19.

90. Ibid., 36–37.

91. Ibid., 23, 29.

92. Ibid., 32–37.

93. Ibid., 251.

94. These episodes are detailed in Ibn Abi Diyaf, *Ithaf ahl al-zaman*, vol. 4, 19–20, 24–28, 65–70.

95. CADN 91, letter dated 18 December 1855.

96. He brought an artisan from Istanbul to make these dishes: Ibn Yusuf, *Chronique tunisienne*, 241, 387.

97. The link between financial disorder and the weakness or decline of the Ottoman Empire has also been rejected: Darling, *Revenue-Raising and Legitimacy*.

98. Issawi, *An Economic History*, 24.

99. His memoirs were dedicated to his children. Brown, *The Tunisia of Ahmad Bey*, 222; Mzali and Pignon, eds., *Khérédine homme d'état*, 256.

100. Oualdi, *Esclaves et maîtres*, 237–275.

101. This was certainly true for the Khedives of Egypt: Kenneth M. Cuno, "Ambiguous Modernization: The Transition to Monogamy in the Khedival House of Egypt," in *Family History in the Middle East: Household, Property and Gender*, ed. Beshara Doumani (Albany: State University of New York Press, 2003).

102. The quote is from Hesse-Wartegg, who borrows liberally from Lubomirski: Hesse-Wartegg, *Tunis*, 93; Josef Lubomirski, *La côte barbaresque et le Sahara, excursion dans le vieux monde* (Paris: E. Dentu, 1880), 64.

103. *The Farmer's Cabinet*, 26 October 1865, page 1.

104. On the politicization of marriage, see also Pollard, *Nurturing the Nation*; Hanan Kholoussy, *For Better, for Worse: The Marriage Crisis That Made Modern Egypt* (Stanford, CA: Stanford University Press, 2010).

CHAPTER 6

1. Observations about the sultan's response from 14 and 17 May and 6 June 1881 and the telegram from Tripoli on 28 May 1881 in CADN, Protectorat-Tunisie, 1st Series, Carton 875. See also the note from 20 May 1881 in Carton 177, the police report on 28 March 1894 in Carton 1217, and the intelligence information dated 18 January 1882 in Carton 194.

2. See Maurice Bompard, *Législation de la Tunisie: Receuil des lois, décrets et règlements en vigueur dans la Régence de Tunis au 1er Janvier 1888* (Paris: Ernest Leroux, 1888), 399–402.

3. The bey was responsible for collecting a war tax imposed on the tribes near the western border; the full text of the treaty is in CADN, Protectorat-Tunisie, 1st Series, Carton 875, in an envelope labeled "Exécution du traité du 12 mai 1881."

4. William H. Schneider, *An Empire for the Masses: The French Popular Image of Africa, 1870–1900* (Westport: Greenwood Press, 1982).

5. On the cultural rationalization and celebration of colonialism, see Todd B.

Porterfield, *The Allure of Empire: Art in the Service of French Imperialism, 1798–1836* (Princeton, NJ: Princeton University Press, 1998); Edward W. Said, *Culture and Imperialism* (New York: Vintage Books, 1993).

6. Uday S. Mehta, "Liberal Strategies of Exclusion," in *Tensions of Empire: Colonial Cultures in a Bourgeois World*, ed. Frederick Cooper and Ann Laura Stoler (Berkeley: University of California Press, 1997). On colonialism in French national identity, see Herman Lebovics, *True France: the Wars over Cultural Identity, 1900–1945* (Ithaca, NY: Cornell University Press, 1992).

7. On how these imperial rivalries played out over jurisdiction, see Mary Dewhurst Lewis, "Geographies of Power: The Tunisian Civic Order, Jurisdictional Politics, and Imperial Rivalry in the Mediterranean, 1881–1935," *The Journal of Modern Political History* 80, no. 4 (December 2008).

8. Scholars of colonialism have long argued for the necessity of viewing relations between the colony and the metropole as a collaborative process; see, for instance, Cooper and Stoler (eds.), *Tensions of Empire*.

9. On the family model within French revolutionary political discourse, see Hunt, *The Family Romance*.

10. Hunt, "The Many Bodies of Marie Antoinette." Targeting royal women and the king's consorts by suggesting that women's political activities were a sign of a weakened monarch, however, had its eighteenth-century precedents; see Sarah C. Maza, *Private Lives and Public Affairs: The Causes Célèbres of Prerevolutionary France* (Berkeley: University of California Press, 1993).

11. Margaret H. Darrow, *Revolution in the House: Family, Class, and Inheritance in Southern France, 1775–1825* (Princeton, NJ: Princeton University Press, 1989). The emphasis on fraternal equality often implied the exclusion of women from public life, as argued by Carla Hesse, *The Other Enlightenment: How French Women Became Modern* (Princeton, NJ: Princeton University Press, 2001).

12. Jo Burr Margadant, "The Duchesse de Barry and Royalist Political Culture in Postrevolutionary France," *History Workshop Journal* 43 (1997).

13. Jo Burr Margadant, "The Perils of the Sentimental Family for Royalty in Postrevolutionary France: The Case of Queen Marie-Amélie," in *Servants of the Dynasty: Palace Women in World History*, ed. Anne Walthall (Berkeley: University of California Press, 2008), 314–315.

14. On the conflicting symbolism of Louis-Philippe and the Queen in relation to gender roles, see Jo Burr Margadant, "Gender, Vice, and the Political Imaginary in Postrevolutionary France: Reinterpreting the Failure of the July Monarchy, 1830–1848," *American Historical Review* 104, no. 5 (1999); Sandy Petrey, "Pears in History," *Representations* 35 (1991).

15. Maza, *Private Lives and Public Affairs*, 169; Porterfield, *The Allure of Empire*.

16. Jean Elisabeth Pedersen, *Legislating the French Family: Feminism, Theater, and Republican Politics, 1870–1920* (New Brunswick, NJ: Rutgers University Press, 2003), 31–32.

17. The quote is from Jean-Marie Roulin, "Mothers in Revolution: Political

Representations of Maternity in Nineteenth-Century France," *Yale French Studies* 101 (2001): 200. See also Maurice Agulhon, "Politics, Images, and Symbols in Post-Revolutionary France," in *Rites of Power: Symbolism, Ritual and Politics Since the Middle Ages*, ed. Sean Wilentz (Philadelphia: University of Pennsylvania Press, 1985).

18. See the 1827 letters quoted in Plantet, ed., *Correspondance des beys*, vol. 3, 646.

19. Whereas Planel views him as a neutral diplomat and supporter of reforms, Clancy-Smith describes him as a double agent, Clancy-Smith, *Mediterraneans*, 54; Planel, "De la nation à la colonie," 203–205.

20. CADN 91, Dépêches confidentielles, 18 December 1855.

21. Direction des Affaires Politiques et Commerciale, 17 October 1860, in CADN, Protectorat-Tunisie, 1st Series, Carton 875, Letter 47.

22. Ibid.

23. See Drouyn de Lhuys, minister of foreign affairs, *Affaires Etrangères, France*. Bibliothèque Nationale de France (BNF), letter dated 13 May 1864 and his letter from 19 December 1864.

24. Marquis de la Valette, minister of foreign affairs, 24 June 1869, in BNF, Affaires d'Orient 1875–1877, Ministère des Affaires étrangères, France, Documents diplomatiques n. XII.

25. Ibid.

26. See his letters dated 25 January and 28 February 1879: Husayn and Ahmad 'Abd al-Salam, *Ras'ail Husayn ila Khayr al-Din* (Qarthaj: al-Mu'assasah al-Wataniyah lil-Tarjamah wa-al-Tahqiq wa-al-Dirasat, Bayt al-Hikmah, 1991), 13 and 16.

27. Ibid., 35–36.

28. CADN, Protectorat-Tunisie, 1st Series, Carton 177.

29. See Letter 103 from the Direction politique, dated 16 May 1881: CADN, Protectorat-Tunisie, 1st Series, Carton 875.

30. Minister of Foreign Affairs, 18 May 1881 in CADN, Protectorats et Mandats, Protectorat-Tunisie, 1st Series, 177.

31. Jules Ferry, *Les affaires de Tunisie: discours de M. Jules Ferry*, preface and notes by M. Alfred Rambaud, ed. (Paris: Imprimerie Gauthier-Villars, 1882), 109.

32. The first mention of this is in Dispatch 125 on 7 October 1882, where it is remarked that "the health of H[is] H[ighness] the Bey is far from satisfactory and has provoked a certain amount of concern among his entourage": CADN, Protectorat-Tunisie, 1st Series, 194.

33. CADN, Protectorat-Tunisie, 1st Series, 194, dispatch dated 18 January 1882.

34. See also the confidential dispatch dated 20 October 1882: CADN, Protectorat-Tunisie, 1st Series, 194, no. 134, and the copies of these in TNA Series F, 1/1/1 Documents 1–5.

35. He served in French Tunisia and later Madagascar: Bompard, *Législation de la Tunisie*, xii.

36. Ibid., xvi.

37. Allan Christelow, *Muslim Law Courts and the French Colonial State in Algeria* (Princeton, NJ: Princeton University Press, 1985). The implications for Tunisia's disparate European populations was equally complex; Lewis, "Geographies of Power."

38. The frequent codification (if not formulation) of tribal laws and Islamic law as distinct from the legal system applied to colonial settlers was a feature of French rule in Algeria and Tunisia and of British rule in Egypt; it was common across the African continent. See Mahmood Mamdani, *Citizen and Subject: Contemporary Africa and the Legacy of Late Colonialism* (Princeton, NJ: Princeton University Press, 1996); Nathan J. Brown, "Law and Imperialism."

39. Dana S. Hale, *Races on Display: French Representations of Colonized Peoples 1886–1940* (Bloomington: Indiana University Press, 2008).

40. Mehta, "Liberal Strategies of Exclusion."

41. David Cannadine, "The Context, Performance and Meaning of Ritual: The British Monarchy and the 'Invention of Tradition,' c. 1820–1977," in *The Invention of Tradition*, ed. Eric J. Hobsbawm and T. O. Ranger (New York: Cambridge University Press, 1983); David Cannadine, *Ornamentalism: How the British Saw Their Empire* (Oxford: Oxford University Press, 2001).

42. Bernard S. Cohn, "Representing Authority in Victorian England," in *The Invention of Tradition*, ed. E. J. Hobsbawm and T. O. Ranger (New York: Cambridge University Press, 1983).

43. This too was removed a few years later when the coins were minted in Paris and based on the French franc: Hugon, *Les emblèmes*, 34–36.

44. The decree appears in an annex of Mohammed el Aziz Ben Achour, ed., *La cour du bey de Tunis* (Tunis: Espace Diwan, 2003), 92–94.

45. See the note dated 20 October 1934, TNA G Series, Subseries SG2, 65/3.

46. Ben Achour, ed., *La cour du bey de Tunis*, 34.

47. Sudhir Hazareesingh, "'A Common Sentiment of National Glory': Civic Festivities and French Collective Sentiment under the Second Empire," *Journal of Modern History* 76, no. 2 (2004).

48. George L. Mosse, "Caesarism, Circuses, and Monuments," *Journal of Contemporary History* 6, no. 2 (1971).

49. Pascal Blanchard, Nicolas Bancel, and Sandrine Lemaire, "Les zoos humains: passage d'un 'racisme scientifique' vers un racisme populaire et colonial en Occident," in *Zoos Humains: XIXe et XXe siècle*, ed. Nicolas Bancel et al. (Paris: La Découverte, 2002).

50. See, for example, Zeynep Celik, *Displaying the Orient: Architecture of Islam at Nineteenth-Century World's Fairs* (Berkeley: University of California Press, 1992); Zeynep Celik and Leila Kinney, "Ethnography and Exhibitionism at the

Expositions Universelles," *Assemblage* 13 (1990); Charles Rearick, "Festivals in Modern France: The Experience of the Third Republic," *Journal of Contemporary History* 12, no. 3 (1977).

51. Great Exhibition and Commissioners for the Exhibition of Great Britain, *Official catalogue of the Great Exhibition of the Industry of All Nations, 1851* (London: Spicer Bros., 1851), 308–310.

52. "The Tunis Court," 31 May 1851, 493–494; "Costume as Portrayed at the Exhibition," 14 June 1851, 564–565; and "Egypt and Tunis," 15 July 1851, 22–23, in *The Illustrated London News*. This organization was similar to the Ottoman exhibit sponsored by Sultan Abd al-Mejid: see Gülname Turan, "Turkey in the Great Exhibition of 1851," *Design Issues* 25, no. 1 (2009).

53. "Paris Universal Exhibition" supplement, 11 May 1867, 470 and 477, and "The Paris Universal Exhibition," 8 June 1867, *The Illustrated London News*.

54. As the French minister of foreign affairs insisted to the Resident General Massicault, "I must remind you that protectorate countries must utilize their own resources for the exposition"; see CADN, Protectorat-Tunisia, 1st Series, 1380A, letter dated 27 January 1887, and later confirmation in 203/05, letter dated 31 May 1889.

55. *Comité d'organisation de l'exposition, process-verbaux,* 1877 in CADN 205/05.

56. *Journal Officiel de la République Française,* 22 May 1889; Lebovics, *True France,* 51.

57. Alfred Picard, *Exposition universelle internationale de 1900 à Paris rapport général administratif et technique* (Paris: Imprimerie nationale, 1902), vol. 4, 328.

58. Saladin, *Tunis et Kairouan.*

59. In many ways creating the "architecture of Islam": Celik, *Displaying the Orient,* 2.

60. Ibn Abi Diyaf, *Ithaf ahl al-zaman,* vol. 4, 30–32.

61. This was a modified version of imperial protocol: ibid., 60–62.

62. CADN, Protectorats, Protectorat-Tunisie, 1st Series, 194, note 160 from the Direction politique dated 29 July 1881.

63. See the articles from *Corriere di Napoli* on 26 May 1890, *L'Unione* on 22 May 1890, and *Courrier Naples* on 19 May 1890, and in the Direction politique Memo 612, 5 August 1891 (also reported in a number of newspapers, including *Daily News* and *El Hadira*) in CADN, Protectorats, Protectorat-Tunisie, 1st Series, 1437.

64. See, for instance, the invitations for numerous foreign powers such as Germany, Greece, and Russia: 3 August 1889 and October 1890, and the note regarding the military cortege: 9 June 1888. Official parade protocols were outlined in Article 6 of the Decree of 24 June 1886. On the specifics of this for Mawlid, see the notes for 14 November 1888 and 4 November 1889: CADN, Protectorats, Protectorat-Tunisie, 1st Series, 1437.

65. These events were subsequently reported in the Arabic and French editions of the official newspaper (*Al-Ra'id* and the *Journal Officiel Tunisien [JOT]*), 1 January 1885. Early accounts of such sorties for Laylat al-qadr and Mawlid, as well as

the reception of visitors at the palace for both ʿid, can be found on 9 August 1883, 10 January 1884, 26 July 1884, 1 January 1885, 9 and 16 July 1885, 1 October 1885, and 24 December 1885.

66. CADN Protectorats, Protectorat-Tunisie, 1st Series, 194, Direction Politique note 35, 6 February 1882.

67. CADN Protectorats, Protectorat-Tunisie, 1st Series, 1437, undated note titled "Le Baïram."

68. The bey and the "princes" in the family attended these; see JOT: 17 July 1884.

69. JOT: 1 November 1882 and Ben Achour, ed., *La cour du bey de Tunis*, 13–15.

70. This is mentioned in a lengthy memo prepared by the Resident General in the 1940s on "investiture protocols": CADN, Protectorat-Tunisia, 1st Series, 60.

71. Ben Achour, ed., *La cour du bey de Tunis*, 46–49.

72. Ibid., 21–23. Said Mestri, *Moncef Bey* (Tunis: ArcsEditions, 1988).

73. See the report 19 April 1894 in CADN, Protectorat-Tunisie, 1st Series, 891 B.

74. Or *darba fi tunis* became *sabarna fi tunis*: Hugon, *Les emblèmes*, 24.

75. Revault, *Palais et résidences d'été*, 311–314.

76. TNA F Series 3/1/1/2.

77. The text of this agreement is in CADN, Protectorat-Tunisie, 1st Series, Carton 1217, and was reprinted in JOT on 9 August 1883. See also the relevant documents in TNA F Series 3/1/1/2 and 3/1/1/4 and 3/1/1/7.

78. See the discussion of these figures based on the palace receipts and expenditures for the three previous years, undated note, CADN, Protectorat-Tunisie, 1st Series, Carton 875.

79. Confidential letter from St. Hilaire to Roustan, No. 65, CADN, Protectorats, Protectorat-Tunisie, 1st Series, 177, Paris, 19 May 1881. See also the 6 August 1881 note that places the stipends of the bey and his family at the top of the list of expenses that could be cut.

80. Undated note, CADN, Protectorat-Tunisie, 1st Series, Carton 875.

81. The Tunisian prime minister served as the obligatory intermediary between the bey, his family, and the French government.

82. These were calculated at an initial sum of 273,600 piasters, which the minister of finances indicated could easily increase during the course of the fiscal year; see TNA F Series 3/1/1/4. A similar request was made that October: TNA F Series 3/1/1/3.

83. TNA F Series 3/1/1/2.

84. TNA F Series 3/1/1/7.

85. This policy is clarified in a footnote: Bompard, *Législation de la Tunisie*, 400.

86. "Note regarding the rules of succession to the Husseinite throne," dated 3 March 1939, CADN, Protectorat-Tunisia, 1st Series, 60.

87. Ibid., CADN, Protectorat-Tunisie, 1st Series, 60.

88. Ibid., CADN, Protectorat-Tunisie, 1st Series, 60.

89. CADN 1217, Protectorat-Tunisie, 1st Series, 1217, and TNA G Series, Subseries SG2, 65/3.

90. Ben Achour, ed., *La cour du bey de Tunis*, 50.

91. The original text does not indicate whether all these princesses were married or adults: ibid., 50–52.

92. Clancy-Smith, *Mediterraneans*, 303.

93. See TNA E Series 550, 30/15, 337, Document 6, a note from the state security agent sent to observe these meetings, dated 26 February 1914.

94. ʿAbd al-ʿAziz Thaʿalibi, *La tunisie martyre: ses revendications*, 2e éd. tirée de l'éd. originale de 1920. ed. (Beyrouth, Liban: Dar al-Gharb al-Islami, 1985).

95. Charles-André Julien, *L'Afrique du nord en marche: nationalismes musulmans et souveraineté française* (Tunis: Cérès Productions, 2001), 111–112.

96. Abdesselem Ben Hamida, *Le syndicalisme tunisien de la deuxième guerre mondiale à l'autonomie interne* (Tunis: Publications de l'Université de Tunis, 1989); Ahmed Ben Miled, *M'hamed Ali, la naissance du mouvement ouvrier Tunisien* (Tunis: Editions Salammbo, 1984); Mustapha Kraiem, *Le Parti Communiste Tunisien pendant la periode coloniale* (Tunis: Institut Supérieur d'Histoire du Mouvement National, 1997); Ilhem Marzouki, *Le Mouvement des femmes en Tunisie au XXe siècle* (Tunis: Cérès Productions, 1993).

97. Julien, *L'Afrique du nord en marche*, 144–145.

98. This is reported by Mestri, *Moncef Bey*, 63.

99. Alice J. Conklin, *A Mission to Civilize: The Republican Ideal of Empire in France and West Africa, 1895–1930* (Stanford, CA: Stanford University Press, 1997).

100. See Cohen, "Gambettists and Colonial Expansion."

101. Reinvented dynastic traditions included court protocol and clothing that dated to the late nineteenth century, a newly composed hymn, and a national flag featuring an Ottoman symbol never used in Morocco but seen by the French as Muslim. Louis Hubert Gonzalve Lyautey, "Politique musulmane: circulaire," *Lyautey l'africain: textes et lettres du maréchal Lyautey*, (Paris: Plon, 1953), quoted in Jonathan Wyrtzen, "Constructing Morocco: The Colonial Struggle to Define the Nation, 1912–1956" (PhD dissertation, Georgetown University, 2009), 62.

102. Elizabeth Thompson, *Colonial Citizens: Republican Rights, Paternal Privilege and Gender in French Syria and Lebanon* (Cambridge, MA: Harvard University Press, 2000), 39–40; Elizabeth Thompson, "Soldiers, Patriarchs, and Bureaucrats: Paternal Republicanism in French Syria and Lebanon," in *Representing Masculinity: Male Citizenship in Modern Western Culture*, ed. Stefan Dudink, Anna Clark, and Karen Hagemann (New York: Palgrave Macmillan, 2007).

103. In a fictionalized memoir set in the early twentieth century, one of the most influential woman in the palace, Lilla Qmar, makes sure to be seen receiving the British consul's wife, since she knew that this would be viewed as a political act by the French: Fayçal Bey, *La dernière odalisque* (Paris: Editions Stock, 2001), 173.

1. These criticisms are summarized in Nicolas Beau and Catherine Graciet, *Le régente de Carthage: main basse sur la Tunisie* (Paris: La Découverte, 2009).

2. The role of force should not be overstated, as the prevalence of corruption and at least nominal regime support led to economic benefits that possibly had a greater impact; Béatrice Hibou, *The Force of Obedience* (Cambridge: Polity Press, 2011).

3. Baron, *Egypt as a Woman*; Najmabadi, "Crafting an Educated Housewife in Iran"; Shakry, "Schooled Mothers and Structured Play."

4. Sanussi had a career in government administration under the bey and the French, though it was briefly interrupted by the French occupations when he went on a pilgrimage. He was a partisan of Afghani; see Green, *The Tunisian Ulama*, 147–154.

5. Muhammad al-Sanussi, *Epanouissement de la fleur, ou Etude sur la femme dans l'Islam*, trans. Mohammed Mohieddin Essenoussi and ʿAbd el Kader Kebaïli (Tunis: Imprimerie Rapide, 1897).

6. Ibid., 13. That women's interests should be secondary to national interests has been illustrated in numerous studies of anticolonial nationalism, many inspired by P. Chatterjee, *The Nation and Its Fragments*. The emphasis on masculinity: Booth, "*Women in Islam*"; Sinha, *Specters of Mother India*.

7. This is the framework used to explain why the Tunisian state successfully passed personal status laws and Morocco and Algeria did not: Mounira M. Charrad, *States and Women's Rights: the Making of Post-Colonial Tunisia, Algeria and Morocco* (Berkeley: University of California Press, 2001).

8. See Abu-Lughod, "Do Muslim Women Really Need Saving?"; Lila Abu-Lughod, "Dialects of Women's Empowerment: the International Circuitry of the *Arab Human Development Report 2005*," *International Journal of Middle East Studies* 41, no. 1 (2009): 89–90; and Fida J. Adely, "Educating Women for Development: The *Arab Human Development Report 2005* and the Problem with Women's Choices," *International Journal of Middle East Studies* 41, no. 1 (2009).

9. Blili Temime, *Histoire de familles*; Charrad, *States and Women's Rights*; Duben, "Turkish Families and Households in Historical Perspective"; Duben and Behar, *Istanbul Households*.

GLOSSARY

'alim (pl. *'ulama'*): Learned scholars, men of religion.

'aljia (pl. *'alaji*): A female slave raised in the palace, including those taken captive in maritime raids around the Mediterranean.

Bardo: An important palace dating to the Hafsid era, located in a small town a few miles from Tunis known by the same name. During much of the Ottoman era it was the political center and main residence of the ruling families.

bey: At the beginning of the seventeenth century this title referred to the commander of the troops who toured the province of Tunisia on the tax-collecting missions. This figure became increasingly important by the mid-seventeenth century during the tenure of Murad Bey, and by its end was the most authoritative position in the province. The title was adopted as a surname by the descendants of Husayn ibn 'Ali, with the feminine form of *beya* used for women.

bit al-muna. See *kummania*.

dar (pl. *diyar*): House, often used in the registers to refer to a domicile as well as to a man's wife.

dey: Literally meaning "maternal uncle" in Turkish, this was a category of officers among the military forces that conquered Tunis in 1574. After the soldiers revolted in 1591, one of the deys served on the military council. By virtue of control of the military corps in the capital, the dey was the preeminent authority in the province in the early seventeenth century, though he subsequently lost power to the bey. For much of the eighteenth and nineteenth centuries this title was largely honorific but was accompanied by a few administrative duties in the city of Tunis and limited judicial authority.

diwan: Military council established with the Ottoman conquest to create continuity in governance while the pasha was reappointed each year.

eyalat-i mumtaze: An Ottoman designation of privileged or favored status accorded to Tunis. The province was not required to pay tribute to the imperial treasury but instead participated in maritime warfare and was accorded a modicum of autonomy in relations with foreign powers.

fez: See *shashia*.

firman: An imperial decree or edict, the orders sent from the sultan.

haml: A unit of measure equivalent to the weight of a load carried by a camel, close to 246 kilograms, though with some variation depending on the product. See *qafiz*.

hanba (pl. *hawanib*): Units of guards often serving at the palace

ihsan: A good deed, used in reference to money distributed to dependents within the palace and members of the extended political network, a type of bonus.

jaria (pl. *juar*): Concubines, or white female slaves in the palace; word sometimes used interchangeably with *'alaji*.

khaznadar: Treasury, or treasurer.

khadem (pl. *khedam*): Literally meaning worker or employee; within the palace, *khedam* was most often used to refer to slaves.

kummania: A space used for storing provisions, also referred to as *bit al-muna*. The servant responsible for the *kummania* was the *kamanja*.

mahalla: Tax-collecting mission that toured the province twice each year.

mamluk: Generally, young boys who were brought to Tunis from the Caucasus as slaves who converted to Islam and were raised within the palace, filling a number of administrative and military functions.

m'amura: Inhabited, populous. *Bardo al-m'amura* was one of the epithets for the palace, indicating its prosperity and ability to support a large population.

manqalji: An employee at the palace who maintained clocks.

metar: Liquid measure used for olive oil, just over 20 liters.

mushir: Military rank roughly the equivalent of a marshal, first accorded to Ahmad Bey in 1840 upon his request.

pasha: Initially the rank of the provincial governor, named by the sultan for one year. By the seventeenth century, it was an honorary position, with the main responsibility of paying the soldiers; later one of the titles of the beys.

piaster: Basic unit of currency in accounting registers, called a *riyal* in Arabic, and broken down into 52 *nasr*.

qafiz: A dry measure used predominantly for grains of approximately 400 kilograms; can be divided into 16 *wiba* or 192 *sa'*.

qaftan: A full-length robe or cloak with sleeves. Made of different fabrics depending on the wealth of the individual, it could include brocade, gold and silver threads, and precious stones. The sultan sent a *qaftan* and *firman* of investiture to confirm the position of the bey in Tunis.

qahwaji: A salaried palace official responsible for matters pertaining to coffee storage, provisions, preparation, and serving, including dishware.

qa'id: The position of a district or town governor.

qazaq (pl. *qazqat*): Christian Europeans serving in the palace, probably ransomed slaves who chose not to return to their countries of origin.

qila: Just over 10 liters or 2.64 gallons; in the palace this measure was used frequently for clarified butter and honey.

qintar: Large unit of measure equaling about 50 kilograms or 100 *ratls*.

qubtan pasha: The admiral of the Ottoman fleet, a position often delegated to one of the sultan's representatives in Algeria who was senior to the beys of Tunis and Tripoli. He also served as an intermediary between these provinces and the sultan.

ratl: Unit of weight divided into *waqa*. The smallest, the *ratl 'attari*, was approximately 500 grams or one pound, consisting of 16 *waqa*, and used to measure spices and metals. The *ratl suqi* that consisted of 18 *waqa* was used for butter, honey, olives, soap, and nuts, and the *ratl khodri* of 20 *waqa* was used primarily for vegetables.

sa': Unit of capacity measuring between two liters for liquids and three liters for dry goods.

sadaqa: Personal charity distinct from obligatory alms or *zakat*.

shashia: Woolen caps manufactured in Tunis and exported across the Ottoman Empire constituting the most important sector in the province. Following the Tanzimat reforms, the *shashia*, or fez, became the official imperial headgear and formed part of the uniform of the *nizami jedid* troops in Tunis.

Sidna: A term of deference used in the archives to refer to the bey, literally meaning "our master" or "our lord."

sqifa: Entranceway. In wealthy homes these were often covered, and tiled, with benches lining the walls for receiving guests and conducting business.

subahi (pl. *subahiya*): Cavalry troops.

Sublime Porte (also Porte): Term used by Europeans to refer to the Ottoman state. It came from the Bab-i Humayun, or Imperial Gate, the main entrance to the Topkapi palace.

'ulama'. See *'alim*.

waqa: Unit of measure, approximately 32 grams.

waqf (pl. *awqaf*): The endowment of properties towards charitable ends.

warda roba: From the Italian for "wardrobe," this refers to individuals within the bey's private entourage probably responsible for his personal affairs.

wiba: Unit of measure; when used for grains equals roughly 25 to 27 kilograms, divided into *sa'*.

zlabia: A pastry made of fried dough dipped in honey, prepared especially during Ramadan.

zawiya (pl. *zawaya*): Shrines dedicated to holy figures. These places of worship often incorporated schools that also served a charitable function when they provided public meals.

BIBLIOGRAPHY

ARCHIVAL COLLECTIONS

Tunisian National Archives (TNA), Tunis, Tunisia

Historical Series (Carton/Dossier)
   1/1–6, 1/8–11, 1/13, 3/3–4, 3/33–35, 3/40–42; 59/653, 72/853, 77/894, 77/898, 78/908, 82/2, 82/4, 82/5, 92/77–80, 92/82, 96/136, 200/348, 205/65, 205/72– 78, 208/127, 209/139, 220/338, 220/340, 220/342, 220/343, 220/346, 220/349, 222/377, 223/400, 1030/184
F Series
   1/1/1, 3/1/1, 3/2, 3/3/1
G Series, Subseries SG2, Carton 65, Dossier 3
Defatir Series
   Annual Expense Registers
      83, 99, 175, 180, 184, 187, 192, 201, 209, 214, 216, 220, 224, 229, 233, 239, 243, 246, 247, 251, 260, 266, 270, 273, 279, 289, 295, 300, 308, 312, 321, 327, 330, 335, 341, 344, 358, 360, 371, 376, 385, 388, 402, 406, 415, 421, 425, 430/4, 436/4, 437, 440/2, 441/2, 442/2, 444/2, 448/2, 451/2, 453/2, 463/2, 470/2
   Income and Expenditures of the Different Beys
      385, 395, 403, 411, 427, 438, 444, 449, 450, 456, 468, 472, 479, 482, 483, 491, 495, 504, 507, 512, 552, 581
   Miscellaneous Registers of the Financial Administration
      1, 2, 28, 30, 85, 94, 101, 111, 211, 221, 229/2, 261, 275, 276, 286, 294, 317, 331, 346, 361, 405, 424, 443, 445, 456, 2143, 2144, 2145, 2155, 2249/2, 2250, 2254, 2276, 2277, 2320, 2321, 2483/2, 2505

Ministry of State Domains Archives, Tunis, Tunisia

Boxes 30, 33, 34, 39, 40, 70, 447

Higher Institute for the History of the
Nationalist Movement, Manouba, Tunisia

Archives of the French Foreign Ministry, Minister of Foreign Relations, Political
Correspondence, Dossier 1, Number 3; New Series on Tunisia, Beylical Family
Roll 116, NS 1

Turba al-bey Museum and Family Mausoleum, Tunis, Tunisia

Center of Diplomatic Archives (CADN), Nantes, France

Archives des Postes
    Constantinople, Embassy: D Series, 2
    Le Caire, Embassy: 20, 467
    Tripoli de Barbarie, Consulate: 104
    Tunis, Consulate: 74, 85, 86, 91, 97, 98, 113–116, 145, 187, 189, 301, 329, 340, 368
Protectorates and Mandates, Tunisia, 1st Series
    32, 60, 62, 133, 177, 188, 194, 202–204, 865B, 875, 884A, 884B, 891B, 956, 1158,
    1168, 1216, 1217, 1380A, 1380C, 1437

PRIMARY SOURCES

Arabic and Tunisian

Husayn, General and Ahmad 'Abd al-Salam. *Ra*s'*ail Husayn ila Khayr al-Din*, vol.
    2. [Letters from General Husayn to Khayr al-Din.] Qarthaj: al-Mu'assasah
    al-Wataniyah lil-Tarjamah wa-al-Tahqiq wa-al-Dirasat, Bayt al-Hikmah, 1991.
Ibn Abi Diyaf, Ahmad. *Min rasa'il ibn abi al-Diyaf.* [From the Letters of ibn al-
    Diyaf.] Edited by Mohammed al-Salah al-Mzali. Tunis: al-Dar al-Tunisiya al-
    Nashr, 1969.
———. *Ithaf ahl al-zaman bi akhbar muluk Tunis wa ahd al-aman*, 8 vols. [Present-
    ing contemporaries the history of the rulers of Tunis and the Fundamental
    Pact.] Edited by Ahmed 'Abd al-Salam. Tunis: Publications de l'Université de
    Tunis, 1971.
———. *Consult Them in the Matter: A Nineteenth-Century Islamic Argument for*
    Constitutional Government. Translated by L. Carl Brown. Fayetteville: Univer-
    sity of Arkansas Press, 2005.
Ibn Yusuf, Muhammad Saghir. *Al-Mashr'a al-mulki fi sultanat awlad 'Ali Turki.*
    [The path of kings in the state of 'Ali al-Turki's sons.] Edited by Ahmed al-
    Twili. Tunis: al-Matb'ah al-'Asriya, 1998.
———. *Mechra el melki, chronique tunisienne (1705–1771) pour servir à l'histoire des*
    quatres premiers beys de la famille Husseinite. Translated by Mohammed Lasram
    and Victor Serres. Tunis: Editions Bouslama, 1978 [1900].
Khayr al-Din. *The Surest Path: The Political Treatise of a Nineteenth-Century Muslim*

Statesman: A Translation of the Introduction to the Surest Path to Knowledge Concerning the Condition of Countries by Khayr al-Din al-Tunsi. Translated by L. Carl Brown. Cambridge, MA: Harvard University Press, 1967.

Mzali, Mohammed Salah, and Jean Pignon, eds. *Khérédine homme d'état: memoires*. Tunis: Maison Tunisienne de l'Edition, 1971.

al-Sanussi, Muhammad. *Epanouissement de la fleur, ou Etude sur la femme dans l'Islam*. Translated by Mohammed Mohieddin Essenoussi and Abd el Kader Kebaïli. Tunis: Imprimerie Rapide, 1897.

al-Tunisi, Khayr al-Din, and Magali Morsy. *Essai sur les réformes nécessaires aux états musulmans*. Aix-en-Provence: Edisud, 1987.

Published Government Documents

Bompard, Maurice. *Législation de la Tunisie: receuil des lois, décrets et règlements en vigeur dans la régence de Tunis au 1er janvier 1888*. Paris: Ernest Leroux, 1888.

Ferry, Jules. *Les affaires de Tunisie: discours de M. Jules Ferry*. Preface and notes by M. Alfred Rambaud ed. Paris: Imprimerie Gauthier-Villars, 1882.

Great Exhibition, and Commissioners for the Exhibition of Great Britain. *Official Catalogue of the Great Exhibition of the Industry of All Nations, 1851*. London: Spicer Bros., 1851.

Picard, Alfred. *Exposition universelle internationale de 1900 à Paris rapport général administratif et technique*. Paris: Imprimerie nationale, 1902.

Plantet, Eugene, ed. *Correspondance des beys de Tunis et des consuls de France avec la cour, 1577–1830*. 3 vols. Paris: Félix Alcan, 1899.

Travel Accounts

Begouen, Vicomte. "La Condamine; Tunis, le Bardo, Carthage." *Revue tunisienne* 5 (1898): 71–94.

Béranger, Nicolas. *La régence de Tunis à la fin du XVIIe siècle: mémoire pour servir à l'histoire de Tunis depuis l'année 1684*. Introduction and notes by Paul Sebag, ed. Paris: Editions L'Harmattan, 1993.

Brunschvig, Robert, Abd-Al-Basit Ibn Halil, and Anselme Adorne. *Deux récits de voyage inédits en Afrique du Nord au XVe siècle*. Paris: Larose, 1936.

Davis, N. *Evenings in My Tent; or, Wanderings in Balad Ejjareed. Illustrating the Moral, Religious, Social, and Political Conditions of Various Arab Tribes of the African Sahara*. 2 vols. London: A. Hall, Virtue, & Co., 1854.

Dunant, Henry. *Notice sur la régence de Tunis*. Tunis: Société Tunisienne de Diffusion, [1858] 1975.

Frank, Louis, and J. J. Marcel. *Histoire de Tunis précédée d'une description de cette régence par le Dr. Louis Frank*. Tunis: Editions Bouslama, [1816] 1979.

Hesse-Wartegg, Ernst von. *Tunis: The Land and the People*. New York: Dodd and Mead, 1882.

Kennedy, John Clark. *Algeria and Tunis in 1845.* London: H. Colburn, 1846.

Lallemand, Charles. *Tunis et ses environs: texte et dessins d'après nature.* Paris: Maison Quantin, 1890.

Latour, Antoine de. *Voyage de S. A. R. monseigneur le duc de Montpensier à Tunis, en Égypte, en Turquie et en Grèce: Lettres.* Paris: Arthus Bertrand, 1847.

Lubomirski, Josef. *La côte barbaresque et le Sahara, excursion dans le vieux monde.* Paris: E. Dentu, 1880.

MacGill, Thomas. *An Account of Tunis, of Its Government, Manners, Customs, and Antiquities, Especially of Its Productions, Manufacturers and Commerce.* Glasgow: J. Hedderwick & Co., 1811.

Monchicourt, Charles. *Documents historiques sur la Tunisie, relations inédites de Nyssen, Filippi et Calligaris (1788, 1829, 1834).* Paris: Société d'Éditions Géographiques, Maritimes et Coloniales, 1929.

Noah, Mordecai M. *Travels in England, France, Spain, and the Barbary States, in the Years 1813-14 and 15.* New York: Kirk and Mercein, 1819.

Perry, Amos. *Carthage and Tunis, Past and Present: In Two Parts.* Providence, RI: Providence Press Company Printers, 1869.

Peyssonel, Jean-André. *Voyage dans les régences de Tunis et d'Alger.* Paris: La Découverte, 1987.

Pückler-Muskau, Hermann von. *Semilasso in Afrika.* Stuttgart: Hallberger, 1836.

———. *Chroniques, lettres et journal de voyage, extraits des papiers d'un défunt.* Paris: Libraries de Fournier Jeune, 1837.

Rousseau, Alphonse. *Les annales tunisiennes.* Tunis: Editions Bouslama, 1983.

Saladin, Henri. *Tunis et Kairouan.* Paris: H. Laurens, 1908.

Shaw, Thomas. *Observations Relating to Several Parts of Barbary and the Levant.* Frankfurt: Publications of the Institute for the History of Arabic-Islamic Sciences, [1738] 1995.

Temple, Grenville T. *Excursions in the Mediterranean: Algiers and Tunis.* London: Saunders and Otley, 1835.

Secondary Sources

'Abd al-Wahhab, Hasan Husni. *Khulasat Tarikh Tunis.* [A summary of the history of Tunisia.] Hammadi al-Sahli, ed. Tunis: Dar al-Jenub lil-Nashr, 2001.

Abou-el-Haj, Rifa'at. "An Agenda for Research in History: The History of Libya between the Sixteenth and Nineteenth Centuries." *International Journal of Middle East Studies* 15, no. 3 (1983): 305-319.

———. "Aspects of the Legitimation of Ottoman Rule as Reflected in the Preambles to Two Early *Liva Kanunameler.*" *Turcica, Revue d'études turques* XXI-XXIII (1991): 371-383.

———. "The Ottoman Vezir and Pasa Households 1683-1703: A Preliminary Report." *Journal of the American Oriental Society* 94, no. 4 (1974): 438-447.

Abou-Hodeib, Toufoul. "Taste and Class in Late Ottoman Beirut." *International Journal of Middle East Studies* 43, no. 3 (2011): 475–492.

Abu-Lughod, Lila. "Dialects of Women's Empowerment: The International Circuitry of the *Arab Human Development Report 2005*." *International Journal of Middle East Studies* 41, no. 1 (2009): 83–103.

———. "Do Muslim Women Really Need Saving? Anthropological Reflections on Cultural Relativism and Its Other . . ." *American Anthropologist* 104, no. 3 (2002): 783–790.

Abun-Nasr, Jamil M. "The Beylicate in Seventeenth-Century Tunisia." *International Journal of Middle East Studies* 6 (1975): 70–93.

———. *A History of the Maghrib in the Islamic Period*. Cambridge: Cambridge University Press, 1987.

Abdesselem, Ahmed. *Les historiens tunisiens des XVIIe, XVIIIe et XIXe siècles: essai d'histoire culturelle*. Tunis: Publications de l'Université de Tunis, 1973.

Adely, Fida J. "Educating Women for Development: The *Arab Human Development Report 2005* and the Problem with Women's Choices." *International Journal of Middle East Studies* 41, no. 1 (2009): 105–122.

Agulhon, Maurice. "Politics, Images, and Symbols in Post-Revolutionary France." In *Rites of Power: Symbolism, Ritual and Politics since the Middle Ages*, edited by Sean Wilentz, 177–205. Philadelphia: University of Pennsylvania Press, 1985.

Allen, Emily. "Culinary Exhibition: Victorian Wedding Cakes and Royal Spectacle." *Victorian Studies* 45, no. 3 (2003): 457–484.

Amanat, Abbas. *Pivot of the Universe: Nasir Al-Din Shah Qajar and the Iranian Monarchy, 1831–1896*. Berkeley: University of California Press, 1997.

Anderson, Lisa. "Nineteenth-Century Reform in Ottoman Libya." *International Journal of Middle East Studies* 16, no. 3 (1984): 325–348.

Appadurai, Arjun. "How to Make a National Cuisine: Cookbooks in Contemporary India." *Comparative Studies in Society and History* 30, no. 1 (1988): 3–24.

———. "Introduction: Commodities and the Politics of Value." In *The Social Life of Things: Commodities in Cultural Perspective*, edited by Arjun Appadurai, 3–63. Cambridge: Cambridge University Press, 1986.

Arberry, Arthur John, Charles Perry, and Maxime Rodinson. *Medieval Arab Cookery = Al-tabikh al-ʿarabi fi al-ʿusur al-wusta*. Devon, England: Prospect Books, 2006.

Artan, Tulay. "Ahmed I's Hunting Parties: Feasting in Adversity, Enhancing the Ordinary." In *Starting with Food: Culinary Approaches to Ottoman History*, edited by Amy Singer, 93–138. Princeton, NJ: Markus Weiner Publishers, 2011.

———. "Aspects of the Ottoman Elite's Food Consumption: Looking for 'Staples,' 'Luxuries,' and 'Delicacies,' in a Changing Century." In *Consumption Studies and the History of the Ottoman Empire, 1550–1992: An Introduction*, edited by Donald Quataert, 107–200. Albany: State University of New York Press, 2000.

Asad, Talal. *Formations of the Secular: Christianity, Islam, Modernity*. Stanford, CA: Stanford University Press, 2003.

Auslander, Leora. *Taste and Power: Furnishing Modern France*. Berkeley: University of California Press, 1996.

Babaie, Sussan. *Isfahan and Its Palaces: Statecraft, Shi'ism and the Architecture of Conviviality in Early Modern Iran*. Edinburgh: Edinburgh University Press, 2008.

Bachrouch, Taoufik. *Formation sociale barbaresque et pouvoir à Tunis au XVIIe siècle*. Tunis: Université de Tunis, 1977.

Baïram, Alia. "Le Bit-El-Mùna ou chambre à provision dans l'habitation traditionnelle à Tunis." *Cahiers des arts et traditions populaires* 7 (1980): 47–58.

Baron, Beth. *Egypt as a Woman: Nationalism, Gender, and Politics*. Berkeley: University of California Press, 2005.

Bates, Ulku U. "Women as Patrons of Architecture in Turkey." In *Women in the Muslim World*, edited by Lois Beck and Nikki R. Keddie, 245–260. Cambridge: Cambridge University Press, 1978.

Beau, Nicolas, and Catherine Graciet. *Le régente de Carthage: main basse sur la Tunisie*. Paris: La Découverte, 2009.

Belkhuja, M'hamed. "Cobbat Mamia." *Revue tunisienne* 26, no. 131 (1919): 163–173.

Ben Achour, Mohammed el Aziz. *Catégories de la société tunisoise dans la deuxième motié du XIXe siècle*. Tunis: Institut Nationale d'Archeologie et d'Art, 1989.

———. "Une famille et sa demeure dans la Medina de Tunis: Dar al-Jalluli (XVIIIe–XXe siècles)." In *L'habitat traditionnel dans les pays musulmans autour de la Méditerranée*, edited by Groupe de recherches et d'études sur le Proche-Orient, 569–598. Le Caire: Institut Francais d'archéologie orientale, 1988.

———. "Al-moassisat al-siyasiya fi 'ahd al-dawla al-Husseiniya (Al-qarnin al-thamin ashr wa al-tisa' ashr)." [The political foundations in the era of the Husaynite state (eighteenth and nineteenth centuries).] *al-Majalla al-tarikhiya al-'arabiya lil-diraset al-'athmaniya* 5–6 (1992): 11–20.

———, ed. "Les 'a'ilat du corpus: notes historiques." In *Hasab wa Nasab: parenté, alliance et patrimoine en Tunisie*, edited by Sophie Ferchiou, 107–136. Paris: Editions CNRS, 1992.

———. *La cour du bey de Tunis*. Tunis: Espace Diwan, 2003.

———. "'Tourbet El Bey' sépulture des deys et de la famille Husaynite à Tunis." *IBLA* 48, no. 155 (1985): 45–84.

Ben Hamida, Abdesselem. *Le syndicalisme tunisien de la deuxième guerre mondiale à l'autonomie interne*. Tunis: Publications de l'Université de Tunis, 1989.

Ben Mami, Mohamed Beji. "Le Dar Rassa'a à Tunis." In *L'habitat traditionnel dans les pays musulmans autour de la Méditerranée*, edited by Groupe de recherches et d'études sur le Proche-Orient, 79–102. Le Caire: Institut Francais d'archéologie orientale, 1988.

Ben Miled, Ahmed. *M'hamed Ali, la Naissance du Mouvement Ouvrier Tunisien*. Tunis: Editions Salammbo, 1984.

Ben Miled, Emna. "'Aicha el Manoubiyya: une tunisienne Libre." *Quaderns de la Mediterrània* 12 (2009): 71–81.

Ben Salem, Lilia. "Introduction à l'analyse de la parenté et de l'alliance dans les sociétés arabo-musulmanes." In *Hasab wa Nasab: Parenté, alliance et patrimoine en Tunisie*, edited by Sophie Ferchiou, 79–104. Paris: Editions du CNRS, 1992.

———. "Structures familiales et changement social en Tunisie." *Revue tunisienne de science sociales* 27, no. 100 (1990): 165–180.

Bennison, Amira K. "The "New Order" and Islamic Order: The Introduction of the *Nizami* Army in the Western Maghrib and Its Legitimation, 1830–1873." *International Journal of Middle East Studies* 36, no. 4 (2004): 591–612.

Bensmaia, Reda. *Experimental Nations: Or, the Invention of the Maghreb*. Princeton, NJ: Princeton University Press, 2003.

Bey, Fayçal. *La dernière odalisque*. Paris: Editions Stock, 2001.

Blanchard, Pascal, Nicolas Bancel, and Sandrine Lemaire. "Les zoos humains: passage d'un 'racisme scientifique' vers un 'racisme populaire et colonial' en Occident." In *Zoos humains: XIXe et XXe siècle*, edited by Nicolas Bancel, Pascal Blanchard, Gilles Boetsch, Eric Deroo, and Sandrine Lemaire, 63–71. Paris: La Découverte, 2002.

Blili Temime, Leïla. "La pratique du habous: fait de structure ou effet de conjoncture? Étude de cas." In *Hasab wa Nasab: parenté, alliance et patrimoine en Tunisie*, edited by Sophie Ferchiou, 271–288. Paris: Editions du CNRS, 1992.

———. *Histoire de familles: mariages, repudiations et vie quotidienne à Tunis, 1875–1930*. Tunis: Éditions Script, 1999.

Booth, Marilyn. *Harem Histories: Envisioning Places and Living Spaces*. Durham, NC: Duke University Press, 2010.

———. "*Woman in Islam*: Men and the 'Women's Press' in Turn-of-the-20th-Century Egypt." *International Journal of Middle East Studies* 33, no. 2 (2001): 171–201.

Boubaker, Sadok. *La régence de Tunis au XVII siècle: ses relations commerciales avec les ports de l'Europe méditerranéenne*. Toulouse: Université de Toulouse, 1978.

Bourqia, Rahma. "Don et théâtralité: reflexion sur le rituel de don (hadiya) offert au sultan au XIXe siècle." *Hespéris-Tamuda* 31 (1993): 61–75.

Bouzgarrou-Largueche, Dalenda. *Watan al-Munastir: fiscalité et société (1671–1856)*. Tunis: Publications de la faculté des lettres de la Manouba, 1993.

Brown, L. Carl. "The Religious Establishment in Husainid Tunisia." In *Scholars, Saints, and Sufis: Muslim Religious Institutions since 1500*, edited by Nikki R. Keddie, 47–91. Berkeley: University of California Press, 1972.

———. *The Tunisia of Ahmad Bey, 1837–1855*. Princeton, NJ: Princeton University Press, 1974.

Brown, Nathan J. *Constitutions in a Nonconstitutional World: Arab Basic Laws and the Prospects for Accountable Government*. Albany: State University of New York Press, 2002.

—————. "Law and Imperialism: Egypt in Comparative Perspective." *Law & Society Review* 29, no. 2 (1995): 103–125.

—————. "The Precarious Life and Slow Death of the Mixed Courts of Egypt." *International Journal of Middle East Studies* 25, no. 1 (1993): 33–52.

Cannadine, David. "The Context, Performance and Meaning of Ritual: The British Monarchy and the 'Invention of Tradition,' c. 1820–1977." In *The Invention of Tradition*, edited by Eric J. Hobsbawm and Terence O. Ranger, 101–164. New York: Cambridge University Press, 1983.

—————. *Ornamentalism: How the British Saw Their Empire*. Oxford: Oxford University Press, 2001.

Celik, Zeynep. *Displaying the Orient: Architecture of Islam at Nineteenth-Century World's Fairs*. Berkeley: University of California Press, 1992.

Celik, Zeynep, and Leila Kinney. "Ethnography and Exhibitionism at the Expositions Universelles." *Assemblage* 13 (1990): 34–59.

Chabbouh, Ibrahim. "La Maison Buras à Kairouan." In *L'habitat traditionnel dans les pays musulmans autour de la Méditerranée*, edited by Groupe de recherches et d'études sur le Proche-Orient, 519–541. Le Caire: Institut Francais d'archeologie orientale, 1988.

Chakrabarty, Dipesh. *Habitations of Modernity: Essays in the Wake of Subaltern Studies*. Chicago and London: University of Chicago Press, 2002.

—————. *Provincializing Europe: Postcolonial Thought and Historical Difference*. Princeton, NJ: Princeton University Press, 2000.

Charrad, Mounira M. *States and Women's Rights: The Making of Post-Colonial Tunisia, Algeria and Morocco*. Berkeley: University of California Press, 2001.

Chater, Khelifa. *Dépendance et mutations précoloniales: la régence de Tunis de 1815 à 1857*. Tunis: Publications de l'Université de Tunis, 1984.

—————. "Le fait Ottoman en Tunisie: mythe et réalité." *Revue d'Histoire Maghébine* 31–32 (1983): 141–148.

Chatterjee, Indrani. *Gender, Slavery, and Law in Colonial India*. Oxford: Oxford University Press, 1999.

Chatterjee, Partha. *The Nation and Its Fragments: Colonial and Post-Colonial Histories*. Princeton, NJ: Princeton University Press, 1993.

Chenoufi, Moncef. "Les deux séjours de Muhammad 'Abduh en Tunisie: et leurs incidences sur le réformisme musulman tunisien (6 Décembre 1884–4 Janvier 1885 et 9–24 Septembre 1903)." *Les Cahiers de Tunisie* 12 (1968): 59–97.

Chérif, Mohamed-Hédi. "La 'déturquisation' du pouvoir en Tunisie: classes dirigeantes et société tunisienne de la fin du XVIe siècle à 1881." *Les Cahiers de Tunisie* 117–118, nos. 3–4 (1981): 177–197.

—————. *Pouvoir et société dans la Tunisie de H'usayn Bin 'Ali (1705–1740)*. 2 vols. Tunis: Publications de l'Université de Tunis, 1984.

Christelow, Allan. *Muslim Law Courts and the French Colonial State in Algeria*. Princeton, NJ: Princeton University Press, 1985.

Clancy-Smith, Julia Ann. *Mediterraneans: North Africa and Europe in an Age of Migration, c. 1800–1900*. Berkeley: University of California Press, 2010.

———. *Rebel and Saint: Muslim Notables, Populist Protest, Colonial Encounters (Algeria and Tunisia, 1800–1904)*. Berkeley: University of California Press, 1994.

Clancy-Smith, Julia A., and Frances Gouda, eds. *Domesticating the Empire: Race, Gender and Family Life in French and Dutch Colonialism*. Charlottesville: University Press of Virginia, 1998.

Clancy-Smith, Julia A., and Cynthia Gray-Ware Metcalf. "A Visit to a Tunisian Harem." *Journal of Maghrebi Studies* 1–2 (1993): 43–49.

Cleveland, William L. "The Municipal Council of Tunis, 1858–1870." *International Journal of Middle East Studies* 9 (1978): 33–61.

Cohen, William B. "Gambettists and Colonial Expansion before 1881: The *République Française*." *French Colonial Studies* 1 (1977): 54–65.

Cohn, Bernard S. *An Anthropologist among the Historians and Other Essays*. Oxford: Oxford University Press, 1987.

———. "Representing Authority in Victorian England." In *The Invention of Tradition*, edited by Eric J. Hobsbawm and Terence O. Ranger, 165–210. New York: Cambridge University Press, 1983.

Conklin, Alice J. *A Mission to Civilize: The Republican Ideal of Empire in France and West Africa, 1895–1930*. Stanford, CA: Stanford University Press, 1997.

Cooper, Frederick, and Ann Laura Stoler, eds. *Tensions of Empire: Colonial Culture in a Bourgeois World*. Berkeley: University of California Press, 1997.

Cuno, Kenneth M. "Ambiguous Modernization: The Transition to Monogamy in the Khedival House of Egypt." In *Family History in the Middle East: Household, Property and Gender*, edited by Beshara Doumani, 247–270. Albany: State University of New York Press, 2003.

———. "Joint Family Households and Rural Notables in 19th-Century Egypt." *International Journal of Middle East Studies* 27, no. 4 (1995): 485–502.

Darghout, Saloua. "Le dar es-Seqeli à Tunis." In *L'habitat traditionnel dans les pays musulmans autour de la Méditerranée*, edited by Groupe de recherches et d'études sur le Proche-Orient, 103–109. Le Caire: Institut Francais d'archéologie orientale, 1988.

Darling, Linda T. *Revenue-Raising and Legitimacy: Tax Collection and Finance Administration in the Ottoman Empire, 1560–1660*. Leiden: E. J. Brill, 1996.

Darrow, Margaret H. *Revolution in the House: Family, Class, and Inheritance in Southern France, 1775–1825*. Princeton, NJ: Princeton University Press, 1989.

De Grazia, Victoria, and Ellen Furlough, eds. *The Sex of Things: Gender and Consumption in Historical Perspective*. Berkeley: University of California Press, 1996.

Demeerseman, André. "Inventaire des biens d'un Caïd en 1826: Bakkar Djellouli, traduction annotée." *IBLA* 45 (1982): 281–302.

Deringil, Selim. "'They Live in a State of Nomadism and Savagery': The Late Ottoman Empire and the Post-Colonial Debate." *Comparative Studies in Society and History* 45, no. 2 (2003): 311–342.

Djait, Hichem. "Influences ottomanes sur les institutions, la civilisation et la culture tunisiennes du XVIᵉ au XIXᵉ siècles." *Revue d'Histoire Maghébine* 6 (1976): 150–156.

Doumani, Beshara. "Introduction." In *Family History in the Middle East: Household, Property, and Gender*, edited by Beshara Doumani, 1–19. Albany: State University of New York Press, 2003.

———. *Rediscovering Palestine: Merchants and Peasants in Jabal Nablus, 1700–1900.* Berkeley: University of California Press, 1995.

Duben, Alan. "Turkish Families and Households in Historical Perspective." *Journal of Family History* 10, no. 1 (1985): 75–98.

Duben, Alan, and Cem Behar. *Istanbul Households: Marriage, Family and Fertility 1880–1940.* Cambridge: Cambridge University Press, 1991.

Duindam, Jeroen Frans Jozef. *Vienna and Versailles: The Courts of Europe's Dynastic Rivals, 1550–1780.* Cambridge: Cambridge University Press, 2003.

Ener, Mine. "Getting into the Shelter of Takiyat Tulun." In *Outside in: On the Margins of the Modern Middle East*, edited by Eugene L. Rogan, 53–76. London: I. B. Tauris, 2002.

———. *Managing Egypt's Poor and the Politics of Benevolence, 1800–1952.* Princeton, NJ: Princeton University Press, 2003.

Enloe, Cynthia. *Bananas, Beaches and Bases: Making Feminist Sense of International Politics.* Berkeley: University of California Press, 2000.

Ennaji, Mohammed. *Soldats, domestiques et concubines: l'esclavage au Maroc au XIXe siècle.* Tunis: Cérès Productions, 1994.

Exertzoglou, Haris. "The Cultural Uses of Consumption: Negotiating Class, Gender, and Nation in the Ottoman Urban Centers during the 19th Century." *International Journal of Middle East Studies* 35, no. 1 (2003): 77–101.

Fahmy, Khaled. *All the Pasha's Men: Mehmed Ali, His Army and the Making of Modern Egypt.* Cairo: University of Cairo Press, 1997.

Fakhfakh, Munsif. *Mujaz al-dafatir al-idariya wa al-jabaʿiya bi-al-arshif al-watani al-Tunisi (Sommaire des registers administratifs et fiscaux aux archives nationales tunisiennes).* Tunis: Publications of the Tunisian National Archives, 1990.

Faroqhi, Suraiya. *The Ottoman Empire and the World around It.* London: I. B. Tauris, 2004.

———. "Research on the History of Ottoman Consumption: A Preliminary Exploration of Sources and Models." In *Consumption Studies and the History of the Ottoman Empire, 1550–1922: An Introduction*, edited by Donald Quataert, 15–44. Albany: State University of New York Press, 2000.

———. *Subjects of the Sultan: Culture and Daily Life in the Ottoman Empire.* London: I. B. Tauris, 2000.

Faroqhi, Suraiya, and Christoph K. Neumann, eds. *Ottoman Costumes: From Textile to Identity.* Istanbul: Eren, 2004.

Farrugia de Candia, J. "Monnaies husseinites." *Revue tunisienne* 11–12, nos. 3–4 (1932): 379–398.

Fay, Mary Ann. "Women and Households: Gender, Power and Culture in Eighteenth-Century Egypt." PhD dissertation, Georgetown University, 1993.

Fendri, Mounir. "L'audience de 9 mai 1835, le Prince de Pückler-Muskau chez Hussine Bey." *Les Cahiers de Tunisie* 30, nos. 121–122 (1982): 187–231.

Ferchiou, Sophie. "Catégorie des sexes et circulation des biens habous." In *Hasab wa Nasab: parenté, alliance et patrimoine en Tunisie*, edited by Sophie Ferchiou, 251–270. Paris: Editions du CNRS, 1992.

———. "Structures de parenté et d'alliance d'une société arabe: les *'aylat* de Tunis." In *Hasab wa Nasab: parenté, alliance et patrimoine en Tunisie*, edited by Sophie Ferchiou, 137–168. Paris: Editions du CNRS, 1992.

Findley, Carter Vaughn. "An Ottoman Occidentalist in Europe: Ahmed Midhat Meets Madame Gulnar, 1889." *American Historical Review* 103, no. 1 (1998): 15–49.

Fleischer, Cornell H. *Bureaucrat and Intellectual in the Ottoman Empire: The Historian Mustafa Ali (1541–1600)*. Princeton, NJ: Princeton University Press, 1986.

Frierson, Elizabeth B. "Cheap and Easy: The Creation of Consumer Culture in Late Ottoman Society." In *Consumption Studies and the History of the Ottoman Empire, 1500–1922: An Introduction*, edited by Donald Quataert, 243–260. Albany, NY: State University of New York Press, 2000.

Gallagher, Nancy Elizabeth. *Medicine and Power in Tunisia, 1780–1900*. Cambridge: Cambridge University Press, 1983.

Ganiage, Jean. *Les origines du protectorat français en Tunisie (1861–1881)*. Paris: Presses Universitaire de France, 1959.

Gibb, H. A. R., and Harold Bowen. *Islamic Society and the West: A Study of the Impact of Western Civilization on Moslem Culture in the Near East*. 2 vols. London: Oxford University Press, 1950.

Gobert, Ernest-Gustave. *Usages et rites alimentaires des tunisiens: leur aspect domestique, physiologique et social; [suivi de] les références historiques des nourritures tunisiennes*. Tunis: MediaCom, 2003.

Göçek, Fatma Müge. *Rise of the Bourgeoisie, Demise of Empire: Ottoman Westernization and Social Change*. New York: Oxford University Press, 1996.

Grandchamp, Pierre. "Documents concernant la course dans la régence de Tunis de 1764 à 1769 et 1783 à 1843." *Les Cahiers de Tunisie* 19–20, nos. 3–4 (1957): 269–340.

———. "A propos du sejour à Tunis de Caroline de Brunswick, Princesse de Galles (4–12 Avril, 1816)." *Revue tunisienne* (1934): 59–70.

Grangaud, Isabelle. *La ville imprenable: une histoire sociale de Constantine au 18e siècle*. Paris: Éditions de l'École des Hautes Études en Sciences Sociales, 2002.

Green, Arnold H. *The Tunisian Ulama, 1873–1915: Social Structure and Response to Ideological Currents*. Leiden: E. J. Brill, 1978.

Grehan, James. *Everyday Life & Consumer Culture in 18th-Century Damascus*. Seattle: University of Washington Press, 2007.

Hale, Dana S. *Races on Display: French Representations of Colonized Peoples 1886–1940*. Bloomington: Indiana University Press, 2008.

Hamli, Mohsen. "The 1890 Legal Wrangles over Sudanese Slaves in Tunisia." *Journal of North African Studies* 16, no. 3 (2011): 421–429.

Hanna, Nelly. *Making Big Money in Cairo in 1600: The Life and Times of Isma'il Abu Taqiyya, Egyptian Merchant*. Syracuse, NY: Syracuse University Press, 1998.

Hareven, Tamara K. "The History of the Family and the Complexity of Social Change." *American Historical Review* 96, no. 1 (1991): 95–124.

Hartman, Mary S. *The Household and the Making of History: A Subversive View of the Western Past*. Cambridge: Cambridge University Press, 2004.

Hathaway, Jane. *The Politics of Households in Ottoman Egypt: The Rise of the Qazdaglis*. Cambridge: Cambridge University Press, 1997.

Hattox, Ralph S. *Coffee and Coffeehouses: The Origins of a Social Beverage in the Medieval Near East*. Seattle: University of Washington Press, 1985.

Hayes, Jarrod. *Queer Nations: Marginal Sexualities in the Maghreb*. Chicago: University of Chicago Press, 2000.

Hazareesingh, Sudhir. "'A Common Sentiment of National Glory': Civic Festivities and French Collective Sentiment under the Second Empire." *Journal of Modern History* 76, no. 2 (2004): 280–311.

Hejaiej, Monia. *Behind Closed Doors: Women's Oral Narratives in Tunis*. New Brunswick, NJ: Rutgers University Press, 1996.

Henia, Abdelhamid. "Circulation des biens et liens de parenté à Tunis (XVIIᵉ–début XXᵉ siècle)." In *Hasab wa Nasab: parenté, alliance et patrimoine en Tunisie*, edited by Sophie Ferchiou, 217–250. Paris: Editions du CNRS, 1992.

———. *Le grid et ses rapports avec le Beylik de Tunis (1676–1840)*. Tunis: Publications de l'Université de Tunis, 1980.

———. "Origine et évolution d'un patrimoine familial Tunisios (XVIIᵉ–XIXᵉ siècles)." *IBLA* 17, no. 154 (1984): 201–247.

Hess, Andrew C. *The Forgotten Frontier: A History of the Sixteenth-Century Ibero-African Frontier*. Chicago: University of Chicago Press, 1978.

Hesse, Carla. *The Other Enlightenment: How French Women Became Modern*. Princeton, NJ: Princeton University Press, 2001.

Hibou, Béatrice. *The Force of Obedience*. Cambridge: Polity Press, 2011.

Hisako, Hata. "Servants of the Inner Quarters: The Women of the Shogun's Great Interior." In *Servants of the Dynasty: Palace Women in World History*, edited by Anne Walthall, 172–190. Berkeley: University of California Press, 2008.

Hoexter, Miriam. *Endowments, Rulers and Community: waqf Al-Haramayn in Ottoman Algeria*. Leiden: Brill, 1998.

Hoodfar, Homa. *Between Marriage and the Market: Intimate Politics and Survival in Cairo*. Berkeley: University of California Press, 1997.

Hourani, Albert. *Arabic Thought in the Liberal Age, 1789–1939*. Cambridge: Cambridge University Press, 1983.

———. "Ottoman Reform and the Politics of Notables." In *The Modern Middle*

East: *A Reader*, edited by Albert Hourani, Philip S. Khoury, and Mary C. Wilson, 83–109. Berkeley: University of California Press, 1993.

Hudson, Leila. "Investing by Women or Investing in Women? Merchandise, Money, and Marriage and the Formation of a Prenational Bourgeoisie in Damascus." *Comparative Studies of South Asia, Africa and the Middle East* 26, no. 1 (2006): 105–120.

——. *Transforming Damascus: Space and Modernity in an Islamic City*. London: Tauris Academic Studies, 2008.

Hugon, Henri. *Les emblèmes des beys de Tunis; étude sur les signes d'autonomie husseinite*. Chalon-sur-Seine: Imprimerie E. Bertrand, 1913.

Hunt, Lynn. *The Family Romance of the French Revolution*. Berkeley: University of California Press, 1992.

——. "The Many Bodies of Marie Antoinette: Political Pornography and the Problem of the Feminine in the French Revolution." In *Eroticism and the Body Politic*, edited by Lynn Hunt, 108–130. Baltimore: Johns Hopkins University Press, 1991.

Ibn Sayyar al-Warraq, al-Muzaffar ibn Nasr, Nawal Nasrallah, Kaj Öhrnberg, and Sahban Muruwah. *Annals of the Caliphs' Kitchens: Ibn Sayyar Al-Warraq's Tenth-Century Baghdadi Cookbook*. Leiden; Boston: Brill, 2007.

Issawi, Charles. *An Economic History of the Middle East and North Africa*. New York: Columbia University Press, 1982.

Jdey, Ahmed. *Ahmed Ibn Abi Dhiaf son oeuvre et sa pensée: essai d'histoire culturelle*. Zaghouan: Publications de la Fondation Temimi, 1996.

Jerad, Medhi. "La famille Djellouli de la deuxième moitié du XVIIIᵉ siècle à 1830." *al-Majalla al-tarikiyya al-Maghribiyya (li-al-'ahd al-hadith wa-al-mu'asir). Revue d'histoire maghrébine*, no. 117 (2005).

Julien, Charles-André. *L'Afrique du Nord en marche: nationalismes musulmans et souveraineté française*. Tunis: Cérès Productions, 2001.

Kabbani, Rana. *Europe's Myths of Orient*. Bloomington: Indiana University Press, 1986.

Kafadar, Cemal. *Between Two Worlds: The Construction of the Ottoman State*. Berkeley: University of California Press, 1995.

Khater, Akram Fouad. *Inventing Home: Emigration, Gender and the Middle Class in Lebanon, 1870–1920*. Berkeley: University of California Press, 2001.

Kholoussy, Hanan. *For Better, for Worse: The Marriage Crisis That Made Modern Egypt*. Stanford, CA: Stanford University Press, 2010.

Khoury, Dina Rizk. *State and Provincial Society in the Ottoman Empire: Mosul 1540–1834*. Cambridge: Cambridge University Press, 1997.

Khuri-Makdisi, Ilham. *The Eastern Mediterranean and the Making of Global Radicalism, 1860–1914*. Berkeley: University of California Press, 2010.

Kolodziejczyk, Dariusz. "Polish Embassies in Istanbul or How to Sponge on Your Host without Losing Your Self-Esteem." In *The Illuminated Table, the Prosperous House: Food and Shelter in Ottoman Material Culture*, edited by Suraiya

Faroqhi and Christoph K. Neumann, 51–59. Würzburg: Ergon in Kommission, 2003.

Kraiem, Mustapha. *Le Parti Communiste Tunisien pendant la periode coloniale.* Tunis: Institut Supérieur d'Histoire du Mouvement National, 1997.

Krieken, G. S. Van. *Khayr Al-Din et la Tunisie, 1850–1881.* Leiden: E. J. Brill, 1976.

Kuchta, David. *The Three-Piece Suit and Modern Masculinity: England, 1550–1850.* Berkeley: University of California Press, 2002.

Kunt, I. Metin. *The Sultan's Servants: The Transformation of Ottoman Provincial Government.* New York: Columbia University Press, 1983.

Kwass, Michael. "Ordering the World of Goods: Consumer Revolution and the Classification of Objects in Eighteenth-Century France." *Representations* 82, no. 1 (2003): 87–116.

Lal, Ruby. *Domesticity and Power in the Early Mughal World.* Cambridge: Cambridge University Press, 2005.

Larguèche, Abdelhamid. *Les ombres de la ville: pauvres, marginaux, et minoritaires à Tunis (XVIIIe et XIXe siècles).* Tunis: Centre de Publications Universitaire Facultés des Lettres de Manouba, 1999.

Larguèche, Abdelhamid et Dalenda. *Marginales en terre d'Islam.* Tunis: Cérès Éditions, 1992.

Larguèche, Dalenda. "The *Mahalla*: The Origins of Beylical Sovereignty in Ottoman Tunisia during the Early Modern Period." In *North Africa, Islam and the Mediterranean World: From the Almoravides to the Algerian War*, edited by Julia A. Clancy-Smith, 105–115. London: Frank Cass, 2001.

———. *Territoire sans frontières: la contrebande et ses réseaux dans la régence de Tunis au XIXe siècle.* Tunis: Centre de Publications Universitaire, 2002.

Lebovics, Herman. *True France: The Wars over Cultural Identity, 1900–1945.* Ithaca, NY: Cornell University Press, 1992.

Lewis, Mary Dewhurst. "Geographies of Power: The Tunisian Civic Order, Jurisdictional Politics, and Imperial Rivalry in the Mediterranean, 1881–1935." *The Journal of Modern Political History* 80, no. 4 (December 2008): 791–830.

Lewis, Reina. *Gendering Orientalism: Race, Femininity and Representation.* London: Routledge, 1996.

Lockman, Zachary. *Contending Visions of the Middle East: The History and Politics of Orientalism.* Cambridge: Cambridge University Press, 2004.

Lucas, Philippe, and Jean-Claude Vatin. *L'Algérie des anthropologues.* Paris: François Maspero, 1975.

Lydon, Ghislaine. "Writing Trans-Saharan History: Methods, Sources and Interpretations across the African Divide." *Journal of North African Studies* 10, nos. 3–4 (2005): 293–324.

Mahmood, Saba. *Politics of Piety: The Islamic Revival and the Feminist Subject.* Princeton, NJ: Princeton University Press, 2005.

Makdisi, Ussama. *The Culture of Sectarianism: Community, History and Violence in*

Nineteenth-Century Ottoman Lebanon. Berkeley: University of California Press, 2000.

———. "Ottoman Orientalism." *American Historical Review* 107, no. 3 (2002): 768–796.

Mamdani, Mahmood. *Citizen and Subject: Contemporary Africa and the Legacy of Late Colonialism.* Princeton, NJ: Princeton University Press, 1996.

Mantran, Robert. "L'évolution des relations entre la Tunisie et l'empire Ottoman du XVIᵉ au XIXᵉ siècle." *Les Cahiers de Tunisie* 26–27, nos. 2–3 (1959): 319–333.

———. *Inventaire des documents d'archives turcs du Dar El-Bey (Tunis).* Tunis: Presse Universitaire, 1961.

Margadant, Jo Burr. "The Duchesse de Barry and Royalist Political Culture in Postrevolutionary France." *History Workshop Journal* 43 (1997): 23–52.

———. "Gender, Vice, and the Political Imaginary in Postrevolutionary France: Reinterpreting the Failure of the July Monarchy, 1830–1848." *American Historical Review* 104, no. 5 (1999): 1461–1496.

———. "The Perils of the Sentimental Family for Royalty in Postrevolutionary France: The Case of Queen Marie-Amélie." In *Servants of the Dynasty: Palace Women in World History*, edited by Anne Walthall, 299–326. Berkeley: University of California Press, 2008.

Marin, Manuela. "Beyond Taste: The Complements of Colour and Smell in the Medieval Arab Culinary Tradition." In *A Taste of Thyme: Culinary Cultures of the Middle East*, edited by Sami Zubaida and Richard Tapper, 205–214. London: Tauris Parke Paperbacks, 2000.

———. "Cuisine d'orient, cuisine d'occident." *Médiévales* 16, no. 33 (1997): 9–21.

Marsans-Sakly, Silvia. "Extracting Revenue and Legitimating Power: The Mahalla in the Regency of Tunis." Paper presented at the 17th Annual Middle East History and Theory (MEHAT) Conference, University of Chicago, 2002.

———. "The Revolt of 1864: Power, History and Memory." PhD dissertation, New York University, 2010.

Marzouki, Ilhem. *Le mouvement des femmes en Tunisie au XXe siècle.* Tunis: Cérès Productions, 1993.

Matar, Nabil. *Britain and Barbary, 1589–1689.* Gainesville: University Press of Florida, 2005.

———. *Turks, Moors & Englishmen in the Age of Discovery.* New York: Columbia University Press, 1999.

Matthee, Rudi. *The Pursuit of Pleasure: Drugs and Stimulants in Iranian History, 1500–1900.* Princeton, NJ: Princeton University Press, 2005.

Maza, Sarah. "The Diamond Necklace Affair Revisited (1785–1786): The Case of the Missing Queen." In *Eroticism and the Body Politic*, edited by Lynn Hunt, 63–89. Baltimore: Johns Hopkins University Press, 1991.

———. *Private Lives and Public Affairs: The Causes Célèbres of Prerevolutionary France.* Berkeley: University of California Press, 1993.

McClintock, Anne. *Imperial Leather: Race, Gender and Sexuality in the Colonial Context*. New York: Routledge, 1995.

Mehta, Uday S. "Liberal Strategies of Exclusion." In *Tensions of Empire: Colonial Cultures in a Bourgeois World*, edited by Frederick Cooper and Ann Laura Stoler, 59–86. Berkeley: University of California Press, 1997.

Melman, Billie. *Women's Orients, English Women and the Middle East, 1718–1918: Sexuality, Religion and Work*. Ann Arbor: University of Michigan Press, 1992.

Meriwether, Margaret L. *The Kin Who Count: Family and Society in Ottoman Aleppo, 1770–1840*. Austin: University of Texas Press, 1999.

Mestri, Said. *Moncef Bey*. Tunis: Arcs Editions, 1988.

Micklewright, Nancy. "Personal, Public, and Political (Re)Constructions: Photographs and Consumption." In *Consumption Studies and the History of the Ottoman Empire 1550–1922: An Introduction*, edited by Donald Quataert, 261–288. Albany: State University of New York Press, 2000.

Mikhail, Alan. "The Heart's Desire: Gender, Urban Space and the Ottoman Coffee House." In *Ottoman Tulips, Ottoman Coffee: Leisure and Lifestyle in the Eighteenth Century*, edited by Dana Sajdi, 133–170. New York: Tauris Academic Press, 2007.

Milani, Farzaneh. "On Women's Captivity in the Islamic World." *Middle East Report* 246 (2008): 40–46.

Milanich, Nara. *Children of Fate: Childhood, Class, and the State in Chile, 1850–1930*. Durham, NC: Duke University Press, 2009.

———. "Review Essay: Whither Family History? A Road Map from Latin America." *American Historical Review* 112, no. 2 (2007): 439–458.

Mintz, Sidney W. *Sweetness and Power: The Place of Sugar in Modern History*. New York: Penguin Books, 1985.

Mitchell, Timothy, ed. *Questions of Modernity*. Minneapolis: University of Minnesota Press, 2000.

———. *Rule of Experts: Egypt, Techno-Politics, Modernity*. Berkeley and Los Angeles: University of California Press, 2002.

Moalla, Asma. *The Regency of Tunis and the Ottoman Porte, 1777–1814*. London: Routledge Curzon, 2004.

Moatti, Lucien. *La Mosaïque Médicale de Tunisie: 1800–1950*. Paris: Editions Glyphe, 2008.

Mohanty, Chandra. "Under Western Eyes: Feminist Scholarship and Colonial Discourses." In *Dangerous Liaisons: Gender, National and Postcolonial Perspectives*, edited by Anne McClintock, Aamir Mufti, and Ella Shohat, 255–277. Minneapolis: University of Minneapolis Press, 1997.

Monod, E. *L'Exposition Universelle de 1889*. Paris: E. Dentue, 1890.

Montague, Joel. "Notes on Medical Organization in Nineteenth-Century Tunisia: A Preliminary Analysis of the Materials on Public Health and Medicine in the Dar El-Bey in Tunis." *Medical History* 17, no. 1 (1973): 75–82.

Moors, Annelies. *Women, Property and Islam: Palestinian Experiences 1920–1990.* Cambridge: Cambridge University Press, 1995.

Mosse, George L. "Caesarism, Circuses, and Monuments." *Journal of Contemporary History* 6, no. 2 (1971): 167–182.

———. *The Image of Man: The Creation of Modern Masculinity.* Oxford: Oxford University Press, 1996.

———. *Nationalism and Sexuality: Respectability and Abnormal Sexuality in Modern Europe.* New York: Howard Fertig, 1985.

Murphey, Rhoads. *Ottoman Warfare, 1500–1700.* London: UCL Press, 1999.

Najmabadi, Afsaneh. "Crafting an Educated Housewife in Iran." In *Remaking Women: Feminism and Modernity in the Middle East*, edited by Lila Abu-Lughod, 91–125. Princeton, NJ: Princeton University Press, 1998.

Necipoğlu, Gülru. "Framing the Gaze in Ottoman, Safavid, and Mughal Palaces." *Ars Orientalis* 23 (1993): 303–342.

———. "An Outline of Shifting Paradigms in the Palatial Architecture of the Pre-Modern Islamic World." *Ars Orientalis* 23 (1993): 3–24.

Osmanoglu, Aïché. *Avec mon père le Sultan Abdulhamid de son palais à sa prison.* Translated by Jacques Jeulin. Paris: L'Harmattan, 1991.

Oualdi, M'hamed. *Esclaves et maîtres: les Mamelouks des beys de Tunis du XVIIe siècle aux années 1880.* Paris: Publications de la Sorbonne, 2011.

Pamuk, Sevket. *A Monetary History of the Ottoman Empire.* Cambridge: Cambridge University Press, 2000.

Pedersen, Jean Elisabeth. *Legislating the French Family: Feminism, Theater, and Republican Politics, 1870–1920.* New Brunswick, NJ: Rutgers University Press, 2003.

Peirce, Leslie. *The Imperial Harem: Women and Sovereignty in the Ottoman Empire.* Oxford: Oxford University Press, 1993.

———. "Seniority, Sexuality, and Social Order: The Vocabulary of Gender in Early Modern Ottoman Society." In *Women in the Ottoman Empire*, edited by Madeline C. Zilfi, 169–196. Leiden: Brill, 1997.

Petrey, Sandy. "Pears in History." *Representations* 35 (1991): 52–71.

Petry, Carl F. "Class Solidarity Versus Gender Gain: Women as Custodians of Property in Later Medieval Egypt." In *Women in Middle Eastern History: Shifting Boundaries in Sex and Gender*, edited by Beth Baron and Nikki R. Keddie, 122–142. New Haven, CT: Yale University Press, 1991.

Planel, Anne-Marie. "De la nation à la colonie: la communauté française de Tunisie au XIXᵉ siècle d'après les Archives Civiles et Notariées du Consulat Général de France à Tunis." PhD dissertation, École des hautes études en sciences sociales, 2000.

Pollard, Lisa. *Nurturing the Nation: The Family Politics of Modernizing, Colonizing, and Liberating Egypt, 1805–1923.* Berkeley: University of California Press, 2005.

Poncet, Jean. "Un problème d'histoire rurale: le habous d'Aziza Othmana au Sahel." *Les Cahiers de Tunisie* 31, no. 3 (1960): 137–156.

Porterfield, Todd B. *The Allure of Empire: Art in the Service of French Imperialism, 1798–1836*. Princeton, NJ: Princeton University Press, 1998.

Powell, Eve M. Troutt. *A Different Shade of Colonialism: Egypt, Great Britain, and the Mastery of the Sudan*. Berkeley: University of California Press, 2003.

Pratt, Keith L., Richard Rutt, and James Hoare. *Korea: A Historical and Cultural Dictionary*. Richmond, Surrey: Curzon Press, 1999.

Quataert, Donald. "Clothing Laws, State, and Society in the Ottoman Empire, 1720–1829." *International Journal of Middle East Studies* 29, no. 3 (1997): 403–425.

———, ed. *Consumption Studies and the History of the Ottoman Empire, 1550–1922: An Introduction*. Albany: State University of New York Press, 2000.

Rahimi, Babak. "*Nahils*, Circumcision Rituals and the Theatre State." In *Ottoman Tulips, Ottoman Coffee: Leisure and Lifestyle in the Eighteenth Century*, edited by Dana Sajdi, 90–116. New York: Tauris Academic Press, 2007.

Rawski, Evelyn Sakakida. *The Last Emperors: A Social History of Qing Imperial Institutions*. Berkeley: University of California Press, 1998.

Raymond, André, ed. *Artisans et commerçants au Caire au XVIIIe siècle*. 2 vols. Damas: Institut français de Damas, 1973.

———. "Les problemes du café en Egypte au XVIIIᵉ siècle." In *Le café en Mediterranée: histoire, anthropologie, economie, XVIIIe-XXe siècle*, edited by J.-L. et al. Miège, 31–71. Aix-en-Provence: Université de Provence, CNRS, 1981.

———. "Tunisiens et Maghrébins au Caire au dix-huitième siècle." *Cahiers de Tunisie* 7, nos. 26–27 (1959): 335–371.

———. *Tunis sous les Mouradites: la ville et ses habitants au XVIIe siècle*. Tunis: Cérès éditions, 2006.

———, ed. *Ithaf ahl al-zaman bi-ahbar muluk Tunis wa 'Ahd al-Aman chapitres IV et V: règnes de Husain Bey et Mustafa Bey*. 2 vols. Tunis: IRMC-ISHMN, 1994.

Rearick, Charles. "Festivals in Modern France: The Experience of the Third Republic." *Journal of Contemporary History* 12, no. 3 (1977): 435–460.

Reindl-Kiel, Hedda. "The Chickens of Paradise: Official Meals in the Mid-Seventeenth Century Ottoman Palace." In *The Illuminated Table, the Prosperous House: Food and Shelter in Ottoman Material Culture*, edited by Suraiya Faroqhi and Christoph K. Neumann, 59–88. Würzburg: Ergon in Kommission, 2003.

Revault, Jacques. "L'habitation traditionelle d'après le Dar El-Hedri." In *L'habitat traditionnel dans les pays musulmans autour de la Méditerranée*, edited by Groupe de recherches et d'études sur le Proche-Orient, 111–126. Le Caire: Institut Francais d'archéologie orientale, 1988.

———. *Palais et demures de Tunis (XVIIIe et XIXe siècles)*. Paris: Editions du CNRS, 1971.

———. *Palais et résidences d'été de la région de Tunis, XVIe–XIXe siècles*. Paris: Editions du Centre national de la recherche scientifique, 1974.

Rouissi, Moncer. *Population et société au Maghreb*. Tunis: Cérès Productions, 1977.

Roulin, Jean-Marie. "Mothers in Revolution: Political Representations of Maternity in Nineteenth-Century France." *Yale French Studies* 101 (2001): 182–200.

Rousseau, Alphonse. *Relation de la prise de Tunis et de la Goulette par les troupes otto-manes en 981 de l'Hegire*. Translated by Alphonse Rousseau. Alger: Imprimerie de Gouvernement, 1845.

Roy, Bernard. *Extrait du catalogue des manuscrits et des imprimés de la Bibliothèque de la Grande Mosquée de Tunis*. Histoire avec la collaboration de Mhammed bel Khodja et de Mohammed el Hachaichi, ed. Tunis: Imprimerie Générale (J. Picard et Cie), 1900.

Ruffin, Bartholomeo. "Journal de L'ambassade de Suleiman Aga à la cour de France (janvier-mai 1777)." *La Revue tunisienne* (1917).

Russell, Mona L. *Creating the New Egyptian Woman: Consumerism, Education, and National Identity, 1863–1922*. New York: Palgrave Macmillan, 2004.

Saadaoui, Ahmed. "Palais et résidences des Mouradites: apport des documents des archives locales (la Tunisie au XVIIᵉ s.)." *Comptes-rendus des séances de l'Acadé-mie des Inscriptions et Belles-Lettres* (2006): 635–656.

———. *Tunis, ville ottomane: trois siècles d'urbanisme et d'architecture*. Tunis: Publi-cations de l'Université de Tunis, 2001.

Said, Edward W. *Culture and Imperialism*. New York: Vintage Books, 1993.

———. *Orientalism*. New York: Vintage Books, 1978.

Sajdi, Dana. *Ottoman Tulips, Ottoman Coffee: Leisure and Lifestyle in the Eighteenth Century*. London: Tauris Academic Series, 2007.

Salzmann, Ariel. "The Age of Tulips: Confluence and Conflict in Early Mod-ern Consumer Culture (1550–1730)." In *Consumption Studies and the History of the Ottoman Empire, 1550–1922: An Introduction*, edited by Donald Quataert, 83–106. Albany: State University of New York Press, 2000.

Samanci, Özge. "Culinary Consumption Patterns of the Ottoman Elite during the First Half of the Nineteenth Century." In *The Illuminated Table, the Pros-perous House: Food and Shelter in Ottoman Material Culture*, edited by Suraiya Faroqhi and Christoph K. Neumann, 161–184. Würzburg: Ergon in Kommis-sion, 2003.

Schilcher, Linda Schatkowski. *Families in Politics: Damascene Factions and Estates of the 18th and 19th Centuries*. Wiesbaden: F. Steiner, 1985.

Schmid, Andre. *Korea between Empires, 1895–1919*. New York: Columbia Univer-sity Press, 2002.

Schneider, William H. *An Empire for the Masses: The French Popular Image of Africa, 1870–1900*. Westport and London: Greenwood Press, 1982.

Sebag, Paul. *Tunis au XVIIe siècle: une cité barbaresque au temps de la course*. Paris: L'Harmattan, 1989.

Sebaï, Nadia. *Mustapha Saheb Ettabaa: un haut dignitaire beylical dans la Tunisie du XIXe siècle*. Carthage, Tunisia: Carthaginoiseries, 2007.

Sethom, Samira. "Étude de quatre contrats de mariage Sfaxiens du XIXᵉ siècle." *Cahiers des arts et traditions populaires: revue du Centre des Arts et Traditions Popu-laires* 6 (1977): 19–36.

Sfar, Béchir. *Assistance publique musulmane en Tunisie*. Tunis: Imprimerie Rapide, 1896.

Shakry, Omnia. "Schooled Mothers and Structured Play: Child Rearing in Turn-of-the-Century Egypt." In *Remaking Women: Feminism and Modernity in the Middle East*, edited by Lila Abu-Lughod, 126–170. Princeton, NJ: Princeton University Press, 1998.

Shields, Sarah D. *Mosul before Iraq: Like Bees Making Five-Sided Cells*. Albany: State University of New York Press, 2000.

Shuval, Tal. "The Ottoman Algerian Elite and Its Ideology." *International Journal of Middle East Studies* 32 (2000): 323–344.

Singer, Amy. "Charity's Legacies: A Reconsideration of Imperial Endowment Making." In *Poverty and Charity in Middle Eastern Contexts*, edited by Michael Bonner, Mine Ener, and Amy Singer, 295–315. Albany: State University of New York Press, 2003.

———. *Constructing Ottoman Beneficence: An Imperial Soup Kitchen in Jerusalem*. Albany: State University of New York Press, 2002.

———. "The 'Michelin Guide' to Public Kitchens in the Ottoman Empire." In *Starting with Food: Culinary Approaches to Ottoman History*, edited by Amy Singer, 69–92. Princeton, NJ: Markus Weiner, 2011.

Sinha, Mrinalini. *Specters of Mother India: The Global Restructuring of an Empire*. Durham, NC: Duke University Press, 2006.

Spivak, Gayatri Chakravorty. "Can the Subaltern Speak?" In *Marxism and the Interpretation of Culture*, edited by Cary Nelson and Lawrence Grossberg, 271–313. New York: Macmillan Education, 1988.

Sraïeb, Noureddine. *Le Collège Sadiki de Tunis, 1875–1956: enseignement et nationalisme*. Paris: CNRS, 1995.

Stoler, Ann Laura. *Race and the Education of Desire: Foucault's History of Sexuality and the Colonial Order of Things*. Durham, NC: Duke University Press, 1995.

Tavakoli-Targhi, Mohamad. *Refashioning Iran: Orientalism, Occidentalism and Historiography*. Hampshire: Palgrave, 2001.

Tha'alibi, 'Abd Al-'Aziz. *La tunisie martyre: ses revendications*. 2e éd. tirée de l'éd. originale de 1920. ed. Beyrouth, Liban: Dar al-Gharb al-Islami, 1985.

Thompson, Elizabeth. *Colonial Citizens: Republican Rights, Paternal Privilege and Gender in French Syria and Lebanon*. Cambridge, MA: Harvard University Press, 2000.

———. "Soldiers, Patriarchs, and Bureaucrats: Paternal Republicanism in French Syria and Lebanon." In *Representing Masculinity: Male Citizenship in Modern Western Culture*, edited by Stefan Dudink, Anna Clark, and Karen Hagemann, 213–234. New York: Palgrave Macmillan, 2007.

Tlili, Béchir. *Études d'histoire sociale tunisienne du XIXe siècle*. Tunis: Publications de l'Université de Tunis, 1974.

Toledano, Ehud R. "The Emergence of Ottoman-Local Elites (1700–1900): A Framework for Research." In *Middle Eastern Politics and Ideas: A History from within,* edited by Moshe Ma'oz and Ilan Pappé, 145–162. London: Taurus Academic Studies, 1997.

———. *Slavery and Abolition in the Ottoman Middle East.* Seattle: University of Washington Press, 1998.

———. *State and Society in Mid-Nineteenth-Century Egypt.* Cambridge: Cambridge University Press, 1990.

Tucker, Judith. *In the House of the Law: Gender and Islamic Law in Ottoman Syria and Palestine.* Berkeley: University of California Press, 1998.

———. *Women in Nineteenth-Century Egypt.* Cambridge: Cambridge University Press, 1985.

Tugay, Emine Foat. *Three Centuries: Family Chronicles of Turkey and Egypt.* London: Oxford University Press, 1963.

Turan, Gülname. "Turkey in the Great Exhibition of 1851." *Design Issues* 25, no. 1 (2009): 64–79.

Valensi, Lucette. "Consommation et usages alimentaires en Tunisie aux XVIIIᵉ et XIXᵉ siècles." *Annales. Histoire, Sciences Sociales* 30, no. 2 (1975): 600–609.

———. "Esclaves chrétiens et esclaves noirs à Tunis au XVIIIᵉ siècle." *Annales, Economies, Sociétés, Civilisations* 22, no. 6 (1967): 1267–1288.

———. *Fellahs Tunisiens: l'économie rurale et la vie des campagnes au 18ème et 19ème siècles.* Paris: Mouton & Co., 1977.

———. "Islam et capitalisme: production et commerce des chéchias en Tunisie et en France aux XVIIIᵉ et XIXᵉ siècles." *Revue d'histoire moderne et contemporaine* 16, no. 3 (1969): 376–400.

Van Der Haven, Elisabeth Cornelia. "The Bey, the Mufti and the Scattered Pearls: Shari'a and Political Leadership in Tunisia's Age of Reform, 1800–1864." PhD dissertation, Leiden University, 2006.

Vehel, J. *La veritable cuisine tunisienne: manuel pratique et complet.* Presentation by Yassine Essid, ed. Tunis: MediaCom, 2003.

Walthall, Anne. "Introducing Palace Women." In *Servants of the Dynasty: Palace Women in World History,* edited by Anne Walthall, 1–21. Berkeley: University of California Press, 2008.

———, ed. *Servants of the Dynasty: Palace Women in World History.* Berkeley: University of California Press, 2008.

Weber, Caroline. *Queen of Fashion: What Marie Antoinette Wore to the Revolution.* New York: Henry Holt and Company, 2006.

White, Joshua M. "Catch and Release: Piracy, Slavery, and Law in the Early Modern Mediterranean." PhD dissertation, University of Michigan, 2012.

Winkler, Jean-Claude. *Le Comte Raffo.* Berlin, 1967.

Womble, Theresa Liane. "Early Constitutionalism in Tunisia, 1857–1864: Reform and Revolt." PhD dissertation, Princeton University, 1997.

Wyrtzen, Jonathan. "Constructing Morocco: The Colonial Struggle to Define the Nation, 1912–1956." PhD dissertation, Georgetown University, 2009.

Yonan, Michael E. "Veneers of Authority: Chinese Lacquers in Maria Theresa's Vienna." *Eighteenth-Century Studies* 37, no. 4 (2004): 652–672.

Zaouali, Lilia. *Medieval Cuisine of the Islamic World: A Concise History with 174 Recipes*. Berkeley: University of California Press, 2007.

Zmerli, Sadok. *Les précurseurs*. Tunis: Éditions Bouslama, 1979.

Zouari, Ali. "Le dar Jalluli et le dar Hintati à Sfax." In *L'habitat traditionnel dans les pays musulmans autour de la Méditerranée*, edited by Groupe de recherches et d'études sur le Proche-Orient, 127–164. Le Caire: Institut Francais d'archéologie orientale, 1988.

Zubaida, Sami. "National, Communal and Global Dimensions in Middle Eastern Food Cultures." In *A Taste of Thyme: Culinary Cultures of the Middle East*, edited by Sami Zubaida and Richard Tapper, 33–45. London: Tauris Parke Paperbacks, 2000.

INDEX

A lowercase "t" after a page number indicates a table. Italicized page numbers indicate illustrations.

Bardo palace, 10–12, 55–56, *69*, *80–81*, *82*, 91; family life in, 12, 18, 21, 44, 47, 70, 93, 97, 100; French ceremonial use of, 164, 165, 166, 169; furnishing and remodeling of, 75, 79, 81, 87, 131; harem, 15, 82, 101, 106; world fairs model of, 161, *162*, *163*. *See also* family, palace; women, palace

Barudi, Muhammad ibn Husayn al-, 57. *See also* bint al-Barudi

Bayram, Muhammad, 91

Behar, Cem, 17, 175

Beja, 69, 112, 116

Berner, Madame, 101–105, 215n86

bey (Ottoman title), 3, 9, 34–35, 36, 37, 39, 47, 56, 119

beys, protectorate era: 'Ali (1882–1902), 157, 165, 166–167, 169; Muhammad al-Hedi (1902–1906), 160; Muhammad al-Nasser (1906–1922), 168, 169–170; Munsef (1942–1943), 170. *See also individual beys*

bint al-Barudi (wife of Hammuda Pasha), 3, 57, 65t, 68t, 89t, 91

Binzart, 6, 69, 112

bit al-muna. See *kummania*

Blili [ben] Temime, Leila, 17, 92, 175

Brunswick, Caroline of (Princess of Wales), 101

Bu 'Attur, Muhammad al-'Aziz, 167

Bu 'Aziz, 45, 198n66; granddaughter of, 45–46

Burteghiz, Imam Yusuf, 41, 43, 60, 197n44

Calligaris, Louis (Luigi), 29, 99, 101, 130, 209n136, 215n78

charity, 6, 26, 90, 98, 111–122, 146; and Tunisian elite, 110. See also *waqf*; *and individual beys*

Charrad, Mounira, 175

children, palace, 41, 47, 57, 59, 86t, 90,

92, 96; constitutional regulation of, 135–138; education of, 41, 61, 87; under French colonial rule, 168; infant and child mortality, 84–85

China: and Empress Dowager Cixi, 25, 107; marriage practices of, 38; Qing Empire, 5, 15, 54

circumcision, celebration of, 26, 90, 118; as charitable act, 113–114, 118, 121–122; under French colonial rule, 163; in Istanbul, 109

Clancy-Smith, Julia, 22, 107

clothing, palace, 28, 55, 99, 100; cost of, 62, 103; economic importance of, 62; European descriptions of, 103, 104, 106, 130, 140; under French colonial rule, 158–159, *160*; reform of, 130–131; as stipend, 13, 57, 62, 87–88, 137, 199n69; women's embroidery of, 84. *See also* trousseau; uniforms

coffee, 68–69, 70, 71, 72, 74, 77, 102, 104, 110, 208n120; price of, 207n105; trade in, 59, 68–69. See also *qahwaji*

colonialism: familial models of, 151, 154, 158, 161, 170–171, 177; legal system, 158. *See also* France

concubines, 13, 30; and early modern courts, 4, 25, 38, 219n39; gifting of, 46, 60, 197n44; and ruling family in Tunis, 42, 57, 60, 66, 84–87, 100. See also *'aljia; jaria*; slaves

constitution of 1861, 26, 127, 133–138, 143, 148, 150; under French colonial rule, 150, 167–168; French opposition to, 155, 176–177; and nationalism, 169; popular opposition to, 134

consumption: critique of, 122, 139–142, 144, 146–147; economic role of, 55, 62; of European goods, 74–76, 78, 177; and modern state, 128,

158, 160–161. *See also* court culture, early modern

court. *See* tribunal, Bardo

court culture, early modern: consumption and display in, 3–4, 12, 25, 54–55; palace personnel, 54, 56; slavery in, 13–14, 17, 30, 38, 73, 122; women and family in, 4–5, 14–15, 18–19, 23, 38–39, 105–106, 107, 176

Dar al-Bey, 76, 79, 101, 166

Davis, Nathan, 69, 74, 110

debt: 136, 137, 138, 147, 167, 224n59, 225n67; ibn Dhiaf's views on, 125; Khayr al-Din's views on, 146. *See also* International Financial Commission

dey (Ottoman title), 34–35, 39, 47

divorce, 31, 42, 45–48, 85, 88, 93, 148, 174; in France, 154

diwan, 33, 34, 36, 47, 58, 71, 79, 163

doctors, palace, 61–62, 72, 84, 132, 203n45, 210n14

Duben, Alan, 17, 175

education, reform of, 131, 132, 145–146

Egypt, 21; Ottoman rule in, 24, 26, 30, 32; reform era in, 129, 141; ruling elite in, 87, 148; ties with Tunis (commercial, cultural, and religious), 6, 53, 68–69, 207n104, 205–206n80; women and family life in, 18, 43, 213n51. *See also* family: Middle East; Muhammad 'Ali Pasha of Egypt

endogamy, 16–17, 39, 43–44, 93, 168

European powers: commercial relations with Tunis, 6, 32, 55, 138, 140, 156; diplomatic and political relations with Tunis, 33, 125–128, 139, 143, 152, 196n10; Europeans in the palace, 12, 21, 42, 58, 60–61, 74, 87, 102, 201n25, 203n43, 222n34; and

reactions to French colonialism, 152, 157, 164–165. *See also* International Financial Commission

European royal families, 3–5, 17, 19, 38–39, 107

family: and household politics, 24, 30, 31, 34, 38, 43–44, 47, 176; Middle East, 16–20, 173–175, 191–192n34, 213n47, 213n51

family, palace: emotional ties in, 42, 59, 97–99, 107, 211n16; French colonial use of, 9–10, 157, 166–169, 176; organization of, 11, 56–58, 70, 77–78, 84–88, 93; political nature of, 5, 9, 12–15, 18–20, 23–24, 31, 38, 42, 44–49, 83, 106–108, 121–122, 128, 169, 173–174, 176; reform of, 135–138, 148–149; relations with local notables, 3, 43, 57, 59–60, 83, 91, 93–96, 175; relations with subject population, 6, 55, 62, 87, 109–110, 112, 115, 118–121, 203n50; study of, 14–16, 83. *See also* Bardo palace; marriage; patriarchy; stipends; succession; women, palace

family, Tunisia, 15, 17, 92–93; household organization of, 73, 91, 94–95; slave ownership in, 13, 73, 91, 94

family life and private sphere, 14–15, 20, 27, 106, 108, 148–149, 152–154, 177

Fatma bint Husayn ibn 'Ali, 41, 65t, 67, 68t, 88, 89; economic activities of, 42; family life of, 57, 79, 86, 90, 116–117

Fatma bint 'Uthman Dey, 39, 40, 113; family relations of, 42; palace politics, 42–43, 96

Ferchiou, Sophie, 93, 114

fez, 6, 130, *131*, 159. See also *shashia*

firman, 36, 37, 44, 130

food and diet: of common people, 63,

71–72, 76, 113; of wealthy, 53, 71, 72–73, 208n120. *See also* coffee; provisions; sweets; *zlabia*

France: Ahmad Bey's visit to, 74; colonial ceremonials of, 158–166; colonial rule of, 22–23, 126, 150–152, 154, 156–158, 170–171; festivals in, 160; interference in Ottoman affairs, 125–127; royal family and politics in, 3–4, 39, 56, 107, 152–154. *See also* European powers

funerals, 96, 115; of palace families, 58, 84, 90, 117, 118, 207n99

Gabes, 6

gender: and modernity, 19, 23, 173, 176; roles, women's, 18, 20, 43, 97, 99, 174; segregation, 14–15, 100, 174. *See also* masculinity; women, palace

Ghar al-Milh, 69

Ghazalia, Fatma, 40, 42

Ghazali, Shaykh Muhammad al-, 40

Ghazalia, Mna, 45, 57, 64t, 65t, 67t, 68t, 88, 89t, 211n21; economic activities of, 114; family life of, 84, 90

gifting: and celebrations, 86, 95, 118, 137; and European diplomacy, 75, 139–140; Ottoman politics of, 32, 36–37, 44; of property, 114–115; and social relations, 14, 46, 100, 105, 110, 119, 121

Habsburg dynasty, 3, 17, 54; and rivalry with Ottomans, 24, 32–33; Schonbrunn palace, 12

Hafsia bint Husayn Bey (wife of 'Allala), 13, 98, 137

Hafsia bint Husayn ibn 'Ali, 41; economic activities of, 42; marriage to 'Ali Pasha, 42, 45, 85, 213n56

Hafsid dynasty, 10, 32, 34, 53

Halq al-Wad palace, 81

Hammam-Lif palace, 81, 166

Hammuda Bey al-Muradi. *See* Muradite family

Hammuda Pasha Bey, 57, 64t, 65t, 66, 68t; charitable activities of, 115–116; family life of, 3, 60, 84–85, 86t, 91, 97, 118, 212n39; government of, 36, 59, 96, 98, 119, 173, 219n61; nationalist view of, 169

Hanansha, 45–46

hanba, 58, 72, 119, 200n19

harem: domestic aspects of, 12–16, 58, 63, 68–69, 81–83, 84–90; Orientalist tropes of, 12, 15–16, 106, 154; political and social role of, 14, 83, 99–105, 106–108. *See also* court culture, early modern; *saraya*; women, palace

Hassan Bey of Constantine, 46

Henana bint Ahmad Mestiri, 93, 98

Hesse-Wartegg, Ernst von, 29, 75, 148

Hijaz, 6, 141

holiday celebrations, 66–67, 70, 73, 87, 161–162. *See also* France: festivals in

household: composition and organization of, 12–16, 21, 34, 35, 55, 56–58, 77, 87–88, 89t, 90, 221n10; and food distribution, 62–70; networks, 30–31, 34–36, 39–41, 45–48, 61–62, 174; and reform era, 127–128, 133, 137–138, 148, 173. *See also* family; family, palace; harem; Ottoman Empire

Hurrem (wife of Sultan Suleiman), 25, 107

Husayn, General (mamluk), 132, 156

Husayn Bey, 58, *131*; charitable activities of, 117, 120; dispute with 'Uthman Bey, 97–98; European critiques of, 140, 224n64; European guests of, 101, 104–105; family life of, 13, 79, 84–86, 93, 99, 118, 215n78; relations with Ottomans, 125, 130; Tripoli affair, 126. *See also* Mestiri, Fatma

Husayn Khoja, 89, 132

ibn 'Ali, Husayn, 9, 40, 79; charitable activities of, 112; dispute with 'Ali Pasha, 44–48; family life of, 30, 39, 85–86, 119; nationalist views of, 22, 31; ties to Muradite households, 31, 40–41

ibn 'Ashur, Muhammad al-Tahir, 74–75

ibn Ayad, Mahmud, 138, 224n51

ibn Ayad, Muhammad, 142

ibn Dhiaf, Ahmad, 28, 60, 74, 127, 198n58, 202n38; accolades of beys, 120; on assassination of 'Uthman, 97–98, 214n65; critique of spending, 141–143, 145, 146–147; on palace women, 60, 98, 107, 134, 148, 174, 223n35

ibn Ismail, Mustafa, 145

ibn Mami, Mahmud, 41

ibn Mami, Muhammad, 41

ibn Yusuf, Muhammad Saghir, 43, 44, 48–49, 60, 72–73, 100, 174, 198n58

'Ilij 'Ali, 32–33

India: British colonial rule in, 19, 159; marriage practices of, 38; Mughal dynasty, 14, 15, 17

infertility, 84, 117

International Financial Commission, 138, 145–146, 155–156

Ismail Bey, 57, 64t, 65t, 67t, 68t, 86, 88, 89t, 118, 119, 206n86

Ismail Kahia, 96, 114, 214n71

Italian: community in Tunis, 28, 61, 126; cultural influence on the palace, 74, 75, 77, 128, 131, 162. *See also* European powers; International Financial Commission; Raffo, Giuseppe

Jalluli family, 59, 72, 212n39; Bekkar, 59, 74; Farhat, 138; Mahmud, 59

Jamal al-Din (*qa'id* of Sousse), 45

janissaries, 33, 34, 35

Jannat bint Mustafa Khaznadar (wife of Khayr al-Din), 75, 143

Japan, 20; Tokugawa shogunate, 14

jaria, 59–60; children of, 86–87; distribution of household provisions, 63–68; marriages with, 95. See also *'aljia*; concubines; slaves

Kalthum bint Mustafa Bey, 125, 134, 143, 212n40, 223n35

Kebura bint Husayn Bey, 89

Kennedy, John Clark, 29, 71, 72, 131–132

khadem, 58, 59, 62, 201n21. *See also* slaves

Khadija (Khaduja) bint 'Ali Bey, 57, 85, 89t, 96, 98

Khadija (Khaduja) bint Yusuf Darguth, 113–114

Khadija bint Husayn ibn 'Ali, 41–42

Khayr al-Din (the corsair), 32, 36

Khayr al-Din (the minister), 127, 140, 143–148, 156; family and personal life of, 75, 148

Khayr al-Din Kahia, 98

Khenis, 69

Khuri-Makdisi, Ilham, 21

Korea: Choson dynasty, 15; Queen Min, 107

kummania, 63, 67t, 73, 91, 94–95

Laz, Mustafa, 39

Mabruka, 40, 43

Maghrib. *See* North Africa

mahalla, 86, 109; food and provisions during, 67, 69, 74; and French colonial rule, 165; interaction with population, 118–121; as source of political authority, 34, 44, 119

Mahbuba bint Mustafa Bey, 59
Mahmood, Saba, 18, 175
Mahmud II (Ottoman Sultan), 75, 134
Mahmud Bey, 64t, 65t, 67t, 68t,
89t, 118, 119, 211n20; dispute with
'Uthman, 96–98, 214n60; family
life of, 86t, 91, 93; government of,
59, 98, 101. See also Amina bint 'Ali
Bey
Mahmud ibn Husayn Bey, 44, 46, 84
Mahrizi, Muhammad ibn Qasim al-,
74
Mamia, Fatma, 41
Mamia, Kebira, 41; charitable activities of, 113; influence on 'Ali Pasha,
42–43, 96
mamluks: as component of household, 30, 41, 62, 71–72; marriages
with palace women, 13, 41, 59, 89,
93–94, 98, 148, 168; origins, size,
and distribution of, 13, 56, 58–59,
201n25; political influence of, 96,
98, 118; and reform era, 137, 148.
See also individual mamluks; slaves
manqalji, 61, 203n47
Manuba, 69, 116
Manubia, Saida 'Aisha, 116–117, 121
marriage: companionate, 19; political
role of, 23–24, 30–31, 34, 42, 47–49,
85, 96, 98; and social alliances, 3,
13, 39–43, 60, 83, 93–94, 173; and
status, 87, 90–91, 136. See also court
culture, early modern; divorce; endogamy; family; palace; polygamy;
weddings
masculinity: and financial responsibility, 70, 77; relation to public
sphere, 14, 107–108; and women's
status, 19, 174. See also family life
and private sphere; patriarchy
Mater, 69
Menana bint Shelebi, 91, 104

Mestiri, Ahmad, 93, 98. See also
Henana bint Ahmad Mestiri
Mestiri, Fatma, 84; family relations,
93; palace politics, 79, 98–99,
215n78
Mestiri, Muhammad, 98
Mintz, Sidney, 54
mixed courts. See reforms in Tunis:
judicial
modernity: colonialism and, 22–23,
76, 150–152; relevance of family to,
19–20, 23, 29, 128, 147–149, 153, 173–
176. See also consumption; nahda;
Ottoman Empire; reforms in Tunis
Moknine, 69
Monastir, 6
monogamy, 15, 17, 92, 148–149, 173, 175
Morocco, 22, 130, 220n64; French
colonization of, 27, 155, 170–171,
232n101; religious ties to Tunis, 6
Muhammad 'Ali Pasha of Egypt, 7, 56,
129–130, 216n105
Muhammad al-Mimun Bey, 89t, 119;
family of, 57, 67t, 86t, 89t, 117
Muhammad al-Rashid Bey, 44; charitable activities of, 117–118; family
life of, 41, 45, 57, 60, 65t, 67t, 68t,
79, 84, 86t, 88t, 89t, 90, 198n65,
212n39, 213n56; government of, 46,
47. See also Ghazalia, Mna
Muhammad al-Sadoq Bey: debts of,
137–138; family life of, 85, 87, 91,
93, 98, 148–149, 215n78; French relations with, 155, 157; government
of, 73, 132, 134, 145, 173; ibn Dhiaf's
critique of, 142–143; nationalist
views of, 169; palaces of, 166, 210n5
Muhammad Bey, 70, 131; family life of,
91, 215n78; French view of, 146, 155;
reforms of, 133, 169
Muhammad Saghir (of Hanansha),
45, 46